...am
inspired by the Bible and the saints

Christian
Names

Christian

Christian Names

Baby names inspired
by the Bible and the Saints

Martin H. Manser

Collins

Collins
A division of HarperCollins*Publishers*
77–85 Fulham Palace Road, London W6 8JB

www.collins.co.uk

First published in Great Britain in 2009 by
HarperCollins*Publishers*

1

A catalogue record for this book is available
from the British Library.

ISBN 978 000 729721 4

Typeset and designed by M.A.T.S., Southend-on-Sea, Essex
Printed and bound in Great Britain by Clays Ltd, St Ives plc

Contents

v

Acknowledgements

Quotations from the Bible text come from the New Revised Standard Version unless otherwise specified.

Extracts from the *Collins Dictionary of the Bible* (by Martin Selman and Martin Manser) and *Collins Dictionary of Saints* (edited by Martin Manser) are used by permission.

I wish to express my thanks to my daughter Hannah for her typing up of the text, to Sam Richardson of the publishers for his encouragement during the compilation of the text, and to Debra Reid and Pieter Lalleman for their advice on the derivation of certain names.

Martin H. Manser

Aylesbury, 2009

vi

Key to pronunciation

a as in ham
ah as in father
ai as in air
aw as in saw
ay as in bay
b as in big
ch as in chin
d as in dog
e as in bet
ee as in see
eer as in beer
er as in her
ew as in too
ewr as in pure
f as in fish
g as in go
h as in hot
i as in it
j as in jam
k as in keep
ks as in mix
l as in leg
m as in man
n as in no
ng as in long, finger

o as in top
oh as in go
oo as in too
oor as in poor
ow as in cow
oy as in boy
p as in pad
r as in red
s as in sit
sh as in ship
t as in too
th as in thin
th as in then
u as in cup
uh as in driver, China
uu as in bull
v as in vase
w as in win
y as in cry, yes
yoo as in you
yr as in tyre
z as in zoo
zh as in vision
Stress is shown in capital
letters: sister: SIS-tuh

Introduction

Christian Christian names are back in fashion. In 2008, over half the top 100 most popular boys' and girls' names in the UK had a religious background. Names like Noah, Isaac and Jacob have been steadily returning to popularity over a number of years.

Religious names also stand the test of time. Research compiled for this book shows that in the last 100 years, in both the UK and the US, names with a religious background were 50 per cent more likely than other names to have remained in the top 100 charts.

Even in an increasingly secular culture, the popularity of religious names isn't surprising. Parents of all beliefs are looking for names with a genuine meaning and story behind them, and they are finding that names with a Christian background fit the bill perfectly.

Christian christian names come from two main sources: the Bible and the saints through church history. This compilation gives the background to these names. It lists some well-known names from the Bible: *David*, *Noah*, *Ruth* and *Sarah* alongside the less familiar *Chloe* and *Susannah*. The names of saints such as *Anthony*, *Bernadette*, *George* and *Martin* and many others are also included, as are Christian virtues such as *Joy* and *Faith*.

Names appear in alphabetical order under their most common spelling, with their gender (m or f) in brackets. The following line explains the typical pronunciation (for a guide see page vii) and the derivation of the name (if known). The main body of the text details the stories of the most famous person or people to have borne that name, and is followed by any common variants or opposite gender form of the name.

This book contains over 2,000 names with a Christian background, but we hope it isn't just used as a reference – but rather as a source of ideas and inspiration. For some parents, choosing baby names can be remarkably easy; for others (especially teachers, for whom every name is a reminder of a wayward child) it can be a huge challenge. Whatever your situation, we hope that *Christian Christian Names* will help you on your way.

Christian
Christian Names

Aaron (m)
[AIR-uhn, A-ruhn] from Hebrew or Egyptian, possibly meaning 'bright' or 'mountaineer'.

Aaron, Moses' elder brother and Israel's first high priest, whose main role was to assist Moses. He served as spokesman for Moses, because Moses was 'slow of speech'. Aaron held up Moses' hands in battle (Exodus 17:12). He was involved in several controversies, especially in making and worshipping the golden calf (Exodus 32), and in publicly criticising Moses (Numbers 12). Later, God confirmed his leading role through the rod that budded ('Aaron's rod') (Numbers 17).

Abel (m)
[AY-bull] from Hebrew, meaning 'breath'.

Abel, Adam and Eve's second son, who worked as a shepherd. He offered a sacrifice that was acceptable to God, through faith (Genesis 4:1–16; Hebrews 11:4), but was murdered by his brother Cain. When God asked where Abel was, Cain replied, 'Am I my brother's keeper?' God judged Cain by making him 'a fugitive and a wanderer on the earth'.

Variant: **Abe**.

Abigail (f)
[AB-i-gayl] from Hebrew, meaning 'father's joy'.

A woman of beauty, wisdom and faith who saved her first husband Nabal, a rich shepherd, but one who was surly and mean. When David sent his men to Nabal, seeking supplies of food, Nabal insulted them. When David's men returned to David, he prepared to destroy him. Abigail lost no time in humbly coming to David with a kind offer of food. Her gracious wise diplomacy persuaded David not to attack. She married David after Nabal died (1 Samuel 25).

The name and occupation came into more general use from the 'waiting gentlewoman' in the play *The Scornful Lady* by Sir Francis Beaumont and John Fletcher, first performed in 1610. Swift, Fielding and other novelists of the period used the name further and it became popularised by the notoriety of *Abigail Hill, lady-in-waiting to Queen Anne, 1704–14*, who used her friendship with the queen to try to secure personal favours.

Variants: **Abbey, Abbie, Abby, Gail, Gale**.

Abner (m)
[AB-nuh] from Hebrew, meaning 'father is light'.
Saul's cousin and commander-in-chief in Saul's army. After Saul died, Abner temporarily upheld the authority of the king's family. He was murdered by David's commander Joab who was suspicious when Abner tried to join David (2 Samuel 3:22–38). After Abner's death, David mourned him, saying, 'A prince and a great man has fallen in Israel this day.'

Abraham (m)
[AY-bruh-ham] from Hebrew, meaning 'father of many'.
The chief recipient of God's promises in the Old Testament and regarded by Jews as the father of their people. Abraham lived in the early centuries of the second millennium BC. His original name was Abram ('the father is exalted'). The story of Abraham in Genesis is organised around the theme of how God began to fulfil some of the promises he had made to him. When God called Abraham at Ur in Southern Iraq and at Haran, he promised him a land, many descendants, a great name, and said he would become a

blessing to many peoples (Genesis 12:2–3). Abraham's continuing childlessness, however, was a serious threat to all these promises, and during the period of waiting, he attempted to find his own ways of producing an heir (Genesis 15:1–4; 16:1–4, 15–16), though he also grew in faith as God confirmed his intentions in a covenant (Genesis 15:1–6; 17:1–27). Isaac was eventually born when Abraham was 100 years old, but God continued to test Abraham, commanding him to offer his son as a sacrifice.

Abraham's obedience to God and his confidence that 'The Lord Will Provide' (Genesis 22:14) make him the supreme example of faith in the New Testament. Abraham's final actions in buying a family burial ground and obtaining a wife for Isaac point to a future fulfilment of the promises of land and descendants.

Variant: **Abe**.

Absalom (m)

[AB-suh-luhm] from Hebrew, meaning 'father of peace'.
David's third son, who overthrew his father and was king for a brief time while David fled across the Jordan. David regained the throne as a result of Absalom receiving bad advice, but despite all this, David was grief-stricken at Absalom's tragic death in an accident (2 Samuel 15:1–18:33): 'O my son Absalom, my son, my son Absalom! Would I had died instead of you, O Absalom, my son, my son!'

Adam (m)

[AD-uhm] from Hebrew, closely related to the word for 'man'.
The name of the first man as well as the Hebrew word for 'human race'. He was in the Garden of Eden and given Eve as a helper. They disobeyed God and so brought sin into the world. In the New Testament, Adam usually represents the human race in its sinful rebellion against God (Romans

5:12–21), though he is also the first man and 'the son of God' (Luke 3:38). Jesus Christ is described as 'the last Adam' (1 Corinthians 15:45).

Variant: **Edom**.

Adelaide (f)
[a-duh-LAYD] from an Old German name meaning 'nobility'.
French empress of Germany (931–999). The daughter of Rudolf II of Burgundy, Adelaide became the wife of Prince Lothair of Italy and, after his death, married Otto the Great of Germany in 951. Otto was crowned emperor by Pope John XII shortly afterwards, with Adelaide as his empress. Otto's family, led by his daughter Theophano, resented Adelaide's influence and, after Otto's death, spent the next 20 years working to alienate Otto's son the emperor Otto II from his mother, finding fault for instance with her unstinting generosity to the poor. Adelaide was obliged to live for a time in retirement from the court but was reconciled with her son Otto before his death, after which she had again to go into retreat.

After Theophano's death in 991 Adelaide finally returned as regent and used her authority to revitalise the religious establishment, founding and restoring monasteries and promoting the evangelisation of the Slavs. She died at a convent she had founded at Seltz in Alsace.

Variant: **Ada**.

Adlai (m)
[AD-lay] from Hebrew, meaning 'my adornment'.
The father of Shaphat, who was responsible for David's cattle in the valleys (1 Chronicles 27:29).

Adrian (m)
[AY-dree-uhn] from Latin *Hadrianus*, meaning 'of Adria' (the town in Italy that gave its name to the Adriatic Sea).

Adrian (died c.304), martyr of Nicomedia. According to legend, Adrian was a Roman officer stationed at Nicomedia who was so moved by the courage of the Christians he persecuted that he declared himself to be a Christian also. He was thrown into prison, where he was visited by his Christian wife Natalia. Further visits were barred after Adrian was sentenced to death, but Natalia continued to see him by disguising herself as a boy and bribing the gaoler. She attended her husband's execution and retrieved his remains.

Also the name of the *African-born English abbot Adrian of Canterbury (died 710)*. While serving as abbot of the monastery at Nerida in Italy he was twice offered the post of Archbishop of Canterbury by Pope Vitalian, but turned down the offer both times. On the second occasion, however, he agreed to accompany the eventual choice, the Greek monk Theodore, to England and once there accepted the post of abbot of the monastery school of St Peter and St Paul (later renamed St Augustine's) in Canterbury. Over the following 40 years he went on to consolidate his reputation as a scholar and administrator and to bolster the standing of Canterbury as a centre of religious learning.

5

Variant: **Hadrian**.

Feminine forms: **Adriana**, **Adrienne**.

Adriana, **Adrienne** feminine forms of **Adrian**.

Agatha (f)
[A-guh-thuh] from Greek, meaning 'good'.
Sicilian martyr (third century). Tradition has it that Agatha was of noble birth but as a young woman incurred the wrath of a consul called Quintian after she refused his advances, having dedicated her virginity to Christ. Charging her with being a Christian, Quintian handed her over to a brothel-keeper but, when she emerged

uncorrupted, had her savagely tortured instead. During the torture, St Peter appeared in a vision to heal her wounds. Her death in prison as she was rolled over hot coals was preceded by an earthquake.

Agnes (f)

[AG-ness] from Greek, meaning 'pure'.

Agnes, Roman martyr (died c.304). Despite her fame, little definite is known about the life of St Agnes beyond the fact that while still a child she died the death of a virgin martyr in Rome and was buried in the cemetery on the Via Nomentana, where a church dedicated to her memory was later erected. Various embellishments have been added to the bare facts of her life story suggesting the reasons for her arrest and execution. According to one of these she was a beautiful young girl of around 12 years old who offered her life voluntarily in exchange for those of other victims of persecution. Another suggests she was put to death as a Christian in revenge after refusing all suitors on the grounds that she had dedicated her virginity to Christ. She became a lasting symbol of chastity and innocence and is honoured today as the patron saint of betrothed couples, virgins and gardeners.

Also the name of the *Italian nun, Agnes of Montepulciano (c.1268–1317).* Born into a wealthy family in Tuscany, Agnes was brought up by the nuns of Montepulciano and in due course became bursar and superioress of a new convent at Proceno. Widely known both for her humble lifestyle (she slept on the ground with a rock for a pillow) and for her visions, she was persuaded back to Montepulciano and there established a new convent in a former brothel, subsequently attaching it to the Dominican order and being appointed prioress in 1306. She became well known for her prophecies and as a worker of miraculous cures.

Aidan (m)
[AY-duhn] from Irish Gaelic, meaning 'small fire'.
Irish missionary (died 651). Aidan served as a monk in the monastery on Iona before being sent to Northumbria as a missionary around the year 635. Raised to the rank of bishop, he chose the island of Lindisfarne as his base and there founded a monastery that became in due course one of the most influential religious centres in Britain. From Lindisfarne he conducted numerous evangelising journeys through the mainland, establishing many churches and monasteries with the support of St Oswald, king of Northumbria, and his successor Oswin.

A gentle and discreet man, according to the Venerable Bede, Aidan won many converts through his generosity towards the needy and through his opposition to slavery.

Variant form: **Aiden**.

7

Alan (m)
[A-luhn] from a Celtic name meaning 'harmony'.
Breton saint ('Blessed Alan de la Roche') who belonged to the Dominican order, and was well known for his accomplished sermons. His special task was to advance devotion to the Blessed Virgin Mary and the practice of the rosary.

Variant forms: **Allan**, **Allen**.

Alban (m)
[ALL-buhn] ultimately from Latin *albus*, meaning 'white'.
Third-century English martyr. Alban was a prominent citizen of the Roman city of Verulamium (modern St Albans) who was beheaded for his faith around the middle of the third century, during the reign of Diocletian.

According to the Venerable Bede, Alban converted to Christianity after offering shelter to a priest hiding from Roman soldiers, impressed by the man's piety and devotion. When the soldiers eventually called at his house to arrest the priest, Alban donned the fugitive's gown and was arrested in his stead, allowing the real priest to escape. When the imposture was discovered, the authorities insisted that Alban should make a sacrifice to the gods and, when he refused, sentenced him to be tortured and put to death. A substantial church (later abbey) was subsequently erected on the site where Alban died, thus becoming the first martyr of the British Isles. He is honoured as the patron saint of converts and victims of torture.

Albert (m)

[AL-buht] from the Old German name *Adalbert*, from *athal* 'noble' and *berhta* 'bright'.

German theologian and bishop, Albert the Great (1206–80). Born into a wealthy family in Swabia, Germany, Albert the Great (or Albertus Magnus) began his career in the church at the age of 16, when he became a Dominican friar. He spent the next 20 years teaching in Paris and at various German Dominican universities, earning a wide reputation as a scholar, his pupils including St Thomas Aquinas.

Today he is recognised as a founder of medieval scholastic philosophy, although he also wrote on a variety of other subjects, including mathematics, physics, astronomy, geography, mineralogy, chemistry, biology, botany, politics, economics and alchemy. His conclusions included the revolutionary notion that the world was spherical rather than flat. He held a number of ecclesiastical posts between 1254 and 1262, among them theologian to the pope and bishop of Regensburg, but felt he was not suited to administrative roles and eventually gave up his see. He passed his final years teaching in Cologne, although he also returned to Paris (1277) in order to conduct a defence of the work of his recently deceased student Thomas Aquinas. He is honoured as the patron saint of students of natural science.

Variants: **Al**, **Bert**, **Bertie**.
Feminine form: **Alberta**.

8

Alberta feminine form of **Albert**.

Aldo (m)
[AL-doh] from an Old German name, from *ald*, meaning 'old'.
An eighth-century saint and native of Siena, Italy, who after her husband's death gave away all her possessions and dedicated her life to helping the poor and sick. During her life, she saw ecstatic visions.
   Variant: **Aldous**.

Alexander (m)
[a-LEX-ahn-duh] from Greek, meaning 'defender of men'.
Bishop of Alexandria (died 326). As bishop of Alexandria from 312, Alexander faced opposition from Meletius of Lycopolis, who disagreed with his lenient attitude towards lapsed Catholics. Further problems arose through the activities of a priest named Kolluth who had assumed the power to ordain deacons and priests and, even more seriously, from another priest called Arius, whose ideas about Christ's divinity and sinless nature diverged from those of the orthodox church and in due course evolved into full heretical form under the title Arianism.

   Alexander's initial approach to Arius was gentle persuasion, but when this did not work, he summoned a synod of Egyptian bishops to condemn and excommunicate him. Arius whipped up support throughout the East and it was not until 325, when Emperor Constantine sided with Alexander at the council of Nicea, that the Arian heresy was officially condemned. Alexander died soon afterwards, naming Athanasius as his successor.
   Variants: **Al**, **Alasdair**, **Alastair**, **Alec**, **Alex**, **Alexis**, **Alistair**, **Lex**, **Sacha**, **Sachy**, **Sandy**, **Xan**, **Xander**, **Zander**.
   Feminine forms: **Alexandra**, **Alexia**, **Sandra**.

Alexandra, **Alexia**, **Alexa**, feminine forms of **Alexander**.

Alexis (m, f)
[uh-LEK-sis] from Greek, meaning 'defender'.
Beggar of Mesopotamia (fifth century). The life of Saint Alexis is largely a matter of legend. Tradition has it that he was the son of a wealthy Roman nobleman who abandoned his bride on their wedding day to go on pilgrimage and ultimately chose a life of poverty in Syria. He willingly shared everything he received with other needy people. A further legend claims that he spent the last years of his life living incognito as a servant in his father's household in Rome.

Sometimes considered as a variant or feminine form of
Alexander.

10

Aleydis (f)
[uh-LAY-dis] from Germanic, meaning 'noble cheer'.
Thirteenth-century Cistercian saint. Born at Shaerbeck, near Belgium, Brussels, she entered the Cistercian convent there at the tender age of seven, staying for the remainder of her life. She was noted for her humility and kindness. At a young age, however, she contracted leprosy and so had to be treated in isolation, with the illness eventually paralysing and blinding her. She received much divine help and assurance including ecstatic visions.

Variants: **Alice**, **Alicia**, **Alison**, **Allison**.

Aloysius (m)
[al-uh-WISH-uhs] Latinised form of *Aloys*.
Italian Jesuit student (1568–91). Born Aloysius Luigi Gonzaga into a noble family of Lombardy, he attended military school before experiencing life at the court of the duke of Mantua. He felt such disgust at the immorality of the court that he refused to accept his inheritance and chose instead a life of prayer and self-denial. He defied the wishes of his family and in 1585 joined the Jesuits, who succeeded in persuading him to give up the more excessive

practices of mortification that he favoured. Though he himself never enjoyed the best of health because of a kidney complaint, he dedicated himself to tending victims of the plague in Rome and in due course died of the disease himself, aged just 23.

Alphonsine feminine form of **Alphonsus**.

Alphonsus (m)

[al-FON-suhs] from the Spanish name *Alfonso*, from the Old German *athal* 'noble' and *funsa* 'ready'.

Alphonsus de Orozco (1500–91), Spanish mystic and spiritual writer. Born in Oropesa, Avila, in Spain, he spent much of his early life in solitude, responding from a command received in a vision of the Virgin Mary to write extensively about prayer and the Christian way of living. His works include his *Confessions*, in which he recounts his own spiritual journey. He became an Augustinian friar at Salamanca in 1522 and dedicated much of his time to prayer. He spent many years of his life preaching to the Spanish nobility in Madrid and hearing their confessions, exercising a strong influence on many prominent figures in public life.

The Italian bishop, theologian and mystic Alphonsus Liguori (1696–1787). Born in Marianella, near Naples, Alphonsus Marie Liguori pursued a highly successful career as a lawyer in Naples before losing a high-profile court case in 1723 and giving up the profession in humiliation. As the result of a vision he defied the wishes of his family and joined the Fathers of the Oratory, being ordained in 1717 and earning a wide reputation as a preacher. In 1732 he founded his own order, called the Congregation of the Most Holy Saviour, popularly known as the Redemptorist Congregation. Appointed Bishop of Sant' Agata dei Goti at the age of 66, he was always a controversial figure within the church establishment and some time before his death was

11

even excluded from the Redemptorist community he had founded. He wrote numerous books and pamphlets, of which the most influential included *Moral Theology* and *Victories of the Martyrs*.

Also the name of the *Spanish Jesuit lay brother Alphonsus Rodriguez (1533–1617)*. Born in Segovia in Spain, Alphonsus Rodriguez had a troubled childhood, having to help his mother run the family wool business after the death of his father when he was 14. He married at the age of 23 but his wife died three years later, shortly followed by his mother and his two children. When his business failed, he attempted to join the Jesuits at Valencia but was refused because of his lack of education. Despite his relatively advanced age, he took up Latin studies and in 1571 was finally admitted by the Jesuits as a lay brother. He spent the next 45 years serving as doorkeeper at the Montesione College on Majorca, earning a wide reputation as a spiritual adviser. Those who profited from his guidance included St Peter Claver, who was inspired by the advice of Alphonsus to take up missionary work.

Variants: **Al**, **Alfonso**, **Alphonse**, **Alphonsus**.
Feminine form: **Alphonsine**.

Alva (m)
[AL-vah] probably from Hebrew, meaning 'exalted'.
Mentioned, in the form *Alvah*, in the Old Testament as a descendant of Esan and clan leader of the Edomites (Genesis 36:40; 1 Chronicles 1:51).

Amanda (f)
[uh-MAN-duh] feminine form of *Amandus*, meaning 'worthy of love'.
Seventh-century French saint. Born into a noble family, he became a monk at the abbey of St Martin near Tours. King Clotaire II requested him to undertake missionary work in

Flanders and Holland. Under his later ministry, many people were converted.

Variant: **Mandy**.

Ambrose (m)
[AM-broze] from Greek, meaning 'immortal'.
German-born bishop (c.339–397). Born in Trier in Germany, Ambrose was the son of the prefect of Gaul and studied law, literature, philosophy and Greek in Rome. His appointment as Bishop of Milan in 374 came as a considerable surprise as Ambrose had not even been baptised, having been sent to Milan simply to maintain peace between rival Catholics and supporters of the Arian heresy. As bishop, however, he gave away his possessions and dedicated himself to the study of Christianity. He soon earned a reputation as a powerful preacher and scholar and also emerged as the leading opponent of Arianism in the West, driving its adherents out of Milan. His writings advanced the cause of Christianity in Western Europe. Notable figures who were deeply influenced by his example included St Augustine who met him in Milan in 386 and was inspired by him to convert to Christianity. He is honoured today as the patron saint of learning and of beekeepers and candlemakers.

Variant: **Emrys**.

Amity (f)
[AM-i-tee] from English *amity*, meaning 'friendship'.
The name stands for the qualities of friendship, kindness and fondness.

Amos (m)
[AY-MOSS] from Hebrew, meaning 'burden-bearer'.
Prophet active about 760 BC. Like his contemporary Hosea, he was unpopular for criticising the kingdom of Israel, predicting its downfall unless the people repented. His

warnings were fulfilled when Israel fell to the Assyrians in 722 BC.

Amy (f)
[AY-mee] from Old French *amée*, 'beloved'. The name has been in use in the English-speaking world for several centuries. Originally it was known in its Latin form *Amatus*, after the thirteenth-century St Amatus, a Dominican nun of Bologna, Italy.
   Variant: **Aimee**.

Ananaias (m)
[an-uh-NY-uhs] from Hebrew, meaning 'the Lord is gracious'.
The name of three individuals in the New Testament. First, the husband of Sapphira who died suddenly because they lied to the church and God (Acts 5:1–11). Also a believer in Damascus who healed Paul's blindness and told him of God's plan to be a missionary (Acts 9:10–19). Third, a high priest before whom Paul was tried (Acts 23:2).

Anastasia (f)
[an-uh-STAY-zhuh] from Greek, meaning 'resurrection'.
Martyr of Sirmium. Little is known of her life beyond the tradition that she was tortured and burnt alive for her faith in Sirmium (Srem Mitrovica in modern Serbia) in 304. Legend adds that earlier in her life she was twice rescued from death by the reformed prostitute St Theodota, who on one occasion piloted Anastasia's ship to safety after she was abandoned at sea.
   Variants: **Stacey**, **Stacy**.

Andrea, **Andreana**, **Andrée** feminine forms of **Andrew**.

Andrew (m)
[AN-drew] from Greek, meaning 'manly, brave'.

14

One of the twelve apostles and the brother of Simon Peter. A fisherman like his brother, he had an important role in introducing people to Jesus (John 1:35–42). With his brother Simon (Peter), he responded to Christ's summons to become 'fishers of people'. Andrew became one of the leaders of the disciples and played a role at the miracle of the feeding of the five thousand and later in Jerusalem.

Also the name of several saints, including: *Andrew of Crete (c.660–740), monk and Bishop of Jerusalem*. Widely respected as a preacher and sacred poet, his poetic output included numerous hymns, some of which are still in use in the Byzantine church today.

Andrew Bobola (1591–1657), Polish Jesuit martyr. Born into an aristocratic Polish family, he joined the Jesuit order at Vilna in 1609 and in due course became head of the house at Bobruysk. He distinguished himself by his service to plague victims and dedicated himself to missionary work.

Andrew Corsini (1301–73), Italian bishop. Born in Florence, he had an unruly youth before reforming and becoming a Carmelite friar in Florence in 1318. He soon earned a reputation as a preacher and healer and in 1360 was chosen as the new bishop of Fiesole. He was much loved for his humility and his generosity towards the poor and lived in conditions of considerable austerity himself. As well as being patron saint of Russia and Scotland, which commemorates Andrew's crucifixion in the X-shaped saltire of the national flag, he is also honoured as patron saint of Greece, of fishermen and of old maids.

Variants: **André**, **Andreas**, **Andy**, **Drew**.

Feminine forms: **Andrea**, **Andreana**, **Andrée**.

Angela (f)
[AN-juh-luh] from Greek, meaning 'angel' or 'messenger'. The name of two saints: *Angela of Foligno (c.1248–1309), Italian visionary*. Born at Foligno in Italy, Angela married a wealthy husband and as a young adult indulged in a life of

luxury and sensuality. In 1285, however, she suddenly repented of her sinful ways and dedicated herself to penance and prayer. After the death of her husband, mother and sons from plague she joined the Franciscan Third Order in 1291. She demonstrated a special sympathy for the poor and the sick and became well known for her visions.

Angela Merici (c.1474–1540), Italian foundress of the Ursuline order. Born at Desenzano in Lombardy and orphaned at an early age, Angela Merici emerged as a leading figure in the Catholic Reformation in northern Italy. Though a laywoman herself, she spent much of her life occupied with the establishment of communities of unmarried women of all classes who desired to live a celibate Christian life. From these communities evolved the Company of St Ursula.

Variants: **Angel**, **Angie**, **Angelica**, **Angelina**, **Angeline**.
Male variant: **Angelo**.

Angelo male variant of **Angela**.

Ann, **Anne** (f)
[an] from the name **Hannah**, from Hebrew meaning 'favour' or 'grace'.
Tradition names Ann as the mother of the Virgin Mary. According to the *Protevangelium of James*, Ann came from Bethlehem. Ann and her husband Joachim were devout and generous to the poor. They failed, however, to conceive any children for some 20 years, prompting them to promise God that if they did have a child they would consecrate the child to him. An angel appeared to Ann to announce that their prayer had been heard. Ann duly conceived and gave birth to Mary. Ann is honoured as the patron saint of Canada, Brittany, housewives, women in labour and cabinetmakers.

Variants: **Anita**, **Annette**, **Annie**, **Annika**, **Nan**, **Nancy**, **Nanette**, **Nina**.

Anna (f)

[AN-uh] from the name *Hannah*, from Hebrew meaning 'favour' or 'grace'.

An elderly widow and prophet from the tribe of Asher. Anna recognised the baby Jesus as the Messiah when he was brought into the temple (Luke 2:36–38).

Variants: **Ania**, **Anya**.

Anne see **Ann**.

Anselm (m)

[AN-selm] from the Old German name *Ansehelm*, from *ans* 'god' and *helm* 'helmet'.

17

Italian bishop (c.1033–1109). Born into a noble family of Piedmont in Italy, he attended monastery school from the age of five. In 1060 Anselm was admitted as a monk to the Benedictine order at Bec Abbey in Normandy, where he established a reputation as a preacher, scholar and teacher. In 1093 he was appointed Archbishop of Canterbury, in which role he proved a vigorous defendant of the English church against secular interference, frequently resisting the wishes of William II and Henry I and even having to go into temporary exile on two occasions because of his outspoken criticism. Anselm was a dedicated opponent of slavery and in 1102 secured a resolution of the ecclesiastical council at Westminster condemning the practice. Among those profoundly influenced by his writings were such notable figures as St Thomas Aquinas.

Variants: **Ansel**, **Ansell**.

Anthony, **Antony** (m)

[AN-tuh-nee] (an English form of the Roman clan name *Antonius*, with the *h* being added because of the incorrect association with Greek *anthos* 'flower').

The name of several saints, including *the Egyptian hermit Antony (251–356)*. Born at Coma near Memphis in Egypt,

Antony had an intense religious experience while listening to the proclamation of the gospel at mass at the age of 20. He responded to this by giving away all his considerable possessions and taking up the life of a hermit in a hut just outside Memphis, dedicating himself to prayer and contemplation and resisting the torments and temptations of daily life. After 15 years there he felt the need for greater solitude and withdrew to an isolated mountain in the Libyan desert, thus becoming one of the founders of the monastic tradition. Aged 55 he founded a loose community of monks who met for worship and teaching.

18

Also *Antony of Padua (c.1196–1231), Portuguese preacher and theologian.* Born in Lisbon, Antony of Padua entered an Augustinian monastery at Coimbra near Lisbon in 1210 and earned a reputation as a scholar and preacher. At the age of 25 he joined the Franciscans with the ambition of serving as a missionary with them. Illness, however, prevented him from performing such work overseas and he had to content himself with preaching in central Italy. He became one of the most celebrated preachers of his day, attracting huge audiences wherever he went. Impressed by Antony's gifts, St Francis appointed him teacher of theology to the Franciscan order (the first person to be given the post). He spent his final years in Padua before his premature death at the age of 36, preaching and promoting reform there.

He is honoured today as the patron saint of Portugal and of lost articles (a reference to the legend that when a young friar stole a valuable manuscript from the saint a terrifying demon menaced the youth, obliging him to return the manuscript to its owner).

Variants: **Antoine**, **Anton**, **Antonio**, **Tony**.
Feminine forms: **Antoinette**, **Antonia**, **Toni**.

Antoinette, **Antonia** feminine forms of **Anthony**.

Antony see **Anthony**.

Apollonia (f)
[a-puh-LO-nee-uh] from Greek, meaning 'of Apollo'.
Martyr of Alexandria (died 249). Tradition has it that Apollonia was an elderly deaconess of Alexandria who was among the Christians put to death by a rioting mob. Her attackers knocked out several of her teeth before moving to burn her alive if she did not renounce her faith. Before they could manhandle her further Apollonia offered a brief prayer and then walked willingly into the fire. She is honoured today as the patron saint of dentists.
   Variants: **Appolina**, **Appoline**.

19

Apollos (m)
[a-POL-uhs] from Greek, meaning 'destroyer'.
A gifted teacher in the church at Corinth, but whose initial enthusiasm at Ephesus needed correction (Acts 18:24–28).

Aquila (m)
[uh-KWIL-uh] from Latin, meaning 'eagle'.
With his wife Priscilla he was a close friend of Paul (Acts 18:1–3), who had an influential teaching ministry and travelled widely for the sake of the gospel.

Archelaus (m)
[are-kee-LAY-uhs] from Greek, meaning 'people's chief'.
Archelaus was the son of Herod the Great who ruled Judea, Idumea and Samaria from 4 BC to 6 AD. He was known for his intense cruelty and tyranny. When Mary and Joseph left Egypt with the infant Jesus, they avoided going to Judea and instead went to Nazareth. (Matthew 2:22).

Ariel (m, f)
[AIR-ee-uhl] from Hebrew, meaning 'lion of God', 'hearth of God' or 'altar of God'.

The name is applied in the Old Testament to two bold Moabites who were killed by David's warrior Benaiah ('two lionlike men', 2 Samuel 23:20, KJV). Also the name of one of the men sent by Ezra to met Iddo (Ezra 8:16).

Arnold (m)
[AR-nuhld] from Old German, meaning 'eagle strength'.
Greek by birth, Arnold served in the court of the Emperor Charlemagne. He was known especially for his great devotion and his kind service to the poor. He died in approximately 800.
  Variant: **Arnaud**.

20

Artemis (m)
[ARE-tuh-mis] a Greek name.
A Greek goddess of the moon and hunting whose Latin name was Diana. She had an imposing temple in Ephesus where her statue was thought to have fallen from heaven (Acts 19:27–35).

Asa (m)
[AY-suh, AY-zuh] from Hebrew, meaning 'doctor'.
King of Judah (c.913–873 BC) who led a religious reformation in his early years, but who later put his faith in human resources rather than God (1 Kings 15:9–24).

Asher (m)
[A-shuh] from Hebrew, meaning 'blessed' or 'happy'.
The eighth son of Jacob (Genesis 30:12–13), born by Zilpah, the maidservant of his wife Leah. Also the name of the tribe descended from Asher that lived in the coastal area northwards from Mount Carmel (Joshua 19:24–31).

Audrey (f)
[AW-dree] Variant of **Etheldreda**.
In olden times a fair was held annually in Ely on 17 October

in honour of this saint. The fair was noted for its quality jewellery and fine silk scarves, which in time came to be known as *St Audrey's laces*. Later, however, the fine scarves were replaced by cheap, gaudy imitations and so the word *tawdry* developed, a shortening and alteration of (Sain)*t Audrey*('s laces), a term that is now applied to anything that is showy but of poor quality.

Variant: **Aud**.

Augustine (m)
[AW-guhs-teen, uh-GUS-tin] from Latin, meaning 'great' or 'venerable'.
The name of two saints: *Augustine of Hippo (354–430), bishop and theologian*. Born in Tagaste (modern Algeria) in North Africa the son of a pagan father, Augustine lived a dissolute youth that he subsequently came to repent of. He founded a school of rhetoric in Milan, Italy in 383 and soon began to feel the need to reform, finally converting to Christianity in 386 while in Milan (partly through the influence of the teachings of St Ambrose). He returned to Africa that same year and was ordained a priest at Hippo in 391. He was raised to the rank of bishop in 396 and for the next four decades gained recognition as the most prominent figure in the north African church. He founded a number of monasteries and also defended the orthodox position against various heresies. His extensive writings, which included *Confessions* and *On the City of God*, had a profound and lasting upon Christian theology. He is honoured as the patron saint of theologians.

Augustine of Canterbury (died c.605), Italian missionary bishop. Augustine served as a monk at the monastery of St Andrew in Rome, becoming prior there, before being selected by Pope Gregory the Great to lead a band of 40 missionaries to Britain in 597. Once in England, Augustine won the support of St Ethelbert, King of Kent, who soon set an example for his subjects by converting to Christianity.

Consecrated as Archbishop of the English, Augustine established his see at Canterbury and founded the monastery of St Peter and St Paul (renamed St Augustine's) there. Over the next seven years he went on to organise two further sees, for the East Saxons and at Rochester. Other significant contributions included his role in advising King Ethelbert in drawing up the earliest extant Anglo-Saxon written laws. Augustine is remembered today as the most important figure in the early evangelisation of Britain.

Variants: **Austen**, **Austin**, **Gus**.

Aurelia (f)
[aw-REEL-yuh] from Latin, meaning 'golden'.
Originally a French princess, Aurelia decided to become a hermit. Accepting the advice of St Wolfgang of Regensburg, she spent over 50 years as a recluse in a Benedictine abbey in Salzburg. She died in 1027.

Balthasar (m)
[BAL-tha-zah] from Phoenician *ba'al*, meaning 'protect the king'.
One of the wise men ('Magi') who followed the leading of the star and came from the East to Jerusalem and then Bethlehem to worship the baby Jesus (Matthew 2:1–12). According to tradition, they were three in number and they were named Balthasar, Casper and Melchior.

Barak (m)
[ba-RAK] from Hebrew, meaning 'lightning'.
An Israelite leader who commanded Israel's tribal mercenaries alongside Deborah against Canaanite forces. God gave Israel a famous victory by means of the weather, but the honour went to Jael, a woman who killed the Canaanite's leader Sisera (Judges 4–5).

The names *Barack* and *Baraka* have origins that are different from *Barak*. *Barack* and *Baraka* are Swahili, coming from an Arabic root meaning 'blessing'. They are found especially in East Africa, before the name of Barack Obama (named after his Kenyan father) came to symbolise diversity within the USA.

Barbara (f)
[BAH-buh-ruh] (from Greek, meaning 'strange').
According to tradition, Barbara was a beautiful young virgin who lived in the third or fourth century. To remove Barbara from the attentions of her many admirers, her father Dioscurus confined her in a tower but was subsequently enraged to discover she had become a Christian. He attempted to kill her for her temerity, but was miraculously prevented from completing the act. After Dioscurus reported Barbara to the authorities she was tortured and formally condemned to death by beheading, Dioscurus volunteering himself as her executioner. As Barbara expired her father was struck by lightning and burnt to ashes. She is honoured as the patron saint of gunners, miners and firefighters.

23

Variants: **Bab**, **Babs**, **Barbie**, **Barbra**, **Bobbie**.

Barnabas (m)
[BAH-nuh-buhs] from Hebrew meaning 'son of encouragement'.
A Jewish-Cypriot leader in the early church who had an important ministry in encouraging others. He contributed generously to the Jerusalem church, but his most important action was in persuading the leaders there to accept Saul of Tarsus as a genuine convert (Acts 9:26–27). After leading the young church at Antioch, he was sent out from there with Paul on the church's first missionary journey (Acts 13:1–3). Initially Barnabas was the leader, but soon graciously gave way to his younger colleague's greater gifts. Though he separated from Paul over whether Barnabas' cousin Mark should accompany them on a

second journey and went his own way to Cyprus, Paul continued to express his admiration for Barnabus (Colossians 4:10; 2 Timothy 4:11). Today he is honoured as the patron saint of Cyprus.

Variants: **Barnaby**, **Barney**.

Bartholomew (m)
[BAH-thol-uh-mew] from Hebrew, meaning 'son of Talmai'. One of the twelve apostles, named in Mark 3:18 and often identified as being the same person as Nathanael, whose meeting with Christ is described at John 1:45–51. No other details are known of his life, but he is credited with advancing the cause of Christianity through the Indian subcontinent. Legend has it that he died a martyr in Armenia. His body is said to have been taken to an island in the Tiber at Rome and his church there became a famous centre of medical expertise (hence the naming of Barts hospital in London). He is honoured as the patron saint of tanners and others who work with skins and leather, such as bookbinders, furriers and cobblers.

Variant: **Bart**.

Bartimaeus (m)
[BAH-ti-may-uhs] from Aramaic *bar*, meaning 'son' and Greek *timaios*, meaning 'honourable'.
A blind beggar from Jericho who received his sight from Jesus as a result of his persistence (Mark 10:46–52).

Baruch (m)
[buh-ROOK] from Hebrew, meaning 'blessed'.
Jeremiah's secretary and companion who wrote down Jeremiah's prophecies and read them to the people (Jeremiah 36).

Basil (m)
[BA-zil] from Greek, meaning 'kingly'.

Cappadocian bishop (c.329–379). Born into a wealthy Christian family of Caesarea (in modern Turkey), Basil was persuaded by his older sister Macrina to give up a promising secular career and join the church. Accordingly, in 356 he founded a monastery on the family estate in Pontus (perhaps the first monastery in Asia Minor) and established a monastic rule there that became a model for the development of early monasticism in the East, which is still the basis of Orthodox monasticism. Together with St Gregory of Nyssa, these saints are sometimes known as the 'Three Cappadocians'.

Because of his profound influence upon the growth of early monasticism and for his undoubted leadership qualities, Basil is identified as one of the Doctors of the Church and is often referred to as Basil the Great. He is honoured as the patron saint of Russia.

25

Variants: **Bas**, **Baz**.
Feminine form: **Basilea**.

Basilea feminine form of **Basil**.

Bathsheba (f)
[bath-SHEE-buh] from Hebrew *bath*, meaning 'daughter' and *sheba*, meaning 'seven(th)' or possibly 'oath'.
A beautiful woman with whom David committed adultery while her husband Uriah was fighting in Israel's army (2 Samuel 11:2–5). David's first child by her died at seven days old, but her second son Solomon became David's successor (1 Kings 1:11–40).

Variant: **Sheba**.

Beatrice (f)
[BEER-tris] from Latin, meaning 'bringer of happiness'.
Beatrice da Silva (1424–90), Portuguese abbess. Born into a noble Portuguese family, Beatrice (or Beatrix) spent her childhood in the royal court and accompanied Queen Isabel

of Portugal to the court in Spain. Briefly imprisoned on false charges, she abandoned the life of the court and joined the Cistercian convent of Santo Domingo de Silos in Toledo. Ultimately she founded the Congregation of the Immaculate Conception of the Blessed Virgin Mary. She is honoured as the patron saint of prisoners.

Variants: **Beat**, **Beatrix**, **Beattie**, **Bee**, **Trix**, **Trixie**.

Beauty (f)
[BEW-ti] from Latin *bellus*.
Physical or spiritual attractiveness that delights the senses. The Bible sees God as the creator of beauty: 'He has made everything beautiful in its time' (Ecclesiastes 3:11, NIV). God himself is also worthy of all admiration and enjoyment as the One who is supremely beautiful.

Bel (f)
[bel] from Akkadian, meaning 'master' or 'lord'.
Name or title of the god of Babylon, Marduk (Isaiah 46:1; Jeremiah 50:2). Also features in the apocryphal book Bel and the Dragon, which is one of the Additions to the Book of Daniel. The name is unrelated to *Bell* or *Belle*.

Benedict (m)
[BEN-uh-dikt] from Latin *benedictus*, meaning 'blessed'.
Name of various saints, including *Benedict of Nursia, (c.480–c.547), Italian patriarch and founder of the Benedictine Rule*, considered the father of western monasticism. Beyond the fact that he was born into a prosperous family in Nursia in Umbria, little is known of the details of Benedict's life. Tradition has it that, revolted by the degeneracy of Rome, he opted initially for the life of a hermit, living in a cave near Subiaco. In due course he was asked to assume the leadership of a community of monks nearby, only for them to attempt to poison him when they failed to live up to his high expectations.

Subsequently he organised the disciples he had attracted into 12 new communities, including the monastery of Monte Cassino (founded c.529). For these communities Benedict formulated the *Regula Monarchorum* or Benedictine Rule, to provide practical and spiritual guidance. This profoundly influential rule placed particular emphasis upon the role of the monastery as a place of sanctuary and education and directed monks to spend most of their time praying, studying, working and living on a communal basis. They were also expected to preach and do charitable work among the local population.

The Benedictine Rule provided the foundation for monastic life throughout the Western world and it is still observed in many monasteries today. He is honoured as the patron saint of Europe and also of cave explorers.

27

Benedict the Black (1526–89), Sicilian lay brother. Born to Black African slaves near Messina in Sicily, he was granted his freedom when he reached the age of 18. As a young man his restraint when insulted because of his colour impressed the leader of a community of Franciscan hermits based near San Fratello and he was invited to join the group. In due course he succeeded to the leadership of the community. In 1578, though still a lay brother and unable to read, Benedict the Black (otherwise called Benedict the African) was persuaded to take charge of the friary and set about returning the community to a stricter observance of the rule of St Francis.

Benedict Biscop (628–689), English abbot. Born Biscop Baducing into a wealthy Northumbrian family, he served as a courtier of King Oswy until 653, when he abandoned the secular life with the intention of becoming a monk. Shortly afterwards, he undertook the first of six pilgrimages to Rome. On his way back from the second of these journeys, he took his vows as a monk and assumed the name Benedict (or Benet). After his third trip to Rome he was appointed abbot of St Augustine's in Canterbury under the

Archbishop of Canterbury St Theodore. Around this time he conceived the idea of founding a monastery of his own and in due course returned to Rome in order to conduct a tour of the greatest monasteries already founded.

Once back in England, with the support of King Egfrith, he founded Wearmouth Abbey (the first Romanesque church in northern England) in 674. After a fifth visit to Rome in 678, in the course of which he gathered together a rich treasury of books and relics, a second monastery followed at Jarrow.

As well as furnishing his monasteries with the books, paintings and relics he had brought back from Rome, he also introduced the Gregorian style of singing and chanting that he had heard abroad, thus having a profound and lasting impact upon religious practice in England throughout succeeding centuries. He is also credited with the first use of glass windows in English churches. He is honoured as the patron saint of painters and musicians.

Variants: **Ben**, **Benedick**, **Benito**, **Bennett**, **Benny**.

Feminine forms: **Benedicta**, **Benita**.

Benedicta, **Benita** feminine forms of **Benedict**.

Benjamin (m)

[BEN-juh-min] from Hebrew, meaning 'son of my right hand'.

Jacob's youngest son, whose mother Rachel died in childbirth. Though initially kept at home when his brothers went to Egypt to find food, he became the means by which Joseph was reconciled to his brothers (Genesis 42:20–45:15). Also the name of the tribe descended from Benjamin, from whom Esther (Esther 2:5) and the apostle Paul (Philippians 3:5) came.

Variants: **Ben**, **Benji**, **Benny**.

Bernadette (f)
[BER-nuh-det] feminine form of *Bernard*.

French visionary (1844–79). Born Marie Bernarde Soubirous in Lourdes, the daughter of a poor miller, she was considered sweet natured but backward as a child. In 1858, at the age of 14, she experienced the first of 18 visions of the Virgin Mary in a cave on the bank of the river Gave. Calling herself Mary of the Immaculate Conception, the vision continued to appear to her over a period of two months, both when she was alone and when she was accompanied by others, although only Bernadette could see her. For years the church authorities declined to take her claims seriously and she was the subject of much scorn. She entered the convent of the Sisters of Charity in Nevers in 1866 and remained there until her death at the age of 35, winning respect for her steadfast refusal to acknowledge her own growing fame. In due course the visions of Bernadette established Lourdes as a major centre of pilgrimage, renowned for miraculous cures.

Bernard (m)
[BER-nuhd] from Germanic, meaning 'brave as a bear'.

Bernard of Clairvaux (1090–1153), French abbot. Born into a noble family of Fontaines de Dijon in Burgundy, he became a monk in 1113, entering the newly founded Benedictine abbey of Cîteaux. Intelligent and charming by nature, he earned a reputation for piety and was noted as a preacher. On the strength of his growing reputation, he was sent with 12 other monks to found a new Cistercian monastery at Clairvaux in Champagne. He went on to oversee the foundation or reformation of 68 more subsidiary houses throughout Western Europe, providing the inspiration for a substantial spiritual revival. His many important writings included works on theology, sermons and letters. He is honoured today as the patron saint of cancer victims and also of Gibraltar.

Variants: **Barnet**, **Bernhard**, **Bernie**, **Berny**.
Feminine form: **Bernadette**.

Bernice (f)

[buhr-NEES] from Greek, meaning 'victorious'.
The oldest of Herod Agrippa I's daughters (born AD 28), she lived with her brother Herod Agrippa II. She was with her brother at the time of Paul's defence of his faith (Acts 25:13).
Variants: **Bernie**, **Berny**.

Bertha (f)

30

[BER-thuh] from Old German, meaning 'bright'.
Frankish princess and Queen of England (died c.603). She married Ethelbert, who was then not yet converted. She brought her bishop-chaplin Liudhard to court. Ethelbert was converted and welcomed St Augustine on his arrival in England in 597.
Variants: **Berta**, **Bertie**.

Bethany (f)

[BETH-uh-nee] from Hebrew, meaning 'house of figs'.
The name of two places in the Gospels. The better known is three km east of Jerusalem where Jesus was based during the last week of his earthly life and where Lazarus, and his sisters Mary and Martha lived (Mark 14:3–9). The other is a place east of the Jordan where John baptised (John 1:28).
Variants: **Beth**, **Bethan**.

Beulah (f)

[BEW-luh] from Hebrew, meaning 'married'.
A place name; symbolic name given to Israel, to refer to its future prosperous state. Instead of being 'Forsaken' and 'Desolate', Israel would be called 'My Delight Is in Her [Hebrew, *Hephzibah*]' and 'Married [Hebrew, *Beulah*]' (Isaiah 62:4).

Blaise (m)
[blayz] probably from Latin *blaesus*, meaning 'lisping'.
Fourth-century Armenian bishop and martyr. Blaise (or **Blase**) is traditionally identified as one of the Fourteen Holy Helpers who enjoyed cult status in certain parts of medieval Europe. Tradition claims that he was a bishop of Sebastea in Armenia, born into a wealthy Christian family, who died a martyr's death during the reign of the Emperor Licinius.

Blane (m)
[blayn] probably from Gaelic *bláán*, meaning 'yellow'.
Scottish bishop (late sixth century). Blane (or Blaan) was born on the island of Bute and studied for the priesthood in Ireland under St Comgall and St Canice before returning to Scotland. He founded a monastery at Dunblane (now the site of Dunblane Cathedral, where a bell alleged to be his is still preserved) and also performed missionary work among the Picts.
   Variant: **Blaine**.

31

Boaz (m)
[BOH-az] from Hebrew, meaning 'strength'.
A wealthy and kind man who married his widowed relative Ruth according to the custom of levirate marriage (Ruth 3–4). Their son Obed was an ancestor of David.

Boniface (m)
[bon-ee-FAS] from Latin, meaning 'doer of good'.
Boniface of Crediton (c.680–754), English missionary and martyr. Born at or near Crediton in Devon, he was baptised Winfrith and was ordained a priest at the age of 30. Pursuing the quiet life of a monk at Exeter and then at Nursling near Southampton for many years, he earned a reputation as a scholar and won respect as a preacher. In 715, however, he decided to undertake missionary work in

Germany, believing this was God's will. Changing his name to Boniface, he received a papal commission from Pope Gregory II to evangelise in Germany and began his mission in Hesse in 718. Such was the success of his work that in 722 he was raised to the rank of bishop and given charge of all the German territories. The Pope also secured for him the protection of Charles Martel, leader of the Franks.

With this support Boniface won vast numbers of converts and effectively established the church in Germany, founding many monasteries as centres of education and evangelisation and staffing them with fellow-missionaries from England. He also did much to revive the church in France. He is honoured as the patron saint of brewers and tailors.

32

Boris (m)
[BO-ris] from Russian, meaning 'fight'.
Both Russian martyrs (died 1015), Boris and his half-brother Gleb were sons of St Vladimir, the first Christian prince of Russia. After their father's death their elder brother Svyatopolk decided to kill Boris and Gleb to forestall any challenge to his claim to the throne. Boris and Gleb met their deaths without attempting to resist, refusing to endanger the lives of their servants or to oppose their own flesh and blood. After their demise they were acclaimed as Christian martyrs and they are still revered in Russia and Ukraine.

Botolph (m)
[BO-tolf] uncertain origin.
Seventh-century saint; formerly chaplain to a convent, about 654 he established a monastery at Icanhoh identified either as Iken (Suffolk) or Boston (Lincolnshire).
   Variants: **Botolf**, **Botulf**.

Brenda see **Brendan**.

Brendan (m)
[BREN-duhn] from Irish *Bréanainn*, from a Gaelic word meaning 'prince'.
Brendan the Voyager (c.486–c.577), Irish abbot. Little definite is known about the life of Brendan beyond the facts that he was born in Kerry, that he was brought up by St Ita at Killeedy and that he founded a monastery at Clonfert in Galway around the year 559. Legend has it that the rule he drew up for use by the monks there was dictated to him by an angel. Other monasteries, such as those at Annadown, Inishdroum and Ardfert, may also have been founded by Brendan.

He is often remembered for the many journeys he made abroad and is said to have visited St Columba in Scotland, where he founded another monastery, to have crossed to Wales, where he served as abbot of a monastery, and to have sailed to Brittany in company with St Malo. He is honoured today as the patron saint of sailors. The feminine form **Brenda** is thought by some to derive from *Brendon*, but *Brenda* is more likely to be a name of an independent origin.

    Variant: **Brandan**.

Brian (m)
[BRY-uhn] perhaps from Irish word for 'hill'.
Blessed Brian Lacey (died 1591). Born in Yorkshire and cousin and assistant of the Venerable Montford Scott, he was betrayed by his brother Richard for being a Catholic.

    Variant: **Bryan**.

Bridget (f)
[BRIJ-it] from the Irish name *Brighid*, meaning 'exalted one'.

The name of two saints: *St Bridget Swedish foundress (1303–73).* Born in the province of Upland, Sweden, Bridget (or Birgitta) lived as a married woman for 28 years and bore eight children to her wealthy land-owning husband Ulf Godmarsson before his death in 1344. During this time she rose to the rank of principal lady-in-waiting to Queen Blanche of Sweden and in this post did her best to persuade the royal family to give up their immoral way of life. After her husband's death, in defiance of the turbulence and decadence of the contemporary religious establishment, she founded a monastery for men and women at Vadstena, with herself as abbess, and from this institution evolved the Order of the Holy Saviour (popularly known as the Bridgettines). She became well known not only for her zeal as abbess but also for her prophetic visions, through which she offered guidance to popes and crowned heads. Today she is honoured as the patron saint of Sweden.

Also, the *Irish abbess Brigid (c.450–523).* Born the daughter of a slave woman and a Celtic chieftain in the vicinity of Dundalk, Brigid (or Bride) was granted her freedom and determined at an early age to pursue a life in the church. In due course she was accepted as a nun by St Mel, Bishop of Armagh, but defied the usual convention of living at home with her family by imitating the example of St Patrick (by whom she may have been baptised) and founding the first convents for nuns in Ireland. The first of her houses (for both men and women) was established at Kildare in 471 and, with Brigid as its first abbess, this soon became an important religious and academic centre. It also became famous for fine religious ornaments and manuscripts. Many other convents followed throughout Ireland. Brigid herself was celebrated both for her leadership skills and for her generosity towards the needy. Today she is honoured as the patron saint of Irish women, poets, blacksmiths and healers.

Variants: **Biddy**, **Birgitta**, **Bride**, **Bridie**, **Brigid**, **Brigitta**.

Bruno (m)

[BREW-noh] from Germanic 'brown'.

German founder (c.1033–1101). Born into a noble family of Cologne, he studied at the cathedral school in Rheims before being ordained a priest and taking up a post teaching theology in Rheims around 1056. He remained in this post for 20 years but then incurred the disfavour of his arch-bishop, whom he accused of simony. Discharged from his office, Bruno and six companions retreated to the mountains near Grenoble and at a location called the Grande Chartreuse erected a modest church that in due course became the first home of the so-called Carthusian monks. From these humble beginnings grew the entire Carthusian order, which placed emphasis upon solitude, fasting, worship, hard work and repentance.

35

Bryce (m)

[brys] of uncertain origin.

French bishop (died 444), who was born in Touraine and studied for the church under St Martin of Tours at the monastery of Marmoutier, he eventually succeeded Martin as bishop of Tours in 397. He appears to have had an unruly nature, having to apologise to Martin for rash words on at least two occasions and as bishop being obliged to vacate his see around 430 and go into exile for some seven years after he was accused of various omissions and misdeeds. After going to Rome and gaining vindication from the Pope he returned to his post a reformed man and dedicated himself to his work, founding several new religious establishments.

   Variant: **Brice**.

Caedmon (m)

[KAD-muhn] meaning unknown.

English poet (died c.680). According to Bede, Caedmon was a cowherd who lived near the great abbey at Whitby. During a dream one night he was miraculously endowed with a divine poetic gift and was inspired to compose a song in praise of God's creation. This he subsequently performed in front of St Hilda and the monks of the abbey. Suitably impressed, they invited Caedmon to take up religious study and to join them as a monk. He went on to compose various songs based upon the Scriptures and in so doing established a lasting reputation as the first great English poet and the father of English sacred poetry.

Caesar (m)

[SEE-zuh] possibly from Latin *caesaries*, meaning 'hair'.
The title of the Roman emperors from Augustus to Nero. Those mentioned in the New Testament are Augustus (27 BC–AD 14; Luke 2:1), Tiberius (AD 14–37; Luke 3:1), and Claudius (AD 41–54; Acts 11:28), though Nero (AD 54–68) and his persecution of Christians also cast his shadow over the early church.

Cain (m)

[kayn] from Hebrew, meaning 'acquired'.
Adam and Eve's eldest son who murdered his brother Abel. He became a wanderer, but God placed a mark on him for his protection (Genesis 4).

Caleb (m)

[KAY-leb] from Hebrew, meaning 'dog'.
One of the twelve Israelite leaders sent by Moses to explore the Promised Land. Only Caleb and Joshua actually entered the Promised Land because of their wholehearted faith (Numbers 13–14).

Callista (f)

[kuh-LIS-tuh] from Greek *kallistos*, meaning 'beautiful'.
Name derives from the names of the three popes named Callistus (also known as Callixtus) especially Callistus I

(died c.222). Originally a slave, but his master put him charge of a bank, which soon failed. He then fled from Rome, but was captured and sentenced to forced labour of the treadmill. He was eventually freed but when found brawling in a synagogue he was sentenced to work in the mines of Sardinia. He was later released to be made manager of a Christian cemetery. He served well in that capacity and became a deacon. 18 years later he was chosen to be pope and had a short but controversial period of office, especially in that he was considered by some to be too lenient in his treatment of sinners.

Camillus (m)   37
[kuh-MIL-uhs] from Latin, of unknown origin.
Italian priest (1550–1614). Born at Bocchianico in the Abruzzi, he converted to Christianity and became a Capuchin novice only after fighting as a soldier of fortune against the Turks and after overcoming an addiction to gambling. A diseased leg resulting from his military experiences prevented him being admitted to the order so he dedicated himself instead to tending the incurably sick at a hospital in Rome. With the support of St Philip Neri, he became a priest in 1584 and founded the Ministers of the Sick to organise staff at eight hospitals throughout Italy. Today he is honoured as the patron saint of nurses and the sick.

Variant: **Camille**.
Feminine form: **Camilla**.

Candace (f)
[KAN-dis] meaning unknown.
A title of various queens of Ethiopia, one of whom is mentioned in the Bible (Acts 8:27).

Variants: **Candice**, **Candida**, **Candy**.

Carleen, **Carlene** feminine forms of **Charles**.

Carmel (f)
[KAH-muhl] ultimately from Hebrew, meaning 'garden'.
Title of the Blessed Virgin Mary: Our Lady of Mount Carmel. The name of a mountain range stretching south-east from the Mediterranean near Acre, and of its chief peak at the north-west end where Elijah defeated the prophets of Baal (1 Kings 18). The order of Mendicant Friars known as the Carmelites dates from the twelfth century.
Variants: **Carmelita**, **Carmen**.

Carole, **Caroline** feminine forms of **Charles**.

38

Casper (m)
[KAS-puh] from Dutch *Jasper*, perhaps ultimately from Persian, meaning 'treasurer'.
One of the wise men ('Magi') who followed the leading of the star and came from the East to Jerusalem and then Bethlehem to worship the baby Jesus (Matthew 2:1–12). According to tradition, they were three in number and they were named Balthasar, Casper and Melchior.
Variants: **Caspar**, **Jasper**.

Catherine, **Katherine** (f)
[KATH-rin] from Greek *Aikaterina*, of unknown origin.
The name could be linked with the Greek word *aikia*, meaning 'torture' because of its association with Catherine of Alexandria (c.290–c.310), martyr of Alexandria. Legend has it that Catherine of Alexandria was born into a noble family of the city and converted to Christianity at the age of 18. Shortly afterwards she found that neither her high rank nor her beauty protected her when she publicly criticised the worship of pagan idols in front of the Emperor Maxentius. She managed to confound the arguments of 50 philosophers expressed against her on the orders of the emperor to point out the flaws in her Christian faith, upon which all 50 were burnt alive. Still refusing to recant her

Christian belief and turning down an offer of marriage to the emperor on the grounds that she was already 'the bride of Christ', Catherine was thrown into prison, where she was given new strength by visions of Christ in her cell. When she was tortured upon a spiked wheel (from which the circular firework known as a *catherine wheel* takes its name) the wheel miraculously burst apart and several of her torturers were killed by the splinters.

Catherine's courage inspired the conversion of 200 soldiers, who were promptly put to death for their temerity, before she herself was finally beheaded. Angels are said to have carried her body off to Mount Sinai, where a great monastery was subsequently named after her.

Today she is honoured as the patron saint of philosophers, preachers, potters, spinners, hospitals, librarians and young girls. Also the name of other saints, including *Catherine of Bologna (1413–63), Italian abbess; Catherine of Genoa (1447–1510), Italian mystic; Catherine of Siena (1347–80), Italian mystic; Catherine of Sweden (1331–81), Swedish abbess; Catherine dei Ricci (1522–90), Italian mystic; Catherine Labouré (1806–76), French visionary.*

Variants: **Caitlin**, **Cath**, **Catharine**, **Cathy**, **Catriona**, **Kaitlyn**, **Kate**, **Katelyn**, **Katharine**, **Kathleen**, **Katie**, **Katy**, **Kay**, **Kit**, **Kitty**.

Cecil male form of **Cecilia**.

Cecilia (f)
[suh-SEE-lee-uh] feminine of Latin name *Caecilius*, from Latin *caecus*, meaning 'blind'.
Roman virgin martyr (dates unknown). The life of Cecilia (otherwise known as *Cecelia* or *Celia*) is a matter of legend. A devout Christian, she is said to have been forced to marry a non-Christian husband named Valerian. Telling him that she had a guardian angel and that he would be able to see

the angel as well if he agreed to be baptised by Pope Urban I, she managed to persuade Valerian to convert and become as committed to her faith as she was herself. Valerian's brother Tiburtius followed their example and also converted. A further legend claims that the two brothers were beheaded after trying to bury the bodies of Christian martyrs and that Cecilia herself was condemned to death for refusing to worship the gods. An attempt to suffocate her failed and when the executioner tried to behead her he missed his aim and she lingered for another three days, during which time she made arrangements to leave all her property to the church. She is honoured as the patron saint of music, musicians and poetry.

Variants: **Celia**, **Cicely**, **Cissy**.

Male form: **Cecil**.

Celestine (f)

[SEL-es-teen] ultimately from Latin *caelestis*, meaning 'heavenly'.

Celestine I (died 432), Italian Pope. Born in Campania, he succeeded Boniface I as Pope in 422 and devoted most of his energy towards combatting heresies. He is said to have sent St Germanus of Auxerre to oppose Pelagianism in England and to have sent St Patrick as a missionary to Ireland (431).

Also Celestine V (c.1214–96), Italian Pope. Born into a peasant family of Abruzzi, Celestine V was previously known as Peter of Morrone and lived for many years as the head of a community of hermits on Monte Morrone. In 1294, when he was 80 years old, he became the surprise compromise choice for pope after the cardinals failed to agree on any other candidate. Peter of Morrone obediently took office as Celestine V but, despite his personal sanctity, proved unsuited to the position. He fell easy prey to the political machinations of King Charles II of Naples and after just five months despairingly resigned the papal office (becoming the only pope to leave the post voluntarily), to be replaced by Boniface VIII.

Variant: **Celeste**.

Chad (m)

[chad] from Old English name *Ceadda*, possibly from Celtic *cad*, meaning 'battle'.

English bishop (died 672). Chad (or Ceadda) was born in Northumbria and was educated under St Aidan on Lindisfarne alongside his brother St Cedd. He succeeded Cedd as Abbot of Lastingham in Yorkshire before being appointed Bishop of York by King Oswiu of Northumberland's son Alcfrith. He was subsequently removed from the post by Theodore of Canterbury in favour of the rival claim of St Wilfrid, who had been appointed to the same post by Oswiu himself. Chad's dutiful acceptance of the demotion impressed Theodore sufficiently to persuade him to reinstate him some time afterwards, this time as first bishop of Mercia, based at Lichfield. During the remaining three years of his life, Chad continued to be true to his reputation for piety and humility and also founded a monastery in Lincolnshire.

41

Chantal (f)

[shahn-TAL] from Old Provençal *cantal*, meaning 'stone' and associated with French *chant*, meaning 'song'.

Name given to honour *St Jane Frances de Chantal*.

Variant: **Chantelle**.

Charity (f)

[CHA-ri-tee] ultimately from Latin *carus*, meaning 'dear'.

The name stands for the Christian quality of love, alongside Faith and Hope (1 Corinthians 13:13).

Variants: **Charis**, **Charissa**, **Cherie**, **Cherry**, **Cheryl**.

Charlene feminine form of **Charles**.

Charles (m)

[chahlz] from a Germanic word, meaning 'man'.

Name of several saints: *Charles of Sezze (1613–70), Italian mystic.* Born John Charles Marchioni into a humble family in Sezze, Italy, he learnt a love of God from his grandmother but was prevented from entering the priesthood because of his lack of education. He chose instead the role of a Franciscan lay brother at Naziano, subsequently serving in various menial roles at monasteries near Rome. He became well known for his many mystical experiences, which he described in an autobiography, as well as for his simple holiness and was also respected for his wisdom, being consulted on spiritual matters by three popes.

Charles Borromeo (1538–84), Italian archbishop. Born into a wealthy family near Lake Maggiore, he was the nephew of Pope Pius IV and at the age of 22 was raised to the rank of cardinal and appointed administrator for the ruinous see of Milan before he had even been ordained a priest. Further senior posts quickly followed as the Pope's favourite consolidated his reputation as a talented and tireless reformer. He played a prominent role in the final session of the reforming Council of Trent (1562), was made Bishop of Milan (1563) and became archbishop the following year.

Charles de Foucauld (1858–1916), French hermit. The Viscount Charles de Foucauld was born into a wealthy family and lived a dissolute youth as a soldier before turning to the church. He rejoined the church formally in 1886 and spent the next 10 years in Trappist houses. In 1897 he entered into the life of a hermit at Nazareth. He was ordained in 1901 and later resumed his hermit existence in the Algerian desert where he aimed to evangelise the desert tribes. Based at Tamanrasset in Algeria from 1905, he became well known in the region under the nickname 'Little Brother Charles of Jesus'.

Charles Lwanga and Companions (died 1885–86). Martyrs of Uganda. The mentally unstable King Mwanga of Buganda launched a campaign of persecution against Christians in his country after Joseph Mkasa Bali-kuddembe, master of the royal pages and a Catholic, criticised the young king for his dissolute behaviour and specifically for the murder of the Anglican missionary bishop James Hannington in 1885. Balikuddembe was beheaded on the orders of the enraged king and replaced by Charles Lwanga, who was also a Christian. Some months later, when one of the pages refused the king's sexual advances, Mwanga had Lwanga and all the other Christians among the royal pages arrested and con-demned all 32 of them to death. They were duly burnt alive at Namugongo, wrapped in burning reed mats. Despite their youth, the victims of the massacre met their deaths with cheerfulness and with their faith in God intact.

Variants: **Carl**, **Carlo**, **Carlos**, **Carol**, **Charley**, **Charlie**, **Chas**, **Chuck**, **Karl**.

Feminine forms: **Carleen**, **Carlene**, **Carol**, **Carole**, **Caroline**, **Charlene**, **Charlotte**.

Charlotte feminine form of **Charles**.

Chloe (f)
[KLOH-ee] from Greek, meaning 'green shoot'.
Chloe is mentioned in 1 Corinthians 1:11: members of her household (family or people) told Paul about what the church at Corinth was like.

Christian (m, f)
[KRIS-chuhn] from Latin *Christianus*.
First used as a nickname in the mainly Gentile church at Antioch in Syria, with the sense of 'one who belongs to

Christ' (Acts 11:26). It occurs only three times in the New Testament: Acts 11:26; 26:28; 1 Peter 4:16.

Variant: **Chris**.

Feminine forms: **Christiana**, **Christie**, **Christina**, **Kirsty**, **Tina**.

Christiana, **Christie**, **Christina** feminine forms of **Christian**.

Christine (f)

[KRIS-teen] from Old English *Cristen*, meaning 'Christian'. A martyr of the early church, probably in the fourth century. She was born in Bofena, Italy. At the age of puberty she rejected the advances of local nobles. Her pagan father then locked her with servants in a tower, putting in her cell valuable pagan idols, which Christine smashed to pieces after receiving an angelic vision: she then gave the valuable pieces to the poor. When her father discovered what happened, he handed her over to a judge who tortured her, trying to make her renounce her faith: she, however, remained firm even under even more severe forms of torture.

Variants: **Chris**, **Chrissie**, **Chrissy**, **Christian**, **Christina**, **Kirsten**, **Kirsty**, **Kristen**, **Kristina**, **Tina**.

Christopher (m)

[KRIS-tuh-fuh] from Greek *Christophoros*, meaning 'carrying Christ'.

Martyr of Lycia (third century). Nothing is known of the life of St Christopher beyond the belief that he died a martyr's death in Lycia (in modern Turkey) during the reign of the Emperor Decius around the middle of the third century. He was sentenced to be burnt to death but when this failed he was shot with arrows and beheaded.

The substance of the modern legend of Christopher was invented in the medieval period. According to this tradition, he was a great giant who vowed to serve the most powerful king on earth. He swore loyalty initially to a Christian ruler, but subsequently abandoned him to serve the Devil. When the Devil revealed his terror of Christ, Christopher determined to serve the latter instead. He was told by a hermit that Christ might be found on the other side of a particular river. When Christopher reached the river he agreed to carry across a child, only to find that the child – which became heavier and heavier – was Christ (proved when the child made Christopher's staff sprout fruit and flowers). Subsequently he obeyed Christ's command to defend the Christians in Lycia at a time of harsh persecution.

He converted all those who sought to capture him but was eventually put to death for refusing to sacrifice to the gods. Today he is honoured as the patron saint of travellers and motorists, who sometimes carry a medallion bearing his image as a good-luck charm.

45

Variants: **Chris**, **Christie**, **Crystal**, **Kit**.

Clare (f)

[clair] from Latin *clarus*, meaning 'clear' or 'bright'.

From the name of two saints: *Clare of Assisi (1193–1253), Italian founder of the Franciscan Poor Clares.* Born into a noble family in Assisi, she was profoundly influenced when she was 18 by hearing St Francis of Assisi preach in 1212 and resolved to imitate his life of poverty and simple faith. In defiance of her family's wishes, she ran away from home and, with the blessing of St Francis, joined a Benedictine convent, where ultimately she was joined by her mother and sister. At the invitation of St Francis, she founded a community of women who wished to live like Franciscan friars, calling them the Poor Clares and insisting upon the observance of absolute poverty. Members of the Poor Clares were expected to keep to the most rigorous of lifestyles, giving up their possessions, never eating meat, sleeping on the floor and rarely speaking.

Today she is honoured as the patron saint of the blind and also of television (a consequence of the legend that she witnessed a Christmas service by means of a vision when illness prevented her attending in person).

Also *Clare of Montefalco (died 1308), Italian nun.* Born at Montefalco in Italy, Clare of Montefalco (or Clare of the Cross) became a member of a community of Franciscan hermits who observed the rule of St Augustine. She was appointed abbess of the convent in 1291 and became widely known not only for her austere lifestyle but also as miracle worker.

Variants: **Claire**, **Clara**, **Clare**, **Claribel**, **Clarice**, **Clarinda**.
Masculine forms: **Clarence**, **Sinclair**.

46

Clarence masculine form of **Clare**.

Claude (m, f)
[clawd] from a Roman name, from Latin *claudus*, meaning 'lame' or 'crippled'.
Claude La Colombière (1641–82), French Jesuit. Born in Saint-Symphorizen d'Orzen near Lyons, he became a member of the Jesuit Order at Avignon in 1659 and established a widespread reputation as a preacher, noted both for his articulacy and for his intelligence. He became head of the Paray-le-Monial College in 1675 and a leading supporter of St Margaret Mary Alocoque, but a year later was appointed chaplain to Mary of Modena, Duchess of York, in London and became a prominent figure among English Catholics.

In the Bible, *Claudia* (f) was a Christian woman in Rome, among those who sent greetings to Timothy via Paul (2 Timothy 4:21). *Claudius* (m) was the Roman emperor from AD 41 to 54 and he is mentioned in Acts 11:28;18:2.

Variant: **Claud**.
Feminine forms: **Claudette**, **Claudia**.

Claudette, **Claudia** feminine forms of **Claude**.

Clement (m)

[KLE-muhnt] from Latin *clemens*, meaning 'mild'.

The name of several saints, including: *Clement I (died c.100), Roman Pope*. Little is known of the life of Clement I (or Clement of Rome) beyond the fact that he was the fourth bishop of Rome and ranks alongside the apostles as one of the fathers of the early church. He was the probable author of an important letter discussing unrest in the church of Corinth and may be the colleague mentioned by the apostle Paul in Philippians 4:3. Legend has it that he was lashed to an anchor and drowned on the orders of the Roman Emperor Trajan.

Also *Clement of Alexandria (c.150–c.215), Greek theologian and Father of the Church*. Probably born in Athens, he converted to Christianity and studied under Pantaenus in Alexandria, eventually succeeding Pantaenus as head of the celebrated school there around 190. He was forced to flee Alexandria during the persecutions of 202 under the Emperor Severus and moved to Caesarea in Cappadocia, where he was reunited with his old friend and pupil Bishop Alexander. He is honoured as the patron saint of lighthouses.

Variant: **Clem**.

Feminine form: **Clementine**.

Clementine feminine form of **Clement**.

Cleopas (m)

[KLEE-uh-puhs] shortened form of Greek *Cleopatros*, meaning 'fame of the father'.

One of two disciples to whom Jesus appeared on the road to Emmaus on the evening of the first Easter day (Luke 24:13–32). The two friends were discussing Jesus' crucifixion and death but they did not recognise that it was

47

Jesus who was walking with them until he broke bread with them in their house.

Clotilda (f)

[kluh-TIL-duh] from a Germanic name derived from *hloda*, meaning 'famous' and *hildi*, meaning 'battle'.

A Burgundian princess, Clotilde (or Clotilda) (c.474–545) was born in Lyons and in due course became the wife of Clovis, king of the Franks, in 491. The two appear to have enjoyed a strong and possibly loving marriage, the pagan Clovis respecting Clotilde's Catholic faith and, in the face of her powerful arguments, even conceding to her demands that their infant sons be baptised as Christians. Clovis himself resisted his wife's encouragement to become a Christian himself until 496 when the threat of defeat in battle persuaded him to turn to the Christian God for aid. Upon his subsequent victory he agreed to be baptised at Reims and gave his tacit approval to the evangelisation of the Frankish kingdom. This in turn led ultimately to the creation of the first Christian states in northern Europe. Clotilda is honoured today as the patron saint of adopted children, brides, exiles, queens, bereaved or abused parents and the parents of large families.

Colette (f)

[ko-LET] feminine of *Nicholas*, ultimately from the Greek name *Nikolaos*, meaning 'victory of the people'.

French nun (1381–1447). Born Nicolette Boylet, Colette was the daughter of a carpenter of Calcye in Picardy and joined the Franciscan order on the death of her parents, when she was aged 17. She spent some eight years living as a hermit at Corbie Abbey in Picardy before claiming to have had a vision of St Francis, who commanded her to set about restoring the order of the Poor Clares to their original austerity. Colette accordingly emerged from her seclusion and set about her mission of reform. She set about renewing the community of the Poor Clares at Besançon in 1410 and over the next 30 years or so continued her work at 17 convents throughout Europe. She never flagged in her mission, praying daily for the conversion of sinners and securing many converts to her cause.

Columba (m)
[kuh-LUM-buh] from Latin, meaning 'dove'.
Columba of Iona (c.521–597), Irish abbot and missionary. Columba (or Colmcille) was born in Donegal the descendant of two royal Celtic houses and was intended for the church from an early age. In due course he became a monk and spent some 15 years preaching and founding monasteries, including those at Derry and Durrow. He eventually fell out with Finnian over the issue of a transcript he had made of Finnian's copy of St Jerome's Psalter, which Finnian (with the support of King Diarmaid) claimed was rightfully his. Relations with Diarmaid worsened some time later when some of the king's men killed a man seeking sanctuary with Columba.

Columba led members of his clan in a campaign against the king and won a bloody battle at Cooldrevne in which some 3000 warriors died. Through this victory Columba won back his Psalter, but perhaps it was his sense of guilt over the many deaths he had precipitated that persuaded him to go into self-imposed exile from his beloved homeland. Accordingly he and a small band of his relatives sailed to the island of Iona off the Scottish coast in 565. There he founded the famous monastery from which he launched various missionary expeditions into Pictish Scotland and northern England.

The community at Iona became Columba's most enduring legacy, attracting students from all over Europe and becoming an important centre of religious learning and writing. Its founder never overcame his sense of loss at leaving Ireland, however, and his writings included poetry

49

expressing his homesickness. Considered the central figure in Celtic Christianity, Columba is honoured today as the patron saint of Ireland, as well as of bookbinders and poets. See also **Malcolm.**

Feminine forms: **Columbina**, **Columbine**.

Columbina, **Columbine** feminine forms of **Columba**.

Connie feminine form of **Constantine**.

Conrad (m)
[KON-rad] from Germanic *kuon*, meaning 'bold' and *rad*, meaning 'counsel'.
Conrad of Parzham (1818–94), Capuchin lay brother. Born into a peasant family of Parzham in Bavaria, he dedicated himself to a life of Franciscan simplicity as a Capuchin lay brother after the death of his parents in 1849. He took vows in 1852 and subsequently, as porter of the friary at the shrine of Mary at Alltotting, dedicated himself to the care of pilgrims there. Over the years he became widely known for his patient and charitable ways and also earned a reputation for prophecy.

Variants: **Curt**, **Kurt**.

Constance feminine form of **Constantine**.

Constantine (m)
[KON-stuhn-teen] from Latin *constans*, meaning 'steadfast'.
From the name of Constantine the Great (c.285–337), the first Christian emperor of Rome and founder of Constantinople. He presided over the church's first general council at Nicaea in 325. He moved his capital to Byzantium on the Bosporus in 330, renaming it Constantinople (now Istanbul). He was baptised on his deathbed.

Feminine forms: **Connie**, **Constance**.

Consuela (f)
[kon-SWE-luh] from Spanish, meaning 'consolation'.
The name comes from one of the titles of the Blessed Virgin Mary: 'Our Lady of Consolation'.

Cormac (m)
[KAW-mak] from Gaelic, meaning 'charioteer'.
Irish abbot and bishop. He was also the king of Munster and a scholar: he is known for his famous Cashel Psalter. He died in battle in 908.

Cornelia feminine form of **Cornelius**.

51

Cornelius (m)
[kuh-NEE-lee-uhs] probably from Latin *cornu*, meaning 'horn'.
A Roman centurion who became Peter's first Gentile convert and on whom the Holy Spirit came as happened at Pentecost. The whole experience confirmed that the gospel was equally for Gentiles as well as for Jews (Acts 10–11).

Also the name of the *Roman Pope (died 253)*. Nothing is known of the details of Cornelius' early life before he succeeded Fabian as Pope in 251. He faced many challenges as head of a deeply divided church, of which perhaps the most important was the issue of the re-admittance to the church of the lapsed faithful. Cornelius, in opposition to his rival Novatian, favoured forgiveness of apostates and repentant sinners, providing they performed suitable penance. He is honoured as the patron saint of cattle and domestic livestock.

Feminine form: **Cornelia**.

Crispin (m)
[KRIS-pin] from Latin *crispus*, meaning 'curly-headed'.
One of two Roman martyrs (died c.285). According to legend, Crispin and Crispinian were two Roman brothers of

noble birth who brought the gospel to the region of Soissons in France, where they earned their living as shoemakers. Ultimately they were tortured and martyred for their faith. A local English tradition claims that they survived and subsequently settled in Faversham in Kent, which was formerly a site of pilgrimage on their account. Their names are most familiar to modern readers from their mention in the celebrated 'St Crispin's Day' speech before the battle of Agincourt in William Shakespeare's *Henry V*. Today they are honoured as the patron saints of shoemakers and leather workers.

52

Crispus (m)

[KRIS-puhs] from Latin, meaning 'curly-headed'.

In the New Testament, the leader of the synagogue at Corinth (Acts 18:8) who became a Christian and was baptised together with all his household. He was one of the few converts to be baptised by Paul himself (1 Corinthians 1:14).

Cuthbert (m)

[KUTH-buht] from Old English *cuth*, meaning 'famous' and *beorht*, meaning 'bright'.

English bishop (c.634–687). Cuthbert was born in Northumbria and brought up by a foster-mother after the death of his parents. He spent his youth as a shepherd and soldier before wearying of warfare and, after a vision, entering Melrose Abbey at the age of 15 and becoming a monk. Shortly afterwards he narrowly survived a plague that claimed many lives and prompted many Christians to revert to paganism. In response to this, he embarked on a lifetime of missionary work throughout northern England, tirelessly calling on the faithful to maintain their faith and taking the gospel as far as the Picts of northern Scotland.

He eventually became prior at Melrose but from 664 was based at Lindisfarne, acquired a gathering reputation as a worker of miracles and becoming known as the 'Wonder Worker of Britain', being credited with miraculous powers of prophecy and healing. In 676, however, he withdrew from the world and spent the next 10 years living as a hermit in a cell on the isolated Farne islands. In 684 he reluctantly gave up the solitary life when he was elected bishop of Hexham but almost immediately arranged to exchange this position for the see of Lindisfarne. Widely revered for his dedication, compassion and generosity towards his flock, he died on the Farne islands two years later. Today he is honoured as the patron saint of sailors.

Cyprian (m)
[SIP-ree-uhn] from Latin *Cyprianus*, meaning 'of Cyprus'.
Bishop of Carthage (c.200–258). Born Thasius Cecilianus Cyprianus into a wealthy family of Carthage, he became a leading lawyer before converting to Christianity around 246, when he was in his forties. He gave away his wealth, took a vow of chastity and around 248 was elected Bishop of Carthage, though he was obliged to spend much of the rest of his life in hiding. Acknowledged as one of the early Fathers of the Church, he wrote extensively on the Scriptures and the church of his day. He is believed to have died a martyr's death, being beheaded during the persecution instituted by Emperor Valerian after he refused to make sacrifice to the gods. He is honoured today as the patron saint of Algeria and North Africa.

Also *Cyprian and Justina, two martyrs of Antioch (c.300).* According to legend, Cyprian was a sorcerer of Antioch who attempted to win the love of the Christian maiden Justina through his magic. Depressed at his lack of success in this enterprise, Cyprian found himself attracted to the faith that his beloved professed and in due course was baptised himself and became a bishop, while Justina became an abbess. They were both martyred at Nicodemia.

Cyril (m)

[SI-ril] from Greek *kyrios*, meaning 'lord'.

Cyril of Alexandria (c.376–444), Archbishop of Alexandria. Born in Alexandria in Egypt, he supported his uncle Theophilus of Alexandria in deposing St John Chrysostom and ultimately succeeded him as Archbishop of Alexandria in 412. Over the next 32 years he did much to defend the church there against the heresy of Nestorianism but also acquired a controversial reputation for stubbornness and volatility in his defence of the orthodox approach, closing churches that were disloyal to him and driving the Jews out of Alexandria. The mob lynching of the respected Neoplatonist philosopher Hypatia was a particular cause of resentment towards his rule. In 431 he presided over the Council of Ephesus, which formally condemned Nestorianism, and following this victory he showed a little more tolerance towards those who disagreed with his orthodox stance. His status as a Doctor of the Church reflects his undoubted importance as a theologian and scholar.

Also *Cyril of Jerusalem (c.315–c.386), Bishop of Jerusalem.* Born in or near Jerusalem, he became a priest around 346 and ultimately bishop of the city. A gentle man by nature, he faced sustained opposition from the supporters of the Arian heresy almost throughout his bishopric. He was forced into exile three times by the advocates of Arianism and in all spent some 16 of his 37 years as bishop absent from his see. In 381 he took part in the Council of Constantinople, which finally brought an end to the Arian heresy and ensured that the final years of his bishopric were relatively peaceful.

Also *Cyril and Methodius, two Slav missionaries (828–809 and c.815–884).* Cyril (born Constantine) and Methodius were two brothers born in Salonika who were ordained as priests in Thessalonica and later moved to Constantinople. Around 863 they were sent to Moravia to spread the gospel. Being speakers of the Slavic language they enjoyed great success but also incurred the enmity of rival German missionaries. Cyril died while the brothers were on a visit to Rome in 869. Methodius, meanwhile, was consecrated bishop by the pope, but on his return to Moravia was imprisoned at the will of hostile German bishops. He was released two years later and continued his missionary work until 879, when he was obliged to go to Rome to respond to the criticisms of his enemies. He was confirmed in the post of archbishop of Sirmium (Pannonia) and Moravia and on his return introduced the celebration of the liturgy in the Slavonic language.

Known as the 'apostles of the Slavs', the two brothers are remembered chiefly for compiling an early version of what became the Cyrillic alphabet and using it to translate the Bible, so establishing their claim to be the fathers of Slavonic literature. Today they are honoured, alongside St Benedict, as the patron saints of Europe.

55

Cyrus (m)
[SY-ruhs] from Persian *Kurush*, meaning 'sun' or 'throne'.
King Cyrus the Great, a Persian emperor (549–530 BC) who is best known in the Bible for conquering Babylon and allowing the Jewish exiles to return home (Ezra 1:1–4). This latter policy is confirmed by the 'Cyrus cylinder', which shows that it was applied to many subject peoples.

Damaris (f)
[DAM-uh-ris] probably from Greek, meaning 'calf'.
The name of a woman in Athens converted under the ministry of the apostle Paul (Acts 17:34). Since she is mentioned specifically, she may have been a woman of prominence.

Damian (m)
[DAME-ee-uhn] ultimately from Greek, meaning 'to tame'.
Damian, Syrian martyr (died c.303). Little is known of his

life beyond the tradition that he, with his twin brother Cosmas, was martyred for the faith at Cyrrhus in Syria. They became the focus of a cult from the fifth century onwards, the legend being embellished with such details as their performing numerous extraordinary miracles and being nicknamed 'the Moneyless Ones' because they never requested payment for their services. Today they are honoured as the patron saints of physicians, surgeons and barbers.

Also the name of the *Belgian missionary Damien de Veuster (1840–89)*, who left his native Belgium in 1873 after volunteering to work in Hawaii, where an epidemic of leprosy had erupted some eight years before. Sometimes called Damien the Leper, he worked to improve the miserable conditions in which lepers lived in isolation, organising them into groups to do useful work in the community and generally improving facilities in the colony. He went to Hawaii with a sense that he too might die of the disease and in fact he finally contracted leprosy himself after 16 years' tireless effort of helping lepers.

Variant: **Damien.**

Dan (m)
[dan] from Hebrew, meaning 'judge'.
The name is now considered a diminutive form of **Daniel** but is sometimes used as a name in its own right. The fifth son of Jacob (Genesis 30:3–6). His mother was Bilhah, Rachel's servant, and he is the ancestor of one of the twelve tribes of Israel. When Jacob was dying, Jacob blessed his sons and he said Dan would 'provide justice for his people' (Genesis 49:16). One of his descendants was Samson, who was a judge (Judges 13).

Variant: **Danny**.

Dana feminine form of **Daniel**.

Daniel (m)

[DAN-yuhl] from Hebrew, meaning 'God is my judge'.

An Old Testament prophet. Of noble descent, Daniel was exiled to Babylon as a young man and given the Babylonian name Belteshazzar (Daniel 1:1–7). He was appointed to high authority in the Babylonian and Persian kingdoms, but suffered for his faith, being dramatically rescued by God in the lions' den (Daniel 6). Through a gift for interpreting dreams and visions, he held high government posts and told kings of God's plans for them and warned about future persecution of the Jews. He had visions that prophesied the coming of the kingdom of the Messiah (Daniel 7–12).

Syrian-born hermit *Daniel the Stylite (409–493)* lived in a monastery from the age of 12 and lived the life of a monk before being inspired to become a hermit by the example of St Simeon the Stylite. He lived in isolation in a ruined temple near Constantinople for nine years and then, after Simeon's death in 459, installed himself permanently there on a platform supported by two pillars. Over the next 33 years he only descended from his platform on one occasion, when he came down to protest against the rule of the Emperor Basiliscus. He was renowned as a prophet and gave simple, practical advice to countless pilgrims, from emperors to invalids.

57

The *Scottish-born Welsh bishop Deiniol* (or Daniel) is supposed to have been a descendant of Celtic royalty and to have come originally from the Strathclyde region. Rising to the rank of bishop of Bangor in Gwynedd, he is reputed to have been the founder of the monasteries at Bangor Fawr on the Menai Strait and at Bangor Iscoed on the river Dee in Clwyd. By the time of the Venerable Bede the latter of these two establishments had become the most important monastery in Britain, with over 2000 monks. He died c.584 and was buried on the island of Bardsey.

Variants: **Dan, Danny.**

Feminine forms: **Dana, Daniella, Danielle**.

Darius (m)

[da-REE-uhs] Persian *darayavahush*.

Name of three emperors in the Persian dynasty. *Darius the Mede* is mentioned in Daniel 5:31; 9:1; he appointed Daniel as a leading official. He may be either the Persian general Gobryas or the Persian king Cyrus.

Also *Darius the Great (Darius I), king of Persia* (Haggai 1:1; Zechariah 1:1), who revived Cyrus' decree in allowing rebuilding work on the temple to continue (Ezra 4:24–6:22) (521–486 BC).

Also *Darius II, king of Persia* (Nehemiah 12:22) (423–404 BC).

David (m)

[DAY-vid] from Hebrew, meaning 'beloved'.

King David (c.1000–961 BC), Israel's greatest king and the ancestor of Jesus Christ. His greatness is based on two features, his military conquests which resulted in Israel's only empire and on God's promise of an eternal dynasty and kingdom. The first phase of David's life (1 Samuel 16–31) describes Samuel anointing David privately as Saul's successor, and Saul's repeated attempts to kill David after he had become a national hero by defeating the giant Goliath (1 Samuel 17) and attacking the Philistines. After Saul died, David became king, first over Judah and then over all Israel, making Jerusalem his capital after capturing it from the Jebusites. This action united the tribes under his kingship, and he cemented Israel's new-found unity by restoring the ark to the centre of national life in Jerusalem (2 Samuel 1–8).

The final phase of the biblical account (2 Samuel 9–20, 1 Kings 1–2) contains several stories about personal conflict within David's family, which was only resolved when Solomon was established as his successor. David's achievements were considerable. He transformed Israel from a disjointed and defeated group of tribes into an empire which included nations such as the Philistines, Moabites, and several Aramean kingdoms (in modern Syria). For the first time, Israel had a central structure under a king, though David's organization was modest compared with that set up by Solomon.

As a gifted musician he contributed to the Book of Psalms. But David had very real weaknesses, too, as shown by his adultery with Bathsheba and his engineering of her husband Uriah's death. Because David repented, however, the Bible portrays him as a forgiven man. David is also known for God's covenant with him (2 Samuel 7). Through him, God promised to build two houses, one in the form of a dynasty and the other in the form of the temple built by Solomon. Several parts of the Old Testament refer to the idea of a future son of David, and the New Testament repeatedly shows how this hope was fulfilled in Jesus Christ (Romans 1:3).

59

Welsh bishop (c.520–c.601), David (or Dewi) is traditionally supposed to have been born the son of a local chieftain at Henfynw in Cardigan. Legend has it that he founded 12 monasteries throughout south Wales and southwestern England and that he was consecrated bishop while on pilgrimage to Jerusalem. Subsequently he was acknowledged as head of the church in Wales, establishing his see at Mynyw, now renamed St David's in his honour.

Nicknamed 'The Waterman' either because he advised abstinence from alcohol or because he ritually practised total immersion in cold water, he appears to have insisted that the monks at Mynyw follow a relatively strict rule of austerity and manual labour. Many churches were dedicated to St David and today he is honoured as the patron saint of Wales and of poets. The reasons why people traditionally wear daffodils or leeks on St David's Day (1 March) are obscure.

David of Scotland (c.1085–1153) Scottish king. The son of Malcolm III of Scotland and Margaret of Scotland, he was educated at the Norman court in England and in due course succeeded to the throne of Scotland in 1124. As king he proved a fierce defender of Scottish independence from England, leading various armed incursions into northern England before achieving peace with the English and then devoting his attentions to religious and social reform in Scotland. He promoted trade, improved the legal system and promoted the Scottish church. He was also praised for his personal piety and generosity and today is remembered as one of the best of all Scottish rulers.

Variants: *Dai, Dave, Davy.*

60 Feminine form: **Davina**.

Davina feminine form of **David**.

Deborah (f)
[DEB-er-uh] Hebrew, meaning 'bee'.
An outstanding woman who was a prophet and led Israel as a judge. She enabled Barak to defeat occupying Canaanite forces under Sisera at the battle of Megiddo (Judges 4–5). The Song of Deborah (Judges 5), which commemorates the triumph of Israel over the Canaanites, is thought to be one of the oldest pieces of Hebrew poetry. She was praised as a 'mother in Israel' (Judges 5:7).

Variants: **Deb, Debbie, Debra.**

Declan (m)
[DEK-lan] probably Gaelic, meaning 'full of goodness'.
Irish bishop (died early fifth century), near Waterford. Born of a noble family, he founded the church at Ardmore where he had been consecrated bishop. He was one of four bishops who were evangelising Ireland before **Patrick** arrived to establish the Christian church in Ireland.

Delilah (f)

[di-LY-lah] Hebrew, meaning 'delight'.

The name of the Philistine woman who betrayed Samson to the Philistines by persuading him to tell her the secret of his strength (Judges 16:4–21). Delilah seduced Samson and by her persistent nagging eventually persuaded him to reveal the secret of his strength, which lay in the length of his hair. While he was asleep, she had his hair cut, and his strength then left him. He was then handed over to the Philistines who blinded him.

Delphine (f)

[del-FEEN] from Latin *Delphinus*, meaning 'of Delphi'.

Blessed Delphine of Provence (1284–1360). Delhine married the French noble Elzear when they were both in their teens and led a life of deep devotion. She went with her husband to Italy, where the King of Naples entrusted some significant work to him. Her husband died later in Paris in 1323. She is known for giving away most of her great wealth to the poor in Provence.

61

Demetrius (m)

[duh-MEE-tree-uhs] 'belonging to Demeter'.

The name of two people in the New Testament: a silversmith in Ephesus who stirred up a riot against the apostle Paul (Acts 19:23–41) and a Christian disciple commended by the apostle John (3 John 12).

Also, *Demetrius, an early fourth-century Serbian martyr*. Details of the life of Demetrius (or Dmitry) are obscure, but he may have been a deacon, possibly at Salonika. According to legend, he was put to death without a trial at Sirmium (now Mitrovica in Serbia) during the reign of Emperor Maximian on charges of preaching Christianity. Dubbed 'The Great Martyr', he subsequently acquired the reputation of a warrior saint in the tradition of St George and others.

Denis (m)

[DEN-is] from Latin *Dionysius*, ultimately from *Dionysos*, Greek god of wine.

French bishop and martyr (d. c.258). Denis (or Denys) of Paris is traditionally supposed to have been an Italian missionary originally named Dionysius who was sent together with five other bishops to Gaul in 250. According to legend he was beheaded on the orders of the Roman authorities alongside a deacon and another priest in Paris on what became known as Montmartre (meaning 'martyrs' hill'). After execution, the martyrs' remains were recovered from the river Seine and interred on what became the site of the abbey of Saint Denis. The identification of St Denis with other early saints, notably Dionysius, a disciple of the apostle Paul, contributed greatly to the saint's popularity around the nineth century and to the spread of his cult throughout Europe. Today Denis is honoured as the patron saint of France.

Variants: **Den**, **Dennis**, **Denys**, **Dion**, **Dwight**.
Feminine form: **Denise**.

Denise feminine form of **Denis**.

Diana (f)

[dy-AN-uh] Latin name of Artemis, the Greek goddess of the moon and hunting.

She had a great temple in Ephesus where her statue was thought to have fallen from heaven (Acts 19:27–28, 35).

Also *Diana D'Andalo (c.1201–36) Italian nun*. Born into a wealthy family of Bologna, she played an important role in persuading her father against his inclination to give St Dominic land for the foundation of a friary near the University of Bologna. Subsequently she took her vows as a nun before St Dominic and tried to persuade her father to establish a Dominican convent on his land: when he refused to cooperate she joined an Augustinian community.

Eventually, under gentle pressure from Dominic's successor as head of the Dominican Order St Jordan of Saxony, the D'Andalo family made possible the foundation of St Agnes' convent at Bologna to house Diana and four companions. Diana and Jordan fell deeply in love, but stubbornly maintained their vows of celibacy and remained no more than close friends for the next 15 years, writing to each other regularly to offer spiritual support and ultimately dying within a year of each other.

Dinah (f)
[DY-nuh] from Hebrew, meaning 'one who judges'.
Jacob's only daughter. Her brothers attacked the people of Shechem after she was raped by Hamor, the local ruler's son (Genesis 34).

Dionysius (m)
[dy-uh-ni-SEE-uhs] from the Latin name, ultimately from *Dionysos*, Greek god of wine.
Dionysius of Alexandria (c.190–c.265) Alexandrian bishop. Born in Alexandria, he became bishop of the city in 247. He faced many challenges during his 17 years as bishop, having to cope with persecution, famine, plague, schism and violence. On one occasion, threats to his personal safety led to his friends forcibly removing him from Alexandria to seek temporary refuge in the Libyan desert. He soon returned, however, and demonstrated his humanity through his insistence upon leniency towards those who had lapsed under pressure from the authorities. Persecution began again later, resulting in a two-year banishment of the bishop, who nonetheless returned to the city as soon as was practicable.

Active as a preacher and writer upon theological matters, Dionysius was widely respected for his learning and for his varied personal qualities, while his fortitude prompted St Basil to bestow upon him the title Dionysius the Great.

Dolores (f)
[duh-LAW-ris] Spanish, meaning 'sorrow'.
The name comes from *Maria de los Dolores* ('Mary of sorrows'), one of the titles of the Blessed Virgin Mary.
   Variant: **Lolita**.

Dominic (m)
[DOM-i-nik] from Latin *dominicus*, meaning 'of the lord'.
Spanish founder of the Dominican Order of Preachers, (1170–1221). Born into a noble family at Calaruega, Spain, he had a quiet childhood, embarking upon religious study at the University of Palencia in Castile in 1184 and in due course becoming a Franciscan canon regular at the cathedral at Osma. In 1204 he undertook evangelical work among the Albigensians in Languedoc in southern France, accompanying his bishop Diego, and consolidated his reputation as a formidable preacher. Although the Pope was then pursuing military action against the Albigensians, resulting in massacres and civil war, Dominic – a compassionate and intelligent man – came to the conclusion that a better way to defend the faith was to establish monastic communities of men and women dedicated to Christian ideals and concentrate upon peaceful persuasion of heretics.

   Accordingly, he set up his first communities for disciplined men and women at Prouille in France in 1206 and, having established his base at Toulouse, eventually won papal recognition for his new order under the title of the Friars Preachers. Members of the order – commonly called Dominicans and wearing black and white robes – took vows of poverty and devoted their lives to preaching and education, going wherever Dominic ordered them to spread the word. Dominic himself proved energetic in travelling far and wide to oversee the establishment of new houses throughout France, Spain and Italy. The order flourished and numbered 60 friaries around Europe by the

64

time of Dominic's death in Bologna. Today he is honoured as the patron saint of astronomers.

Feminine forms: **Dominica**, **Dominique**.

Dominica, **Dominique** feminine forms of **Dominic**.

Donald (m)
[DON-uhld] from two Celtic words, meaning 'world' and 'powerful'.
Scottish patriarch (early eighth century). Donald (or Domhnall) was supposedly a married man of Ogilvy in Forfarshire, who, following the death of his wife, pursued a devout religious life together with his nine daughters. This quasi-monastic community continued after Donald's death, when the nine women moved to Abernethy. The nine women, sometimes called 'The Nine Maidens', are remembered in the names of various natural features in the Abernethy area.

Variants: **Don**, **Donny**.

Dorcas (f)
[DAW-kus] from Greek, meaning 'deer, gazelle'.
A disciple in Joppa who was known for her good works. She died but was brought back to life by the apostle Peter (Acts 9:36–42). She was also known as Tabitha, the Aramaic word for gazelle.

Dorothy (f)
[DO-ruh-thee] from Greek, meaning 'gift of God'.
Cappadocian martyr (died c.303). The details of the life of Dorothy (or Dorothea) are shrouded in legend. The story goes that she was a virgin who lived in Caesarea in Cappadocia and was arrested for her Christian faith during the persecution instituted under Emperor Diocletian. When two women were sent to obtain a recantation from her, she converted them both to the Christian faith and was

65

duly sentenced to death by beheading. On her way to execution she was mocked by a young lawyer named Theophilus, who requested that she send him flowers and fruit from Paradise. A child immediately appeared bearing a basket of apples and roses, which Dorothy handed to her astounded persecutor. The lawyer declared his instant conversion to Christianity and was accordingly martyred as Dorothy was. She is honoured as the patron saint of brides, midwives and florists.

Variants: **Dora**, **Dot**, **Dorothea**, **Thea**.

Drusilla (f)

66

[droo-SIL-uh] from the Roman family name *Drusus*, possibly ultimately meaning 'strong'.
The third and youngest daughter of Herod Agrippa I. Aged 15, she married Azizus, King of Emesa, but after a year's marriage she left her husband to marry Felix, a Gentile governor of Judea. Felix and Drusilla heard Paul talk about faith in Jesus Christ (Acts 24:24).

Dunstan (m)

[DUN-stuhn] from Old English *dun*, meaning 'hill' and *stan*, meaning 'stone'.
English archbishop (c.909–988). Born near Glastonbury and possibly of royal blood himself, he abandoned a secular career in favour of the church after a serious illness. He lived for a while as a hermit before being appointed royal adviser during the minority of King Edmund. Around 643 he was given responsibility for monastic reform in Glastonbury and largely from his work there came the revival of Benedictine monasticism throughout Britain. Dunstan founded or refounded numerous abbeys in south-west England and around 970 oversaw a conference for the compilation of a national monastic rule.

As well as his work on monastic revival and reform of the church, including the reconstruction of many church buildings and the consolidation of church law, Dunstan played a key role in the secular leadership of the country. Appointed Archbishop of Canterbury in 959, he presided over the coronation of Edgar as king of all England in 973: the service he drew up for this event is still essentially the same coronation ceremony in use today. Today Dunstan is honoured as the patron saint of goldsmiths, jewellers, locksmiths, blacksmiths, musicians and the blind.

Dympna (f)
[DIMP-nuh] Irish martyr, dates unknown.
The story of Dympna (or Dymphna) would appear to owe more to folklore than fact. Inspired by the discovery of the ancient human skeletons of a man and a woman at Gheel, near Antwerp in Belgium, in the thirteenth century, the legend grew that they were the bones of an Irish – or possibly British – princess who fled with her chaplain Gerebernus from her pagan father's incestuous desire (supposedly provoked by her physical similarity to her deceased mother). Her father, however, followed the couple to Gheel and killed them both when she refused to return home. Dympna subsequently became associated with the healing of mental disorders and a hospital for the insane (still extant) was established at Gheel by the end of the thirteenth century. Today she remains the patron saint of the insane and of runaways.
    Variant: **Dymphna**.

Ebenezer (m)
[e-buh-NEEZ-zuh] (from Hebrew, meaning 'stone of help'). The name of a victory that God gave the Philistines. To commemorate the victory, Samuel set up a stone, remembering God's support for Israel (1 Samuel 7:12). Also the site of a Philistine defeat of Israel (1 Samuel 4:1–11).

67

Eden (m, f)

[EE-duhn] from Hebrew, meaning 'pleasure'.

The place where Adam and Eve lived, and from which they were driven as a punishment for disobeying God (Genesis 2:8; 3:24). Reference to the Tigris and Euphrates (Genesis 2:14) flowing from it indicates it was a real place, though things like the trees of life and of the knowledge of good and evil suggest it possessed more than just physical qualities. It is thought to have been located in southern Iraq, or in an area of eastern Syria known in ancient times as Beth-Eden.

Edith (f)

68

[EE-dith] from Old English *ead*, meaning 'rich', 'blessed' and *gyth*, meaning 'war'.

Edith of Wilton (c.961–984), English nun. Born in Kemsing, Kent, the illegitimate daughter of King Edgar and Wulfrida, Edith (or Eadgyth) was brought up at the nunnery at Wilton, near Salisbury, and spent her whole life there. She refused all the privileges that her connections with royalty could have given her and instead became well known for her piety and humility, even turning down offers of the position of abbess at Winchester, Barking and Amesbury in order to remain with the nuns at Wilton. She was particularly noted for her generosity to the poor and for her empathy with wild animals.

Edmund (m)

[ED-muund] from Old English *ead*, meaning 'rich', 'blessed' and *mund*, meaning 'protection'.

English martyr (841–870). The adopted heir of Offa of Mercia, he became king of East Anglia as a young man and ruled in peace before the arrival of an invading Danish army in 865. He was defeated in battle in 870 and taken prisoner by the Danes, who ordered him to renounce Christianity and agree to pay them tribute. Edmund refused these demands and was subjected to torture before being executed. The abbey at Bury St Edmunds (named after him and where his body was taken) became the site of a powerful Benedictine abbey.

Also *Edmund of Abingdon (c.1175–1240), English archbishop.* Born as Edmund Rich into a wealthy merchant family in Abingdon, he was educated at Oxford and Paris before becoming a priest. As a teacher of theology at Oxford, he earned a reputation both for his holiness and his eloquence as a preacher. He was appointed treasurer to Salisbury cathedral in 1222 and ultimately became Archbishop of Canterbury in 1233. He led the church through seven troubled years, preventing war between the king and his nobles and promoting ecclesiastical reform.

69

Edna (f)
[ED-nuh] from Hebrew, meaning 'pleasure'.
In the Apocrypha, the wife of Raguel and mother of Sarah, who married Tobias (Tobit 7:1–16).

Edom see **Esan**.

Edward (m)
[ED-wuud] from Old English *ead*, meaning 'rich' or 'blessed', and *weard*, meaning 'guardian'.
Edward the Confessor (1003–66), English king. The son of King Ethelred II (the Unready), he was educated in Ely until the Danish invasion of 1013, after which he completed his studies in Normandy with his Norman mother Emma. He remained in Normandy after his widowed mother married the new king of England, Cnut, and himself succeeded to the throne on Cnut's death in 1042. Edward married Edith, daughter of the powerful Earl Godwin, but the couple produced no heir (according to popular but unsubstantiated tradition because of Edward's godly chastity). Edward's reign was a time of peace and prosperity and the king himself was praised for his generosity to the poor and for

his firmness towards recalcitrant nobles, gradually acquiring a saintly reputation. Edward was canonised in 1161 and during medieval times was widely considered the patron saint of England until eclipsed by St George.

Also *Edward the Martyr (c.962–978), English king*. The son of King Edgar, he faced rival claims to the throne but acquired it in 975 largely through the influential support of St Dunstan. Unfortunately, the youthful king's reign ended just three years later when he was murdered by assassins at Corfe in Dorset, apparently by supporters of his half-brother Ethelred (popular rumour assigned much of the blame to Ethelred's mother Aelfthryth). Stories of miracles surrounding Edward's name quickly accrued and he was described as a saint and martyr as early as 1001.

Variants: **Ed**, **Eddie**, **Eddy**, **Ned**, **Neddy**, **Ted**, **Teddy**.

Edwin (m)

[ED-win] from Old English *ead*, meaning 'rich', 'blessed' and *wine* 'friend'.

English king (584–633). Edwin spent much of his youth in exile in Wales and East Anglia before defeating and killing his rival King Ethelfrith and claiming the throne of Northumbria for himself in 616. A widower, he found that his advances to Ethelburga of Kent were initially refused on the grounds that he was not a Christian. The marriage eventually took place on condition that Ethelburga should be free to pursue her religion and that Edwin would consider converting to Christianity as well. Encouraged by the missionary bishop St Paulinus of York, he eventually became a Christian himself at Easter 627 (together with many of his nobles), a key event in the expansion of Christianity in northern England.

Variant: **Ed**.

Feminine form: **Edwina**.

Edwina feminine form of **Edwin**.

Egbert (m)

[EG-buht] from Old English *ecg* 'sword' and *beorht* 'bright'. English monk (died 729). Born into a noble family in Northumbria, he became a monk at Lindisfarne and subsequently continued his studies in Ireland. When he and his companion Aethelhun were struck down by the plague, Egbert swore that if he was spared he would go into exile for the rest of his life. Aethelhun died, but Egbert survived and accordingly left Ireland for ever. He went on to organise several evangelical missions to Germany, although he himself remained permanently on Iona from 716.

Eleanor (f)

[EL-i-nuh] probably from *Helen*, ultimately from Greek, meaning 'the bright one'.

Variant of **Helen**, introduced in England in the twelfth century by Eleanor of Aquitaine (c.1122–1204), wife of King Henry II. The name was popularised by Eleanor of Castile (c.1245–90), wife of King Edward I. When she died, a series of 'Eleanor crosses' was set up, one at each stage of the journey where her body rested from Nottinghamshire to London.

Variants: **Ellie**, **Leonora**, **Nell**, **Nelly**.

Eleazar (m)

[e-lee-AY-zuh] from Hebrew, meaning 'God has helped'.

A son of Aaron and his successor as high priest alongside both Moses and Joshua (Numbers 20:26). He led the Levites and had oversight of those responsible for the sanctuary. With Joshua, he apportioned the land (Joshua 14:1).

Variant: **Lazarus**.

Eli (m)

[ee-LY] from Hebrew, meaning 'Yahweh is high'.

A high priest who took responsibility for Samuel. His family was removed from office because of their lack of concern for the ways of God (1 Samuel 1:21–3:21). The fact that this message was conveyed by his young assistant Samuel shows Eli's failure to hear God and also his unfitness to lead Israel.

Elihu (m)
[i-LY-hew] from Hebrew, meaning 'he is my God'.
The fourth and youngest of Job's friends, who advised Job to look to God for an explanation of his suffering rather than to the unhelpful arguments of the three other friends (Job 32–37).

72 **Elijah** (m)
[i-LY-juh] from Hebrew, meaning 'Yahweh is God'.
An important prophet who was active in the northern kingdom of Israel in the ninth century BC. His background is unknown except that he came from Tishbe in Gilead. His ministry was largely spent in opposing the kings of the ruling Omride dynasty, namely Ahab and his sons Ahaziah and Jehoram (1 Kings 17–19, 21; 2 Kings 1–2). Their promotion of Baal worship was a direct threat to Yahweh's supremacy as the God of Israel. Elijah therefore challenged 400 priests of Baal to a contest at Mount Carmel to show the people that Yahweh was the only true God. Elijah was persecuted by Ahab's wife Jezebel, but God protected him and his predictions of the deaths of Ahab and Jezebel were both fulfilled.

The result of his ministry was the preservation of a faithful remnant of people who worshipped God. His work was characterised by several miracles, and he was eventually taken up to heaven in a whirlwind rather than actually dying. Later, his name was associated with the expectation of a forerunner of the Messiah, which Jesus explained was fulfilled in John the Baptist (Malachi 4:5–6; Matthew 11:12–14).

Variant: **Elias.**

Elisabeth see **Elizabeth**.

Elisha (m)
[i-LY-shuh] from Hebrew, meaning 'God is Saviour'.
Elijah's successor as the leading prophet of the northern
kingdom in the latter half of the ninth century BC. His
ministry was different from Elijah's, being more concerned
with leading prophetic guilds and with demonstrations of
God's miraculous power (1 Kings 19:19–21; 2 Kings
2:1–8:15; 13:14–21). He was also more of a seer, com-
municating his message in pictures as well as words. He
emphasised the contrast between true faith and the
unbelief of Israel's kings, and spoke about God's
sovereignty over the nations, as illustrated by his healing of
the Syrian general Naaman and his predictions concerning
the kings of Damascus.

73

Elizabeth, **Elisabeth** (f)
[i-LIZ-uh-beth] from Hebrew, meaning 'God is my oath'.
John the Baptist's mother and a close relative of Jesus'
mother Mary, who encouraged Mary with a prophecy about
her unborn son (Luke 1:42–45). She came from the priestly
family of Aaron. Elizabeth and her husband seemed
destined to remain childless until visited by the angel
Gabriel, who told them that Elizabeth would give birth to
a son who would prove a new Elijah. When Zechariah
refused to believe this he was immediately struck dumb
and did not regain his voice until after the baby was born.
Zechariah's heartfelt words of thanks upon the birth of
John became enshrined as the canticle known as the
Benedictus, which begins 'Blessed be the Lord God of
Israel...'
   Also *Elizabeth of Hungary (1207–31), Hungarian
noblewoman.* The daughter of King Andrew II of Hungary
and wife of Louis IV, Elizabeth was devoted to her husband
and grief-stricken when he died of plague during the

Crusades. Unlike many other saints who sought holiness through chastity and isolation from the world, she was fully committed to her life as a wife and mother (bearing her husband a son and two daughters); she became widely loved for her generosity in distributing the wealth of her family among the poor. Other acts of kindness included the building of hospitals and, on one occasion, nursing a leper. She is honoured as the patron saint of beggars, bakers, charities, lace-makers and the Sisters of Mercy.

Variants: **Beth**, **Bethan**, **Betsy**, **Betty**, **Buffy**, **Elise**, **Eliza**, **Elsie**, **Elspeth**, **Isabel**, **Isobel**, **Libby**, **Lili**, **Lisa**, **Lisbeth**, **Liz**, **Liza**, **Lizzie**, **Lizzy**.

74

Elkanah (m)
[el-KAH-nuh] from Hebrew, meaning 'God has created'. The father of the prophet Samuel and husband of Hannah (1 Samuel 1:1–2:20).

Ellen see **Helen**.

Elmo see **Erasmus**.

Emil male form of **Emily**.

Emily (f)
[EM-uh-lee] feminine form of Roman family name *Aemilius*.
Emily de Rodat (1787–1852), French noblewoman. Born into a wealthy family, as a young woman she occupied herself with charitable works, as well as joining local convents for brief periods. In 1815 she established a free school at Villefranche-de-Rouergue, from which evolved the Congregation of the Holy Family of Villefranche, whose activities soon spread to many parts of the world.

Also, *Emily de Vialar (1797–1856), French foundress*, who spent 20 years looking after her widowed father before inheriting enough money to expand her charitable activities. She used her money to found charities and institutions throughout the world, being known both for her shrewdness and her humanity.

Male form: **Emil**.

Variant: **Millie**.

Emmanuel (m)

[i-MAN-yoo-el] a Hebrew name, meaning 'God with us'.

The use of this name for Jesus Christ shows that he brought God's presence to earth when he was born (Matthew 1:22–23).

Variants: **Manny**, **Manuel**.

Feminine forms: **Emanuelle**, **Emmanuelle**.

Emmanuelle feminine form of **Emmanuel**.

Enoch (m)

[EE-nok] from Hebrew, meaning 'dedicated'.

An ancestor of Noah and father of Methuselah. A prophecy by Enoch is recorded in Jude 14–15. He did not die but was taken up to heaven (Genesis 5:24).

Ephraim (m)

[EE-fruh-im, EE-fray-im, EE-fruhm] from Hebrew, meaning 'double fruitfulness'.

The name of Joseph's second son who was adopted by his grandfather Jacob and given the blessing of the firstborn (Genesis 48:8–20). Later, Ephraim became the most important tribe in the northern kingdom of Israel, occupying a prestigious position among the tribes (Judges 8:2–3). Its name was even used occasionally as an alternative for Israel. It occupied the central highlands west of the Jordan.

Erasmus (m)
[i-RAZ-muhs] from Greek, meaning 'beloved'.
Bishop and martyr (died c.303). Little is known for certain of the life of Erasmus beyond the tradition that he was a bishop in Formiae in the Campagna in Italy who was put to death during the persecutions of Diocletian. Another legend claims that, after many tortures, he was executed at Formiae by having his entrails pulled from his body through the use of a windlass.

The name *Erasmus* is known in the Italian altered form, *Elmo*. 'St Elmo's fire' is the popular name for the luminous light sometimes seen on ships' masts during storms, a result of electrical discharges. According to one legend, in reward for being saved from drowning by a sailor, Elmo is said to have promised that a light would be displayed to indicate an impending storm. He is the patron saint of sailors.

Eric (m)
[E-rik] from Norse, meaning 'ever ruler'.
King of Sweden (died c.1160). Having ascended to the throne of Sweden in 1156, he sought to convert the Finns to Christianity through conquest, but was subsequently killed during a Danish attack upon Uppsala, being wounded in an assassination attempt and then tortured and beheaded.

Variants: **Rick**, **Ricky**.
Feminine forms: **Erica**, **Erika**.

Erica, **Erika** feminine forms of **Eric**.

Ernest (m)
[ER-nist] Old German 'serious'.
The abbot of a Benedictine abbey in Zwiefalten, Germany. He was active in the Crusades, preaching in Persia and

Arabia, where he was captured. He was tortured to death in Mecca in 1148.

Variant: **Ernie** .

Esau (m)
[EE-saw] from Hebrew, meaning 'hairy'.
The elder twin son of Isaac and a hunter. He sold his birthright to his younger brother Jacob, whom he hated (Genesis 25:29–34) and lost the blessing as the eldest son (Genesis 27). Esau and Jacob were eventually reconciled as a result of God's intervention and Esau became the ancestor of the Edomites.

77

Esther (f)
[ES-tuh] from Persian, meaning 'star' or possibly a variant of *Ishtar*, Babylonian goddess of love.
A Jewish woman of outstanding beauty who became queen of the Persian king, Xerxes. Her name is probably Persian, though she also had a Jewish name *Hadassah*, meaning 'myrtle'. Though initially dependent on her uncle Mordecai, her faith, wisdom and courage were crucial in enabling Jews in Persia to escape a plan to kill them (Esther 4:11–17; 7:1–8:8).

Variants: **Ester**, **Hester**.

Ethan (m)
[EE-thuhn] from Hebrew, meaning 'long-lived'.
A man renowned for his great wisdom (1 Kings 4:31) and also credited with being the author of Psalm 89.

Ethelbert (m)
[E-thul-bert] from Old English *aethal* 'noble' and *beorht* 'bright'.
English king (560–616). Having married a Christian, the Frankish princess Bertha, he overcame initial doubts and

converted to Christianity himself after welcoming St Augustine on his arrival in England in 597, so becoming the first Christian Anglo-Saxon king.

He did much to promote Christianity among his subjects through his patronage of St Augustine at Canterbury without actually forcing them to convert. He also ordered the building of St Andrew's cathedral in Rochester and enabled the establishment of the first St Paul's cathedral in the territory ruled by his neighbour King Sabert of the East Saxons, who had also converted to Christianity with encouragement from Ethelbert. With help from Augustine, Ethelbert also drew up the earliest surviving Anglo-Saxon code of law, under which special protection was given to the clergy and the church.

Etheldreda (f)
[e-thul-DREE-duh] from Old English *aethal*, meaning 'noble' and *thryth*, meaning 'strengh'.

English abbess (c.630–679). Born in Suffolk a daughter of King Anna of the East Angles, she married twice, the second time to Egfrid, son of King Oswy of Northumbria. Both marriages remained unconsummated and, after Egfrid gave her up, Etheldreda (or Audrey) became a nun, settling on the Isle of Ely. She founded a double monastery (now the site of the present cathedral) at Ely around 672 and remained abbess there for the rest of her life, devoting herself to penance and prayer. She is honoured as the patron saint of Cambridge University.

Variants: **Audrey, Ethel**.

Eugene (m)
[YOO-zheen] from Greek, meaning 'well-born'.

Eugenius of Carthage (died 505) Carthaginian bishop. Eugenius became bishop of Carthage in 481, at a time of persecution by Arian Vandals. He spent many years in exile in Tunisia and elsewhere, suffering considerable deprivation, and eventually died in exile in southern France.

Variants: **Ewan**, **Ewen**, **Gene**, **Owen**.

Feminine forms: **Eugenia**, **Eugenie**.

Eugenia, **Eugenie** feminine forms of **Eugene**.

Eulalia (f)

[yoo-LAY-lee-uh] from Greek, meaning 'talking well'.

Eulalia of Merida (died c.304) Spanish martyr. Little is definitely known about the life of Eulalia of Merida beyond the fact that she was a 12-year-old girl who was persecuted at Merida in Spain for her Christian faith. Legend has it that she protested against Maximian's punitive policy against the Christians and for her temerity was tortured and, when she refused to recant, burnt to death. A complementary tradition describes how a white dove flew from her mouth as she died and how her body was covered by snow.

79

Eunice (f)

[YOO-nis] from Greek, meaning 'good victory'.

In the New Testament, the mother of Timothy and daughter (or daughter-in-law) of Timothy's grandmother Lois. Eunice was a Jew who was a Christian believer and her husband was a Greek (Acts 16:1; 2 Timothy 1:5). Little is known about Eunice, but she is praised by the apostle Paul for the significant influence she exerted on Timothy in teaching him the Scriptures from his childhood (2 Timothy 3:14–15).

Euodia (f)

[yoo-OH-di-uh] from Greek, meaning 'good journey'.

A prominent woman in the church at Philippi, who was quarrelling with Syntyche, another woman in the church. The apostle Paul urged these two women to resolve their differences in the Lord (Philippians 4:2–3).

Euphemia (f)
[yoo-FEE-mi-uh] from Greek, meaning 'good speech'.
A virgin martyr at Chalcedon, probably during the persecution by the Roman Emperor Diocletian. Many traditions surround her death, including the torture that she is said to have miraculously survived until she was killed by a wild bear c.307.

Eustace (m)
[YOO-stuhs] from Greek, meaning 'fruitful'.
Roman martyr (dates unknown). Legend has it that Eustace was a general who served under the Emperor Trajan. While hunting near Tivoli, he is said to have encountered a stag bearing a glowing crucifix in its antlers. As a result of this vision, Eustace is said to have become a Christian immediately, despite the disgrace and loss of wealth that this would entail. His superiors demanded that he recant his new Christian faith, but he refused and was roasted to death in a brazen bull together with his wife and sons. He is honoured as the patron saint of hunters.
Variants: **Stacey**, **Stacy**.

Evangeline (f)
[i-VAN-juh-leen] from Greek, meaning 'good news'.
The name was first introduced by the American poet Longfellow in his poem 'Evangeline' (1847).

Eve (f)
[eev] from Hebrew, meaning 'life'.
The first woman; wife of Adam, specially created from one of his ribs (Genesis 2:21–23). She was the mother of Cain, Abel and Seth. Adam and Eve disobeyed God; as a punishment, God told Eve that childbirth would be a painful experience and her husband would exercise authority over her (Genesis 3). See also **Zoe**.

Ezekiel (m)
[i-ZEE-ki-uhl] from Hebrew, meaning 'God strengthens'.
Sixth-century BC priest who prophesied to the Babylonian exiles. Little is known of his personal life except that he was struck dumb for a while and not allowed to mourn for his wife (Ezekiel 3:26–27; 24:15–27). His prophecies sometimes involved him in strange behaviour and colourful visions (e.g. of dry bones, Ezekiel 37) but this does not detract from his important contribution to biblical thought at a critical time in Israel's history.

Ezra (m)
[EZ-ruh] from Hebrew, meaning 'help'.

An important reformer in post-exilic Judaism, whose main achievement was to establish the law of God as the basis of the Jewish community. He was appointed by the Persian king, Artaxerxes, probably Artaxerxes I in the mid-fifth century BC, as something like a 'Minister for Jewish Affairs' to teach the Jewish law and ensure that the Jews kept the Persian law (Ezra 7:11–26).

Fabian (m)
[FAY-bi-uhn] from the Roman family name *Fabianus*, possibly meaning 'bean-grower'.
Roman Pope and martyr (died 250). Fabian was a humble farmer who, according to legend, became Pope in 236 when a dove marked him out by settling on his head, so indicating this man of as God's choice. Fabian distinguished himself for his holiness and hard work during his 14 years in office, which ended with his martyrdom when he became the first Christian in Rome to be put to death under the persecution ordered by Decius. It was probably Fabian who took the important step of reorganising the church in Rome into seven deaconries. Today he is honoured as the patron saint of lead-founders and potters.

Faith (f)

[faith] from Latin *fides*, meaning 'trust'.

The name stands for the Christian quality of beliefs and trust, alongside Charity (Love) and Hope (1 Corinthians 13:13).

Also, French martyr (died third century). Born into a Christian family in Agen, Aquitania, Faith dedicated her life to Christ as a child. While still a young girl, she refused to leave her home during the persecution of the Romans and was arrested on the orders of the Roman prefect Dacian. When demands that she should offer sacrifices to the goddess Diana proved fruitless, she was sentenced to be tortured. So extreme was her suffering, however, that her captors took pity on her and she was executed instead alongside other martyrs.

Variants: **Fay**, **Faye**.

Felicity (f)

[fuh-LIS-i-tee] from Latin *felicitas*, meaning 'happiness'.

One of two Carthaginian martyrs Perpetua and Felicity (died 203). They were prominent among a group of martyrs executed as Christians in Carthage on the orders of Septimus Severus. Felicity was a pregnant slave-girl, while Perpetua was a young married noblewoman with a baby. They and seven men were arrested as Christians and thrown into prison, where Perpetua had the first of several visionary dreams in which she saw a ladder reaching to heaven. She and other members of the group had further similarly miraculous dreams and interpreted them as divine reassurances that they would be raised to heaven at their deaths.

Also, *Felicity of Rome (second century), Roman martyr.* Felicity is variously identified as the leader, or possibly the sister or even the mother, of a group of seven Christian men martyred for their faith in ancient Rome during the reign of Antoninus Pius. Evidence for the legend of Felicity and the

82

so-called Seven Brothers is scant but their veneration became well established in the early Roman church. It is said that the group refused to renounce their faith or make sacrifices to pagan gods and so were put to death, with Felicity being the last to die.

Felix (m)
[FEE-liks] from Latin, meaning 'happy'.
Antonius Felix, Roman governor of Judea from AD 52–60.
Felix is mentioned in Acts (chapters 23 to 25), because Paul stood before him at Caesarea during his first trial for his Christian faith. Felix was familiar with the Christian way (Acts 24:22). With his wife Drusilla, he listened to Paul as he explained the Christian faith further, but Felix's response was that he was afraid. Hoping that Paul would bribe him, Felix kept Paul under house arrest for two years and spoke with him regularly (Acts 24:24–27).

83

Also the name of several saints, including *St Felix, Roman martyr (dates unknown)*. According to legend, Felix was a Christian priest in Rome who during the persecution of Diocletian was sentenced to death for his faith. As Felix was being led to his execution a stranger in the crowd declared that he was also a Christian and would die alongside Felix. The two men were killed and buried on the Ostian Way.

Felix of Dunwich (died 648), English bishop. Little is known of Felix's early career beyond the fact that he was born in Burgundy and at some point left Gaul for England. By now a bishop, Felix was ordered by Honorius of Canterbury to embark on a mission to promote the Christian church in East Anglia at the request of Sigebert, the Christian king of the region. Felix accordingly settled at Dunwich and did much over the next 17 years to advance the church among the East Angles, his various good deeds including the establishment of a boys' school at Dunwich and the foundation of a monastery at Soham, where Felix was eventually buried. The town of Felixstowe was named in Felix's honour.

Ferdinand (m)
[FER-di-nand] from Old German, meaning 'brave journey'.
Ferdinand III of Castile (1199–1252) Spanish king. Born near Salamanca, the son of Alfonso IX of León and Berengaria of Castile, he became king of Castile in 1217 and of León in 1230, thus uniting the two kingdoms. Under his leadership over the next 27 years his armies seized much of Andalusia from Moorish control and made it Christian. He showed tolerance towards the Muslims and Jews who remained after the ousting of the Moors; he also founded the university of Salamanca and rebuilt the cathedral at Burgos. He is honoured as the patron saint of local rulers, prisoners and the poor.

Fidelis (m)
[fi-DAY-lis] from Latin, meaning 'faithful'.
Fidelis of Sigmaringen, Franciscan friar and martyr (1578–1622). Born as Mark Rey in Sigmaringen, south Germany, Fidelis practised law and became known for his help to the poor. He became a Franciscan Capuchin monk in 1612 and was later sent to preach among Protestants in Switzerland. He was killed by a group of angry peasants in 1622.
   Variant: **Fidel**.

Florian (m)
[FLAW-ree-uhn] from Latin, meaning 'flowery'.
An officer in the Roman army, who was head of the administration in Noricum province and who was martyred in 304 in the period of office of the Roman Emperor Diocletian. He was forcibly drowned in the river Enns, which event him led to be called on to give protection against flooding and fire.

Frances (f)

[FRAHN-sis] feminine form of *Francis*.

Frances of Rome (1384–1440), Italian noblewoman. Born into a wealthy family in Rome, she married at the age of 13 and bore her husband several children but yearned to be a nun. She dedicated herself to charitable activities, helping to alleviate the distresses of the poor and those suffering due to plague and war. In 1433 she founded a Benedictine community of devout women called the Oblates of Tor de' Specchi, to which she retreated after the death of her husband in 1436. Apart from her good works, Frances of Rome was also said to have had many mystical experiences, including visions and visitations by angels.

Also, *Frances Xavier Cabrini (1850–1917), Italian-born US foundress.* Born Frances Cabrini into an Italian farming family in Lombardy, she dreamt as a child of becoming a missionary and adopted the additional name Xavier in honour of the great missionary leader Francis Xavier. She was twice turned down as a nun on health grounds but was instead recruited to help run an orphanage in Codogno. When this failed, she went on to found (1880) the Missionaries of the Sacred Heart to organise schools and orphanages for the poor. Kindhearted but practical and morally strict, she oversaw the rapid growth of this organisation before, in 1889, leading a group of her assistants to New York to undertake work with needy Italian immigrants there. Such was her success that soon the society had opened branches in many other cities around the world, with some 68 houses dedicated to the care of poor orphans by the time of Cabrini's death in 1917. Honoured as the patron saint of immigrants, she became (1946) the first US citizen to be canonised.

Variants: **Fanny**, **Fran**, **Francesca**, **Françoise**, **Frankie**.

Francis (m)

[FRAHN-sis] from Latin *Franciscus*, meaning 'Frenchman'. *Francis of Assisi (1181–1226), Italian founder of the Franciscan order*. Born Francesco Bernadone into a wealthy family of Assisi in Italy, he had a dissolute youth and fought as a soldier before being taken prisoner in 1202 and ultimately returning home because of poor health. After experiencing a vision, he dedicated himself to the service of God, taking a strict vow of poverty and adopting a simple, faithful lifestyle. He travelled extensively in central Italy as an itinerant preacher, attracting many disciples and going on to found the highly influential order of the Friars Minor for men and, with his friend St Clare, a parallel religious community called the Poor Clares for women. Members of these orders were encouraged to give up all their possessions and to imitate the simple lifestyle of Francis himself. In 1224, while praying in retreat on Mount Alvernia, Francis is said to have seen a vision of an angel nailed to a cross and to have received the stigmata of Christ's wounds.

Francis is especially remembered today for his gentleness and for his readiness to see God's presence in all aspects of nature, as evidenced by his love of animals. The Franciscan order (as the movement founded by Francis became known) spread throughout the world and Francis himself became one of the most celebrated and best-loved of all saints. He is honoured today as the patron saint of ecologists and animals.

Francis of Comporosso (1804–66), Italian lay brother. Born Giovanni Croese into a farming family in Liguria, he joined the Franciscan friary at Sestri Ponente near Genoa but subsequently left them to become a member of the more rigorous Capuchin order. In due course he rose to the rank of questor in Genoa, his duties including the begging of food for the other brothers and himself. When cholera broke out in Genoa in 1866 he was unflinching in setting about ministering to the ill and went so far as to offer his own life to God in exchange for a halt in the epidemic. He soon contracted the disease himself and died, upon which the epidemic ceased.

Francis of Paola (1416–1507), Italian founder of the Franciscan Minim Friars. Born in Paola, Calabria, he joined the Franciscan Friars Minor at the age of 13 and undertook pilgrimages to Assisi and Rome before adopting the life of a hermit in a cave near his birthplace. In time he attracted a number of disciples and from these beginnings developed the community known as the Minim Friars, whose lifestyle was based on humility and austerity. Francis himself established a reputation as a miracle-worker and prophet. In 1943 he was named patron saint of seafarers (a reference to a legend that he used his cloak as a boat and other miraculous seafaring stories connected with his name).

Francis de Sales (1567–1622), French bishop. Born into a noble family in Thorens, Savoy, he worked as a lawyer but defied his parents' expectations of a prominent secular career by becoming a priest, being ordained in 1593. He performed missionary work throughout the Chablais region, attracting many converts from Calvinism, and in time rose to the rank of bishop of Geneva, establishing himself as a leading figure of the Counter-Reformation. He was noted both as a priest and as an administrator and educator, numbering among his disciples St Jane de Chantal, with whom he founded the Order of the Visitation in 1610. His many writings included the influential *Introduction to the Devout Life* and *Treatise on the Love of God*. He is honoured as the patron saint of writers and of the Catholic press.

Variants: **Frank**, **Frankie**.
Feminine form: **Frances**.

Freda feminine form of **Frederick**.

Frederick (m)
[FRED-rik] from Old German, meaning 'peaceful ruler'.
Frederic Ozanam (1813–53), Italian founder of the St Vincent de Paul Society. Born in Milan, he studied at the Sorbonne in Paris, establishing a reputation as a steadfast defender of the Catholic faith. He also became known for his charitable work on behalf of the poor, often providing for them out of his own resources, attracting many sympathetic followers, who in due course formed the nucleus of the first conference of the St Vincent de Paul Society. Ozanam himself married and became a professor of literature at the Sorbonne, remaining a prominent figure in French public life until his premature death in Marseilles at the age of 40.

88

Variants: **Fred**, **Freddie**, **Freddy**.
Feminine form: **Freda**.

Fulbert (m)
[FUUL-buht] from Old German, meaning 'very bright'.
French abbot (c.608–85). Born the son of a bishop in Gascony, Fulbert (or Philibert) studied before serving as a monk in the monastery at Rebais. He was promoted to the position of abbot at the monastery but soon resigned in the face of opposition from the other monks and moved to Rouen, where in 654 he was granted land to found the influential abbey of Jumièges. He went on to found the monastery of Noirmoutier, later establishing further houses for monks or nuns throughout Neustria, so consolidating his standing as one of the most important founders of the early monastic tradition. The name was introduced as Filbert at the Norman conquest.

Gabby feminine form of **Gabriel**.

Gabriel (m)
[GAY-bree-uhl, ga-bree-EL] from Hebrew, meaning 'man of God' or 'my strength is God'.

One of the two archangels mentioned in the Bible. He announced the birth of both John the Baptist and Jesus Christ. Gabriel is identified in the Old Testament (at Daniel 8:15 and 9:21) as the angel who appears to Daniel and in the New Testament reappears (at Luke 1:11–20) to Zechariah, father of the unborn John the Baptist, and to Mary (Luke 1:26–38) to announce the coming birth of Christ. In reference to his role as a messenger of God, Gabriel has been honoured as the patron saint of the post office and of telecommunication workers since 1921.

Feminine forms: **Gabby**, **Gabrielle**.

Gabrielle feminine form of **Gabriel**.

Gaius (m)
[GY-uhs] from Latin, meaning 'rejoice'.
Name of four individuals in the New Testament: *Gaius from Macedonia*: One of Paul's travelling companions (Acts 19:29), who along with Aristarchus was caught up in a riot against the Christian message. *Gaius from Derbt*: One of those who went ahead of Paul from Philippi and waited for him at Troas (Acts 20: 4–5). *Gaius from Corinth:* One of those baptised by Paul in Corinth (1 Corinthians 1:14), probably the same Gaius as mentioned in Paul's greetings in Romans 16:23. Also the one addressed in 3 John. In a fourth-century text, the *Apostolic Constitutions*, a reference occurs to a person called Gaius whom the apostle John installed as the first bishop of Pergamum in Asia Minor, together with a Bishop Demetrius of Philadelphia. This is possibly the same Gaius as in 3 John.

Variant: **Caius**.

Gamaliel (m)
[guh-MAY-lee-uhl] from Hebrew, meaning 'God is my reward'.

Paul's Jewish teacher who advised the Sanhedrin to adopt a cautious attitude to the first Christians (Acts 5:33–40).

Gemma (f)
[JEM-muh] from Italian, meaning 'gem'.
Gemma Galgani (1878–1903), Italian laywoman. Gemma was born into a poor family near Lucca and dedicated herself to Christ as a child. While still a girl, she decided upon a life as a nun, but was denied the possibility of joining the Passionist Congregation by chronic illness. She spent many hours in prayer and professed to have had many visions of Christ, the Virgin Mary and a guardian angel. Though such declarations made her an object of ridicule among her family and friends, she insisted upon the truth of these experiences.

Harder to pour scorn on, however, were the displays of Christ's stigmata that appeared on her body periodically in the years 1899–1901, as described by various witnesses. Wounds resembling those suffered by Christ bled freely on her hands, feet and side every Thursday evening and did not heal over until Sunday, causing Gemma much pain. She died of nephritis and tuberculosis of the spine at the age of just 25. She is honoured as the patron saint of tuberculosis sufferers and pharmacists.

Variant: **Jemma**.

Genevieve (f)
[JEN-uh-veev] from French, possibly 'lady of the people'.
Geneviève (c.422–c.500), French laywoman. Born in Nanterre, France, Geneviève (Genevieve or Genovefa) was singled out for future holiness by St Germanus who noticed her in 429 when she was only seven years old in a crowd that had gathered to hear him speak as he passed through Nanterre on his way to Britain. In answer to his questions the girl told him that she was going to dedicate her life to God and accordingly, at the age of 15, she took a vow of

virginity. She decided, however, to remain a laywoman and went to live with her godmother in Paris, where she busied herself praying and working on behalf of the poor (despite hostility from some quarters).

When the Franks besieged Paris, Geneviève saved the city from starvation by leading a convoy of ships up the Seine to find supplies, so becoming a national heroine. Similarly, when Attila the Hun's invading army unexpectedly skirted Paris, the credit was placed on the prayers of Geneviève that the city might be spared. Today Geneviève is honoured as the patron saint of Paris as well as of sufferers from drought and other disasters.

Geoffrey see **Godfrey**.

George (m)
[jawj] from Greek *georgos*, meaning 'farmer'.
George (died c.303), legendary dragon-slayer and martyr. The details of the life of St George have been the subject of considerable debate, but it seems he may have been a Roman soldier who was martyred for his Christian faith during the reign of the emperor Diocletian. Some accounts identify him as a son of the Roman governor of Palestine who trained as a soldier in the Roman army and rapidly rose to the rank of general. He allegedly took part in a campaign against Persia and may even have participated in an expedition to Britain (although there is little evidence for this). He left the army around 298 when only those who worshipped the gods of Rome were allowed to remain in the armed forces but he subsequently spoke up on behalf of beleaguered Christians before the imperial court at Nicomedia. As punishment for his temerity, he was tortured at or near Lydda.

The familiar story of George and the dragon is a later addition to his story, probably conceived some 900 years after his death. According to this, George was a knight from

Cappadocia who happened to meet a young woman who was about to be sacrificed by the people of Silene in Libya to a fierce dragon in order to appease its fury. George wounded the creature and brought it to the town but only killed it after the terrified local populace consented to be baptised as Christians.

Today St George is honoured as the patron saint of both Portugal, Genoa, Spain and Venice. His flag, a red cross on a white ground is now considered the national flag of England.

Variant: **Georgie**.

Feminine forms: **Georgia**, **Georgina**.

92

Georgia (f)

[JAW-juh] feminine form of **George**.

Sixth-century French saint who, having decided to remain unmarried, lived a life of solitude, spending her time fasting and praying. At her death, the congregation at a funeral were surprised to see a flock of white doves that accompanied her body to the church and hovered over the church during her funeral.

Georgina feminine form of **George**.

Gerald (m)

[JE-ruhld] from Old German, meaning 'spear rule'.

Gerald of Aurillac (c.855–909), French nobleman. Born the son of the count of Aurillac in Auvergne, he inherited the family estates and, despite poor health, distinguished himself for his fairness and competency as count in his turn. He was particularly respected for his godly devotion, spending many hours in prayer, and considered becoming a monk himself, but was persuaded he could do more good as a layman. Around 890 he founded the celebrated monastery at Aurillac, which later became the home of the Cluniac order.

Variants: **Gerry**, **Jerry**.
Feminine form: **Geraldine**.

Geraldine feminine form of **Gerald**.

Germaine (f)
[jer-MAYN] from French *Germain*, meaning 'German'.
Germaine of Pibrac (1579–1601), French peasant woman.
Germaine Cousin was born near Toulouse as the daughter
of a poor French farmer. Afflicted with scrofula and
crippled in the right hand, she lost her mother as a child and
was cruelly treated by her stepmother, who made her live
in a stable and eat kitchen scraps. She found some consolation in her religious faith and was well known locally
for her kindness to others. When she died, at the premature
age of 22, she was allegedly witnessed ascending to heaven
on a beam of light, accompanied by angels.

93

Gershom (m)
[GER-shuhm] from a Hebrew verb, meaning 'to drive out'.
One of Moses' sons, by his wife Zipporah. He was given this
name by Moses, who said 'I have become a foreigner in a
foreign land' (Exodus 2:22, TNIV). In Exodus 2:22 the writer
explains the name in terms of it being similar in sound to
two other words *ger* (meaning 'stranger') plus *shom*
meaning 'there'. So in Exodus 2:22 the meaning is given 'a
stranger there'.

Gertrude (f)
[GER-trewd] from Old German, meaning 'strong spear'.
Gertrude (1256–1302), Benedictine nun. Probably born near
Eisleben in Saxony, she began her education in the
Benedictine nunnery of Helfta, becoming a pupil of St
Mechtild. She took her vows as a nun at the age of 25 and
remained at the nunnery for the rest of her life, dedicating
herself to the veneration of the Sacred Heart and to the

study of the Scriptures. Sometimes called Gertrude the Great, she became perhaps the most renowned of all medieval visionaries, claiming to have undergone a profound spiritual conversion aged 26 and subsequently to have experienced numerous mystic revelations while at her devotions. Details of these visions were recorded in the *Revelations of St Gertrude*, the best known of the writings of Gertrude and her mentor Mechtild that have survived. She is honoured today as the patron saint of the West Indies.

Gertrude of Nivelles (626–59), abbess and visionary. While still a young woman she was appointed abbess of the monastery at Nivelles founded by her mother in 640 and despite her youth proved very capable in the post, showing great wisdom in her decisions and offering hospitality to missionaries. She is honoured as the patron saint of travellers, gardeners and the recently deceased.

Variants: **Gert**, **Trudie**, **Trudy**.

Gervase (m)

[JER-vayz] from Old German, meaning 'spear servant'.
Roman martyr (dates unknown). Nothing is known about the circumstances of the martyrdom of Gervase and his fellow martyr Protase, whose remains were discovered in Milan in 386. The search for their decapitated bodies had been ordered by St Ambrose, following some kind of dream or revelation in which he was alerted to their presence. Various miracles accompanied the retrieval of the bodies, which were transferred to the newly-completed cathedral of Milan. Some historians have suggested a link between Gervase and Protase and the legend of Castor and Pollux.

Variants: **Gervais**, **Jarvis**.

Gideon (m)

[GID-ee-uhn] from Hebrew, meaning 'hewer' or 'feller'.
One of the judges who led Israel for 40 years (Judges 6–8). Also called Jerub-Baal, he rose to prominence as a young

man by challenging Israel's humiliating position under the Midianites. His leadership is demonstrated by his initial reluctance to take command, his hatred of idolatry and his courageous faith. Later, he turned down an offer of kingship, though he compromised with pagan worship.

Gilbert (m)
[GIL-buht] from Old German, meaning 'bright hostage'.
Gilbert of Sempringham (c.1085–1189), English founder of the Gilbertine Order. The son of a Norman nobleman, he was physically disabled and so considered unsuitable for a military career. Instead he was appointed parson of Sempringham, which was part of his father's manor in Lincolnshire, and – after being ordained as a priest and turning down the rank of archdeacon – settled there into an austere, devout way of life.

95

In 1131 he founded his own order, assembling a religious community of young women on the Benedictine model. The order prospered with the addition of lay brothers and sisters and with the introduction of chaplains to guide the nuns. In the following years, the order spread with new monasteries being established throughout Lincolnshire and Yorkshire, complete with hospitals and orphanages.

Variant: **Gil**.

Giles (m)
[jylz] from Latin *Aegidus*, from the Greek word for 'young goat'.
French hermit (died c.710), Giles (or Aegidius) is thought to have lived as a hermit near Arles and to have founded a monastery there but the rest of his life is shrouded in legend. The most celebrated story concerning him describes how he was accidentally wounded by an arrow fired by the Visigoth king Wamba while protecting his pet deer, upon which the king's hunting hounds were miraculously rooted to the spot. Other tales describe how

he received the confession of the Emperor Charlemagne and how he received two beautiful doors as a gift from the Pope while on a visit to Rome. Giles ranked among the most popular of all saints during the medieval period, when he was considered the patron saint of cripples, beggars and blacksmiths.

Gillian feminine form of **Julian**.

Gladys (f)
[GLA-dis] from Welsh *Gwladys*, meaning 'ruler'.
Fifth-century Welsh saint who was married to St Gundleus; she was the mother of the Welsh abbot St Cadoc. According to Arthurian tradition, Gundleus is said to have kidnapped Gladys.
Variant: **Glad**.

Gloria (f)
[GLAW-ree-uh], from Latin, meaning 'glory'.
The word *glory* refers to God's majestic greatness. God makes his glory known to people in various ways. It is revealed in the world he has made, and aspects of it are visible to everyone (Romans 1:20). It is also made known through his actions and through the church. In the Old Testament period, specific experiences of God's glory were given to individuals and to Israel (Exodus 33:18–23; 1 Kings 8:10–11), but the supreme revelation of the glory of God is in the person of Jesus Christ (John 1:14).

Godfrey (m)
[GOD-free] or **Geoffrey** [JEF-free]
(from Old German, meaning 'God's peace').
French bishop (died 1115). Godfrey (or Geoffrey) of Amiens attracted attention through his success in reviving the run-down monastery at Nogent-sous-Coucy, which prospered under his disciplined leadership. In 1104 his talents were

officially recognised when he was appointed bishop of Amiens. He proved a stern master in this role, however, stamping out corrupt practices among the local clergy and in the process acquiring many enemies. In 1114 opposition to his reforms had become so fierce that he was obliged to retreat to the monastery of the Grande Chartreuse. He died a year later, before he could return to his troubled diocese.

   Variants: **Geoff**, **Jeff**, **Jeffrey**.

Goliath (m)
[guh-LY-uth] from Hebrew, meaning 'exile; captive' or 'uncovered'.
A Philistine giant warrior who threatened Israel's army but whom David killed with a slingstone in a duel (1 Samuel 17).

Grace (f)
[grays] from Latin *gratia*, meaning 'favour'.
God's undeserved favour to all, shown in that he is slow to anger (Exodus 34:6) and primarily in the sending of Jesus Christ as the Saviour of the world. God provides further grace so that people can accept Christ's love for them (Ephesians 2:8–9).

   Variant: **Gracie**.

Gregory (m)
[GRE-guh-ree] from Greek, meaning 'watchman'.
Gregory I, Gregory the Great (c.540–604), Roman pope.
Beyond the fact that he was born into a noble family in Rome, the son of a senator, and was attracted to the religious life from a young age, little is known of the details of Gregory's early life. He was appointed prefect of Rome in 573 but a year later gave up this prestigious secular post in order to become a monk and then a deacon and an abbot, turning his own home and his six estates in Sicily into monasteries. Subsequently he was appointed ambassador

to the court of Byzantium in Constantinople and became adviser to Pope Pelagius II in Rome. He was elected to the papacy himself in 590, so becoming the first monk to become pope.

As Rome's political leader he provided spiritual and practical support as the population of Rome struggled against famine, floods and plague, made peace with threatening invaders and rebuilt the ravaged city, opposed slavery and withstood the pressure of the rival Byzantine empire. As head of the church he instituted sweeping reforms, promoted the Benedictine monastic movement, sponsored the Christianisation of England and effectively laid the basis for the political power of the medieval papacy. He is honoured today as the patron saint of musicians, singers and teachers.

Also *Gregory II (c.669–731), Roman pope.* Born into a wealthy family in Rome, he became a Benedictine monk and in due course was raised to the rank of subdeacon under Pope Sergius. When Constantine died in 715, he was elected his successor as pope. An able pontiff, he repaired the walls of Rome, recaptured territories from the Lombards, warded off a Lombard invasion of the city, defended the church's independence from interference by the Greek emperor Leo III the Isuarian, and received many notable pilgrims in Rome.

Gregory III (died 741), Syrian-born pope. As a priest in Rome, Gregory became well known both for his scholarship and for his piety. In 731 he was elected pope by acclamation while accompanying the funeral procession of his predecessor as pope, St Gregory II. His ten-year papacy opened with the intensification of the dispute with Emperor Leo III on the use of sacred images in worship and led to the holding of two councils at which Gregory excommunicated those who destroyed such images. Subsequent events included the forging of an alliance with the Frankish king Charles Martel in order to defend the independence of the church and the promotion of missionary activity in Germany and elsewhere.

Gregory VII (c.1021–85), Italian pope. Born into a relatively humble family in Tuscany, and baptised Hildebrand, he became a Benedictine monk and in due course was appointed secretary to Pope Gratian (1045). Within a few months, however, Gratian was deposed and Gregory was obliged to accompany him into exile. In 1047 Gratian died and Gregory returned to monastic life. In 1049 he was summoned to Rome by Pope Leo IX, who made him a cardinal-subdeacon and administrator of the Patrimony of St Peter's. He went on to establish himself as the power behind the throne during the reigns of Popes Victor II, Stephen, Nicholas II and Alexander II before becoming pope himself in 1073.

Gregory of Nazianzus (c.329–c.390), Cappadocian patriarch. Born in Nazianzus, Cappadocia (in modern Turkey), Gregory of Nazianzus (or Gregory Nazianzen) was the son of wealthy Christian converts, his father being the bishop of Nazianzus. He was educated in Caesarea, Alexandria and Athens and was planning a career as a lawyer or rhetorician before being persuaded by his father to enter the church as a monk. Known as one of the three Cappadocian Fathers, alongside Basil the Great and Gregory of Nyssa, Gregory became patriarch of Constantinople in 380.

Gregory of Nyssa (c.330–c.395), Cappadocian bishop. The younger brother of St Basil the Great and St Macrina the Younger, he was born in Caesaria, trained for a career as a rhetorician and married before entering the church. Identified as one of the three Cappadocian Fathers, alongside St Basil and Gregory of Nazianzus, he became bishop of Nyssa in 371 and supported the orthodox position against the Arian heresy. A somewhat rash, tactless man, he was deposed by Arian opponents in 376 but was reinstated in 378 and appointed bishop of Sebaste in 380, playing a prominent role at the Council of Constantinople the following year and becoming a greatly respected figure in the Eastern church.

Gregory of Tours (c.538–c.594), French bishop and historian. Born Georgius Florentius into a wealthy Gallo-Roman family at Clermont-Ferrand, he became bishop of Tours in 573. Despite poor health, he showed great energy in meeting the many challenges he faced as bishop, including civil war and opposition from highly placed political figures. He generally succeeded in avoiding getting enmeshed in political issues and concentrated upon alleviating the suffering of the people. He also oversaw the rebuilding of Tours cathedral. Today, however, he is remembered chiefly as a historian. His most important writings included the *History of the Franks* and various biographical works concerning the lives of the martyrs, among them *Glory of the Martyrs* and *Life of the Fathers*.

Gregory the Wonderworker (213–c.270), Cappadocian bishop. Born into a prominent pagan family of Neocaesarea, Pontus (in modern Turkey), he was converted to Christianity and ultimately was elected bishop of Neocaesarea around 238. As bishop he had a profound impact upon the people of Neocaesarea, converting virtually the entire population to Christianity. He was respected as an orator and also established a reputation for miracle-working, hence his title Thaumaturgus (meaning 'Wonderworker'). Among other celebrated deeds, he was alleged to have diverted rivers, dried up a lake, moved a mountain and assumed the form of a tree in order to deceive his pursuers during the persecution of Christians instituted by Decius in 250. He is sometimes identified as the patron saint of people in desperate situations, especially those threatened by floods or earthquakes.

Variant: **Greg**.

Guy (m)

[gy] from Old German *Wido*, meaning 'wood'.

Guy (also called Vitus), Modestus and Crescentia, Italian martyrs (died *c*.303). The exact details of the lives and martyrdom of Guy, Crescentia and Modestus are shrouded in obscurity. It seems that there may have been two saints called Vitus, the earlier Vitus being martyred in Lucania in southern Italy and the second being put to death after cruel torture with his nurse Crescentia and her husband Modestus in Sicily during the reign of Diocletian.

One version of the legend has Vitus casting an evil spirit out of the son of Diocletian himself, an act that only served to convince the authorities to have the Christian executed. Whatever the truth of the matter, Vitus became particularly associated with various physical ailments, including epilepsy and chorea (also known as 'St Vitus' dance'). He has long been considered the patron saint of people suffering from such nervous disorders as well as from snakebite or rabies. He is also the patron saint of dancers and actors.

Gwen (f)

[gwen] from Welsh, meaning 'white'.

Gwen Teirbron of Brittany. Reported to have married twice, and mother of saints Gwethenoc, James and Winwaloe: this is said to be the reason for her having been born with three breasts. She crossed the English Channel from Britain to flee from a plague, settling in France. She later remarried and was the mother of St Cadfan. She is sometimes identified with Saint Whyte (Candida) who is buried in Whitchurch (Dorset).

Masculine form: **Gwyn**.

Gwyn masculine form of **Gwen**.

Hadrian (m) variant of **Adrian**.

Hagar (f)
[HAY-guh] from Hebrew, probably meaning 'flight'.
Sarah's female servant whom Sarah gave to her husband Abraham to produce a child. Ishmael's subsequent birth led to Sarah's jealousy and Hagar's expulsion from the household, but God granted Hagar a special revelation of himself (Genesis 21:8–19).

Ham (m)
[ham] from Hebrew, meaning 'hot'.
One of Noah's three sons who survived the flood with him and from whom the world was repopulated (Genesis 6:10; 9:18–19).

102

Hannah (f)
[HAN-nuh] from Hebrew, meaning 'favour' or 'grace'.
The mother of the prophet Samuel. She gave birth to him after God heard her desperate prayer because she was barren, and then dedicated him to the service of God (1 Samuel 1).

Harold (m)
[HA-ruuld] from the Old English name *Hereweald*, meaning 'leader of the army'.
Child martyr (died 1168). It is said that he was put to death by Jews in Gloucester. The veneration of child martyrs is often considered as an example of the pervasive anti-Semitism of the period.
   Variants: **Errol**, **Harry**.

Harvey (m)
[HAH-vee] from the French, meaning 'battle-worthy'.
Sixth-century French saint. Born blind, Harvey (also called *Hervé*) became a monk and later abbot of Plouvien. He was well known for his preaching and for the miracles he performed.

Heber (m)

[HEE-buh] from Hebrew, meaning 'associate'.

The name of various men in the Old Testament: a descendant of Jacob (Genesis 46:17) and the ancestor of the Heberites (who are named after him) (1 Chronicles 7:31–32). Also: the husband of Jael, who killed Sisera (Judges 4:11–21); father of Soco (1 Chronicles 4:18); descendant of Benjamin (1 Chronicles 8:17).

Hedwig (f)

[HED-vig] Old German, meaning 'strife'.

Silesian noblewoman (c.1174–1243). Born into a noble family in Bavaria, Hedwig (or Jadwiga) was brought up in the monastery of Kitzingen and was married to Henry, heir to the dukedom of Silesia, at the age of 12. As well as bearing seven children by Henry, she played an active role in the governing of the country and used her wealth to benefit the poor through the foundation of various religious houses and hospitals, including Silesia's first convent. When her husband was captured by his enemy Conrad of Masovia, she acted as peacemaker and restored good relations between the two states.

Variant: **Hedda**.

Helen (f)

[HE-luhn] from Greek, meaning 'the shining one'.

Helen (c.250–330), Roman empress. Helen (sometimes identified as Helena or Ellen) was born the daughter of an innkeeper in Bithynia (Turkey) and in due course became the wife of the Roman general Constantius Chlorus. She bore him a son (later Constantine the Great, the first Christian emperor) but was divorced by her husband when he became emperor. In 312, the year in which she was named empress by her son Constantine, she was converted to Christianity and became well known for her godly devotion and for her generosity to good causes, building

103

churches and doing much to advance the Christian faith throughout the Roman Empire.

Because of her son Constantine's links with Britain (he was in York when he succeeded to the imperial throne) Helen was once supposed to be British herself and her name is preserved in various place names in northeast England.

Variants: **Eileen**, **Elaine**, **Eleanor**, **Elena**, **Ellen**, **Helena**, **Nell**, **Nelly**.

Helier (m)
[HEL-ee-uh]
Sixth-century Belgian-born martyr. He was converted to Christianity as a youth by his tutor, a man named Cunibert, but fled his home when his outraged pagan father killed Cunibert for this act. Helier eventually settled in a cave in Jersey in the Channel Islands and lived there as a hermit. After 15 years he was murdered by some brigands to whom he had attempted to preach. The town of St Helier on Jersey was named in his honour.

Henrietta feminine form of **Henry**.

Henry (m)
[HEN-ri] from Old German, meaning 'home ruler'.
Henry II (973–1024), Holy Roman Emperor. Born in Bavaria, he succeeded to the dukedom of the country in 995 and became emperor of the Holy Roman Empire in 1014. He devoted himself to the consolidation of the Empire, chiefly through waging war with various neighbours, but he also reformed and reorganised the church as a subordinate part of the imperial structure. According to a legend, he really wished to become a monk and agreed a celibate marriage with his wife St Cunegund.

Also: *Henry of Finland (died 1156), English-born bishop and martyr.* Also known as Henry of Uppsala, he was born in England but appointed bishop of Uppsala in Sweden

104

c.1152. He accompanied the army of the Swedish king St Eric against the Finns in 1154 and subsequently set about baptising the defeated Swedish warriors. He built a church at Nousis but fell foul of·a convert Finn, who had taken exception at Henry excommunicating him after he had murdered a Swedish soldier and consequently killed the bishop. He is honoured today as the patron saint of Finland.

Variants: **Hal**, **Hank**, **Harry**.

Feminine form: **Henrietta**.

Hephzibah (f)
[HEF-zi-bah] from Hebrew, meaning 'my delight is in her'. The mother of king Manasseh (2 Kings 21:1) and a symbolic name given to Israel, to refer to its future prosperous state. Instead of being 'Forsaken' and 'Desolate', Israel would be called 'My Delight Is in Her [Hebrew, *Hephzibah*]' and 'Married [Hebrew, *Beulah*]' (Isaiah 62:4).

105

Herbert (m)
[HER-buht] from Old German, meaning 'bright army'. English hermit (died 687). A friend of St Cuthbert, Herbert lived on an island in Lake Derwentwater, where he spent much time in prayer and fasting. Among his prayers was a desire to die on the same day as Cuthbert, a desire that was granted to him.

Variants: **Herb**, **Herbie**.

Hezekiah (m)
[hez-uh-KY-uh] from Hebrew, meaning 'Yahweh is strength'. King of Judah (c.715–687 BC). A king whose faith saved Judah from being incorporated into the Assyrian empire. His anti-Assyrian policy resulted in Sennacherib besieging Jerusalem in 701 BC, but the latter unexpectedly withdrew after Hezekiah's prayer and Isaiah's prophecy (2 Kings 18:5–19:36; Isaiah 36:1–37:37). Later however, Isaiah

criticised him for over-confidence towards the Babylonians. Hezekiah was an enthusiastic builder, constructing the Siloam tunnel to safeguard Jerusalem's water supplies during the siege (2 Chronicles 32:27–30).

Hilary, Hillary (m, f)
[HIL-uh-ree] from Latin, meaning 'cheerful'.
Hilary of Arles (c.400–449), French bishop. Talented and well educated, he was uncertain whether to pursue a secular career or a religious vocation but was persuaded by his elder relative St Honoratus of Arles to train as a monk at the island monastery of Lérins. In 429, aged just 29, he became bishop in succession to Honoratus, about whom he wrote a celebrated memoir. The youthful bishop became well known for his energetic approach to his post, even undertaking manual labour himself in order to earn money for the poor and selling off church possessions to raise ransoms for captives.

Hilary of Poitiers (c.315–367), French bishop and theologian. Born into a wealthy pagan family in Poitiers, he was converted to Christianity in 350 and in due course (despite being a married man with a daughter) became the city's bishop by popular demand, earning a reputation both for his religious zeal and for his gentle manner. He was unswerving in his passionate but controversial opposition to Arianism and as a consequence was eventually exiled to Phrygia by the Arian Emperor Constantius II. He continued to defend orthodoxy and discipline against the Arians in the East and four years later was returned by his exasperated hosts whence he had come.

His many influential writings on the subject of Arianism included *De Trinitate* and *De Synodis*. Sometimes called the 'Athanasius of the West', he is also remembered for his innovative use of metrical hymns in teaching Christian doctrine and through the Hilary term in the calendar of law courts and some universities, which was named after him.

He is honoured as the patron saint of slow learners and of cures for snakebites.

Hilda (f)

[HIL-duh] from Old English, meaning 'battle'.

English abbess (614–680). Born in Northumbria, she was a grand-niece of King Edwin of Northumbria and was baptised at the age of 13. She lived a secular life until the age of 33, then became a nun and in 649 was made abbess of a convent in Hartlepool. She is usually remembered, however, for the work she did at the monastery she founded (or re-founded) at Whitby in 657. Men and women lived separately but prayed together at this establishment, among them such luminaries as the religious poet Caedmon and St John of Beverley. Under her guidance, the monastery became an important centre of religious learning with a fine library and it was there that the highly influential Synod of Whitby took place in 663–664.

Hildebrand see Gregory.

Hildegard (f)

[HIL-duh-gahd] from Old German 'battle' and 'enclosure'.

Hildegard of Bingen (1098–1179), German abbess and visionary. Born in Bokelheim, she was educated with the Benedictines and became a nun herself at the age of 18. In 1136, at the age of 38, she was appointed prioress at Diessenberg. She had claimed to have visions since the age of five but in 1141, at the age of 42, she underwent a profound spiritual transformation and her prophecies became increasingly intense. She went on to record her visions in a book entitled *Scivias*, which comprised a series of 26 revelations, many of them describing the Day of Judgement and warning against sinful ways.

Transferring her expanding community to a new convent at Rupertsberg, near Bingen, around 1147, she became widely renowned for her prophetic powers and offered advice and reproof to several popes and crowned rulers. She also conducted lengthy correspondences with such luminaries as St Bernard of Clairvaux. Other writings included commentaries on the Gospels, books on natural science and medicine, poems, hymns and a morality play.

Hillary see **Hilary**.

Hippolytus (m)
[hi-POL-i-tuhs] from Greek *hippos*, meaning 'horse' and *lyo*, meaning 'to let loose'.

108

Roman priest (died c.235), who was banished by the Roman emperor to the quarries of Sardinia in 235. The rift between Hippolytus and the church was mended before he, together with his fellow exile Pontian, died in exile there. Their bodies were later returned to Rome by St Fabian and the two were declared to be martyrs.

Hiram (m)
[HI-ram] from Hebrew, short form of *Ahiram*, meaning 'my brother is exalted'.
A king of Tyre who was friendly towards David and Solomon and provided materials and workers for building the temple (1 Kings 5:1–12).

Holly (f)
[HO-lee] the name of the evergreen shrub or tree.
A girl born at the time around Christmas.

Hope (f)
[hohp] Old English *hopa*.
The name stands for the Christian quality of hope, alongside Faith and Charity (Love) (1 Corinthians 13:13). In the Bible, hope is a confidence based on God's promises about the future and also the content of those promises.

Hosea (m)
[hoh-ZEER] from Hebrew, meaning 'salvation'.
A prophet who was active in the northern kingdom of Israel in the eighth century BC a few years before it fell to the Assyrians. His life concerns his marriage, separation and reconciliation with the prostitute Gomer, which was all part of his message of God's forgiving love.

Hubert (m)
[HEW-buht] from Old German, meaning 'bright mind'.
French bishop (c.656–727). The circumstances of St Hubert's youth are obscure though it has been suggested he was the son of the Duke of Guienne and, according to fourteenth-century legend, converted to Christianity whilst out hunting on Good Friday after encountering a stag that bore a cross in its antlers and called upon him to repent. He served as a priest under St Lambert and succeeded him as bishop of Maastricht, promoting missionary work in the Ardennes district. Injuries he sustained in a fishing accident in 726 hastened his death the following year. His emblem is a stag and he is honoured as the patron saint of hunters.

109

Hugh (m)
[hew] from Old German, meaning 'heart' or 'soul'.
Little Saint Hugh (died 1255), English martyr. The discovery of the body of a nine-year-old boy in a well in Lincoln in 1255 led to accusations that he had been ritually crucified by local Jews (as in the parallel case of William of Norwich). Some 19 Jews were tortured and hanged on charges of involvement in the boy's death; others were thrown into prison or heavily fined. The legend of Little Saint Hugh is perhaps best known today from an allusion to it in Chaucer's *Canterbury Tales*.

Also *Hugh of Lincoln (c.1135–1200), French-born bishop*. Born into a noble family at Avalon in Burgundy,

Hugh of Avalon (as he was originally styled) received a convent education and while still a young man was appointed prior of a monastery at Saint-Maxim. He joined the Carthusian order in 1160 and was made a procurator at the Grande Chartreuse in 1175. His reputation for piety, combined with his proven administrative abilities, led to him being invited to become prior of Charterhouse in Witham, Somerset. The monastery flourished under Hugh, who was duly appointed bishop of Lincoln (the largest diocese in the country) in 1186. Under his leadership Lincoln became a prominent centre of religious learning and the great cathedral there was considerably extended. He is honoured as the patron saint of sick children.

110

Variants: **Hughie**, **Hugo**, **Huw**.

Huldah (m)
[HUUL-duh] from Hebrew, meaning 'weasel'.
A female prophet who confirmed to King Josiah that the coming destruction of Judah would be postponed because of Josiah's repentance (2 Kings 22:14–20).

Hyacinth (f)
[HY-uh-sinth] from the name of the flower.
Originally a masculine, now a feminine, name. The name of a Roman martyr, with Protus (dates unknown). Little is known for certain about the martyrdom of Protus and Hyacinth, although legend identifies them as two brothers or fellow-teachers who were executed for their Christian faith in the fourth century or earlier. The story of their martyrdom enjoyed a boost in 1845 when the tomb of St Hyacinth was located and found to contain a set of charred bones (supporting the tradition that the saints were burnt to death). The tomb of St Protus was empty (his relics having reportedly been transferred to Rome in the ninth century).

Ignatius (m)

[ig-NAY-shuhs] originally from a Greek name, possibly from Latin *igneus*, meaning 'fiery'.

Ignatius of Antioch (died c.107), Syrian bishop and martyr. Little is known about his life beyond the fact that he became bishop of Antioch around AD 69 and as an elderly man was arrested by the Romans and sent with a military escort to Rome under a sentence of death imposed by Emperor Trajan. After a long journey, during which he was feted by Christians at many of the places that he passed through, he was thrown to wild beasts in the public arena. During his final journey he wrote seven celebrated letters, in which he urged unity within the Christian community and expressed his consolation in being able to demonstrate his devotion to Christ by dying for his faith.

Also *Ignatius of Laconi (1701–81), Capuchin lay brother.* He was born Ignatius Vincent Peis into a poor family in Laconi, Sardinia, and remained in the area all his life, living as a lay brother with the Capuchin Franciscans at Buoncammino near Cagliari from the age of 20 after suffering a severe shock when his horse bolted. As a middle-aged man of 40, after 20 years devoted to prayer and silence, he embarked on some 40 years of begging for alms on behalf of the community, becoming widely revered for his devout, gentle ways and for his kindness towards the poor, the sick and the young.

Ignatius of Loyola (1491–1556), founder of the Jesuit order. Born Iñigo de Recalde de Loyola into a noble Basque family at Loyola Castle near Azpeita in Spain, he trained as a soldier and fought against the French in Castile. In 1521 he sustained a severe leg wound from a cannon shot at the siege of Pamplona and subsequently underwent a spiritual conversion after reading the life of Christ during his convalescence. He retreated for 10 months to a cave at Manresa, spending his time in prayer and penance and later recording his experiences in his celebrated book *Spiritual Exercises* (published in 1548).

He went on pilgrimage to Jerusalem in 1523 but was dissuaded from his intention of evangelising among the Muslims there and went on to spend several years in academic study in Spain. He later joined St Francis Xavier and others in taking vows of poverty and chastity, with the ultimate aim of converting Muslims in Palestine.

When journeying to Palestine proved impossible, the group met once more in Venice in 1537 and resolved to found a new religious order called the Society of Jesus in Rome. The society, which espoused spiritual discipline as well as obedience to Christ and the Pope, won official papal approval in 1540, with Ignatius as its superior general from 1541. The Jesuits, as members of the order became known, went on to play a prime role in the Catholic Reformation throughout Europe, countering the Protestantism of Luther and Calvin, and in succeeding centuries undertook missionary work on behalf of the Catholic church all over the world.

Variant: **Inigo**.

Ira (m)
[Y-ruh] from Hebrew, meaning 'watchful'.
The name of three men in the Old Testament: *Ira the Jairite*, who was David's priest (2 Samuel 20:26); *Ira, son of Ikkesh*, one of David's thirty warriors, who came from Tekoa (2 Samuel 23:26); *Ira the Ithrite*, another of David's warriors (2 Samuel 23:38).

Irene (f)
[Y-reen] from Greek *eirene*, meaning 'peace'.
One of three Macedonian martyrs, the others being Agape and Chionia (died 304). These three sisters of Salonika in Macedonia who were arrested as Christians after they

refused to eat meat that had been offered in sacrifice to the gods. When brought before the governor of Macedonia, Agape and Chionia again refused to eat the food and were accordingly sentenced to death and burnt alive. Because of her youth, Irene was spared and thrown into prison, but subsequently brought before the governor again on charges of possessing Christian texts. Confessing her crime, she was burnt alive, together with her books.

Variant: **Rene**.

Irmina (f)

[ER-mee-nuh] from Old German *ermin*, meaning 'universal'.

Died c.708. The daughter of the Frankish King Dagobert II, she was a nun in the monastery at Öhren near Trier, which was built after the death of the nobleman she was engaged to. She is thought to have helped St Willibrord in his missionary work and gave the land on which the monastery at Echternach (in Luxembourg) was established by Willibrord.

Variants: **Emma**, **Irma**.

Isaac (m)

[Y-zuhk] from Hebrew, meaning 'he laughs'.

Abraham and Sarah's promised son. His name reflects his parents' incredulity at God's announcement of his birth because of their old age (Genesis 17:17; 18:10–15). He is a rather shadowy figure between Abraham and Jacob. Though Isaac sometimes responded positively to God (Genesis 26:23–25; 28:1–5), God was often at work through his passivity, as when he was about to be offered as a sacrifice (Genesis 22) and a wife was found for him (Genesis 24).

Also *Isaac Jogues (1607–46), French missionary and martyr.* Born in Orléans, he joined the Society of Jesus in 1624 and was sent out to Canada as a missionary some 12 years later, spreading the gospel among the Mohawks. He was captured by Iroquois Indians at Ossernenon (modern Auriesville, New York) in 1642 and over the following year of imprisonment was exposed to brutal torture. He escaped with the help of the Dutch but subsequently, after disease broke out among the Bear clan, he was blamed for this misfortune and when he and another priest named John Lalande entered a longhouse supposedly for a peace banquet, they were set upon with knives in the belief that they were sorcerers. Both men were beheaded with tomahawks and their bodies thrown in the Mohawk river.

114   Variant: **Izaak**.

Isabel see **Elizabeth**.

Isaiah (m)
[y-ZY-uh] from Hebrew, meaning 'salvation of Yahweh'.
An important prophet who prophesied in Judah for about 50 years from c.740 BC. His commissioning is recorded in Isaiah chapter 6. His wife was also a prophet and they had two sons whose names were clues to his message (Isaiah 7:3;8:3). Three of Isaiah's most famous prophecies are the coming king (9:6), the death of the servant (chapter 53) and the good news of deliverance (chapter 61): Christians see these prophecies fulfilled in Jesus Christ.

Ishmael (m)
[ISH-may-el] from Hebrew, meaning 'God hears'.
Isaac's half-brother and Abraham's son by his wife's slave Hagar. Though not the main heir of God's promises, God promised Ishmael his descendants would become a great nation (Genesis 17:20; 21:17–18). His descendants the Ishmaelites were a tribal people who lived in Edom (Psalm 83:6), but God's promise has traditionally been thought to be fulfilled through the Arab peoples.

Isidora feminine form of **Isidore**.

Isidore (m)

[IZ-i-daw] from Greek, possibly meaning 'gift of Isis'.

Isidore of Pelusium (died c.450), Egyptian abbot. Probably born in Alexandria, Isidore left his family to become a monk at the monastery of Lychnos near Pelusium and in due course may have become abbot of the monastery. He was widely respected for his devout and austere way of life, dressing in skins and eating only herbs. Remembered as one of the Fathers of the Church, he offered guidance to St Cyril of Alexandria and wrote numerous letters on spiritual matters, of which some 2000 survive.

Isidore of Seville (c.560–636), Spanish archbishop. Variously known as Isidore the Bishop or the Schoolmaster of the Middle Ages, he was born into a noble family of Cartagena in Spain and in due course succeeded his elder brother St Leander as archbishop of Seville in 601. He established a wide reputation as a scholar, writer and teacher and did much to organise and strengthen the Spanish church, presiding over the influential councils of Seville and Toledo. He promoted the conversion of the Visigoths from Arianism and established the cathedral schools from which developed the great universities of the medieval period. Under Isidore's guidance the schools provided instruction in a wide range of subjects, including medicine, law, Hebrew and Greek.

Noted for his austere lifestyle and generosity to the poor, Isidore was also the author of many books, among them the encyclopaedic *Etymologies*, a history of the world, a dictionary of synonyms and biographies of famous men. He is the patron saint of students and computer users.

Isidore the Farmer (born c.1080–1130), Spanish farmer. Born Isidore Merlo Quintana into a peasant family in Madrid, he worked as a farm labourer all his life, combining his love of the land with devotion to God. Various legends tell how the angels, impressed by his faithfulness, assisted him with his ploughing and replaced the gifts he divided amongst the needy, heedless of his own poverty. He is the patron saint of farmers, livestock, dead children and also of Madrid.

Feminine form: **Isidora**.

Israel (m)
[IZ-ray-el] from Hebrew, meaning 'he struggles with God'. The name given to Jacob as he wrestled with God (Genesis 32:28; 35:10). From the time of the exodus, Israel is the usual term for the 12 tribes, underlining their descent from Jacob, though it is used in several different senses. First, it was the name of the nation of Israel, often called literally 'the descendants of Israel'. Second, it had a special religious sense which drew attention to Israel's status as God's covenant people. Third, it became the name of the land which was previously known as Canaan and which the Romans later called Palestine.

When the monarchy divided after Solomon's reign, the northern kingdom was known as Israel for 200 years (c.922–722 BC) while the southern kingdom was known as Judah. Israel in its religious sense was applied to both kingdoms during this period (2 Chronicles 20:29; Amos 3:1). In the New Testament, Israel is almost a synonym for the Jews. It is used particularly by Jews of themselves, and underlines the continuity of God's purposes in election and covenant for his people (Luke 24:21). Occasionally in the New Testament, Israel is a term for the church (Galatians 6:16; Revelation 21:12). The modern state of Israel was established in 1948.

Ives (m)
[yvz] variant of *Ivo*.

Also called Hya. An eighth-century Irish maiden revered in Cornish and Breton tradition. According to Cornish legend, she sailed across the Irish Sea on a leaf and once in Cornwall she persuaded the chieftain Dinan to found a church. Little else is known of her life, although Breton tradition identifies her as a convert of St Patrick who was put to death with her followers in Armorica in 777. She is remembered today as the patron saint of St Ives (formerly called Porth Ia) in Cornwall, where she is supposed to have landed after her voyage from Ireland.

Ivo (m)
[EE-voh] from Old German, meaning 'yew'.
Ivo of Brittany (c.1235–1303) French lawyer, born into a noble family at Kermartin near Tréguier in Brittany, and so also known as *Ivo of Kermartin*, he studied law and theology in Paris and Orléans and was ultimately appointed judge of the church courts at Rennes and Tréguier. He quickly established a reputation for impartiality and honesty and as a champion of the poor, but he later resigned his legal posts in 1287 in order to devote himself to the welfare of his parish, working with the people of Tredez and Lovannec. His many good deeds included the building of a hospital at Lovannec and selfless acts of generosity towards the poor.

117

  Variant: **Yves**.
  Feminine forms: **Yvette**, **Yvonne**.

Jabez (m)
[JAY-bez] sounds like Hebrew word for 'sorrow'.
An honoured member of the tribe of Judah who prayed for God's blessing and protection; God granted his request (1 Chronicles 4:9–10).

Jacob (m)
[JAY-kuhb] from Hebrew, meaning 'supplanter'.
The ancestor of the 12 tribes of Israel through his 12 sons. Family problems plagued much of his life. He stole

(supplanted) his elder brother Esau's birthright and deceived his father into giving him the eldest son's blessing. When he fled to his mother's relatives and married the two sisters Leah and Rachel, his father-in-law continually made life difficult, though God blessed Jacob through these experiences. In old age, favouritism towards his two youngest sons Joseph and Benjamin caused further friction.

He died in Egypt but was buried in the Promised Land as a final sign of his faith in God. God used Jacob to begin to fulfil the promise that Abraham would become the father of a nation (Genesis 25:19–50:26). Particularly through major experiences of God at Bethel (Genesis 28) and Peniel (Genesis 32:22–32), Jacob was transformed from a scheming, arrogant materialist into a person who learnt to trust God for his family as well as for himself (Genesis 47:28–49:28).

Variants: **Jacques**, **Jake**, **James**.
Feminine forms: **Jacoba**, **Jacobina**, **Jacobine**.

Jacoba, **Jacobina**, **Jacobine** feminine forms of **Jacob**.

Jael (f)
[JAY-el] from Hebrew, meaning 'mountain goat'.
The wife of Heber the Kenite. She killed Sisera, the commander of the Canaanite forces (Judges 4:17–22; 5:24–27).

Jairus (m)
[JY-ruhs] from Hebrew, meaning 'he enlightens'.
The synagogue leader whose daughter Jesus raised to life (Mark 5:21–43).

James (m)
[jaymz] variant of *Jacob*.
One of Jesus' brothers who led the church in Jerusalem,

presiding over the Council of Jerusalem (Acts 15) and was probably the author of the letter of James. He was martyred in AD 62.

Also *James, son of Zebedee.* An apostle who was the lesser-known brother of John and one of Jesus' inner circle, (called James the Greater to distinguish him from another apostle, James the Less). He lived as a fisherman alongside his brother John before being called to serve as one of Christ's disciples. Hard physical labour had made him very tough and on account of this (and possibly his fiery temper) he and John were nicknamed Boanerges (meaning Sons of Thunder). James became one of the leaders among the disciples and was present at several of the key episodes of Christ's life, including the agony in the Garden of Gethsemane. Jesus predicted James would suffer for his faith, and he is the first apostle known to have been martyred, c.AD 44 (Mark 10:35-39; Acts 12:2). James the Greater is honoured as the patron saint of pilgrims, blacksmiths and labourers and also of the countries Spain, Chile, Guatemala and Nicaragua.

119

James, son of Alphaeus. An apostle, probably also known as 'James the Younger' or 'James the Less' to distinguish him from James, son of Zebedee (Mark 15:40).

Jane (f)
[jayn] feminine form of *John*.
Jane Frances de Chantal (1572-1641) French foundress. Born Jane Frances Frémyot in Dijon, she was the daughter of the president of the parliament of Burgundy. When she was 20 years old she married Baron Christophe de Rabutin-Chantal of Bourbilly, to whom she was devoted, and went on to bear him seven children before he was killed in a hunting accident 1601. Jane took a vow of celibacy and for a time endured harsh treatment at the hands of her tyrannical father-in-law before hearing St Francis de Sales preaching in 1604 and being inspired to serve as one of his

disciples. She became a nun in 1610 and that same year, in collaboration with her close friend and spiritual adviser St Francis, founded the Order of the Visitation of the Virgin Mary.

Variants: **Janice**, **Janie**, **Jayne**, **Jennie**, **Jenny**.

Janet, **Janice** feminine forms of **Jane**.

Japheth (m)
[JAY-feth] possibly from Hebrew, meaning 'to be spacious'. One of Noah's three sons who survived the flood with him and from whom the world was repopulated (Genesis 6:10; 9:18–19, 27).

120

Jared (m)
[JA-red] from Hebrew, meaning 'descent'.
The father of Enoch and other children; he lived to be 962 years old (Genesis 5:15–20). He is also mentioned in Luke's genealogy of Jesus (Luke 3:37).

Jason (m)
[JAY-suhn] possibly from *Joshua*.
The name of two men in the New Testament: Jewish Christian at Thessalonica, who received and helped Paul. Jason and others were called before the city officials because of their association with the Christian missionaries but were released. Also, a Christian (Paul's 'relative') who is listed among those who send greetings in Paul's letter to the church at Rome (Romans 16:21).

Jasper variant of **Casper**.

Jean, **Jeanne**, **Jeanette**, **Jeannette** feminine forms of **John**.

Jedidiah (m)
[jed-i-DY-uh] from Hebrew, meaning 'beloved of Yahweh'.

The name the prophet Nathan gave from God to the baby Solomon (David's second son by Bathsheba) (2 Samuel 12:24–25).

Jemima (f)
[juh-MY-muh] from Hebrew, meaning 'wild dove'.
The eldest daughter born to Job after his restoration (Job 42:13–15).

Jephthah (m)
[JEF-thuh] from Hebrew, meaning 'he releases/opens'.
One of the judges, who defeated Ammonite forces on both sides of the Jordan and led Israel for six years. He sacrificed his daughter as a result of a careless vow to God (Judges 10:6–12:7).

Jeremiah (m)
[je-ruh-MY-uh] from Hebrew, meaning 'may Yahweh exalt'.
A prophet who was active from 626 BC until after the fall of Jerusalem in 587 BC. Sometimes known as the 'weeping prophet', he was a deeply sensitive man (Jeremiah 8:21–9:1). He faced repeated rejection from his family as well as the people, and was finally taken against his will by some Jewish exiles to Egypt where he is thought to have died.
    Variants: **Jeremy**, **Jerry**, **Jez**.

Jerome (m)
[juh-ROHM] from Greek, meaning 'sacred name'.
Italian biblical scholar (c.341–420). Born Eusebius Hieronymus Sophronius into a wealthy family of Strido in Dalmatia, he established a reputation as a scholar while living in Rome, inspired by classical literature and Cicero, before being baptised by the Pope at the age of 18. Subsequently he rejected the distractions of the material world and lived as a monk for some years. He later

travelled to Antioch, but contracted a serious illness during which he experienced a vision of Christ, who berated him for his failings as a Christian. When he recovered, Jerome spent the next four years as a hermit in the Syrian desert before eventually returning to his scholastic studies in Constantinople under the guidance of St Gregory of Nazianzus.

Of Jerome's many influential writings his translation of the Bible from Greek and Hebrew into Latin was the most important, and the resulting Latin Vulgate Bible remained the authoritative translation until around the middle of the twentieth century by virtue of its clarity and accessibility. Jerome is honoured today both as a Doctor of the Church and as the patron saint of biblical scholars and librarians.

122

Jesse (m)
[JES-ee] from Hebrew, meaning 'Yahweh exists'.
David's father, to whose house in Bethlehem Samuel came to anoint Saul's successor as king (1 Samuel 16:1–13).

Jessica (f)
[jes-i-kuh] from Hebrew, *Iscah*, probably meaning 'she will look out'.
Found in the Old Testament in the form of *Iscah*, Abraham's niece (Genesis 11:29). The name was popularised by Shakespeare who gave this name to Shylock's daughter in *The Merchant of Venice*.
Variants: **Jess**, **Jessie**.

Jesus (m)
[JEE-zuhs] from Hebrew, meaning 'Yahweh saves'.
The founder and centre of Christianity. Jesus was born in or before 4 BC, but little is known of his life before the age of 30 except that he was a carpenter and grew up in a poor family in Nazareth (Matthew 13:55; Luke 2:51–52). His public ministry began with his baptism and his

temptations (Matthew 3:13–4:11). For the next three years, he travelled around Palestine, preaching and teaching and carrying out a wide range of miracles, healing people of various diseases. The central theme of his teaching was 'the kingdom of God': God's powerful activity in the world and his rule over people's lives. He concentrated his attention on the Jewish people, leaving Palestine only rarely to visit Phoenicia and the Decapolis. He lived as a poor person, with no home of his own, and supported by his disciples. Opposition was common, especially from Jewish religious leaders, though his miracles made him popular with ordinary people.

Highlights included the Transfiguration, possibly on Mount Hermon, and Peter's first recognition that Jesus was the expected Messiah (Matthew 16:15–20). The Gospels give special attention to the events of the last week of his life, especially the Last Supper, the garden of Gethsemane, his trial, crucifixion and resurrection. He ascended to heaven 40 days later, but an angel promised he would return again, confirming what Jesus himself had taught. Often generally thought to be too sacred as a first name, it is popular as a first name with Spanish speakers.

123

Jethro (m)
[JETH-roh] from Hebrew, meaning 'abundance' or 'excellent'.
Moses' father-in-law, also known as Reuel and Hobab. He advised Moses of the need to delegate his responsibilities (Exodus 18).

Jezebel (f)
[JEZ-uh-bel] from Hebrew, meaning 'where is the prince' or 'where is the dung'.
A Phoenician woman from Tyre who married Ahab king of Israel. She actively pursued a policy of promoting the worship of Baal and of opposing the worshippers of the

Lord, especially the prophet Elijah (1 Kings 18:13–14; 19:1–2). Her death was prophesied by Elijah (1 Kings 21:23), which was ultimately fulfilled (2 Kings 9:30–37). Also the name of a woman prophet in the church at Thyatira who led believers astray (Revelation 2:20).

Joachim (m)
[JOH-uh-kim, yoh-AH-kim] from Hebrew, meaning 'may Yahweh exalt'.
Tradition names Joachim as the father of the Virgin Mary. See **Ann**.

124   **Joan** (f)
[john] feminine form of *John*.
Joan of Arc (c.1412–31), French heroine otherwise known as the Maid of Orléans. Born into a poor peasant family, she received a revelation in 1425 when, at the age of 13, she heard what she identified as the voice of St Michael. She went on to hear his voice, and that of various other angels, many more times and in 1428 reported that St Michael had instructed her to raise the English siege of Orléans and achieve the crowning of the Dauphin Charles at Rheims.

Believing this to be the will of God, the illiterate 16-year-old Joan embarked on her mission, initially provoking scorn and admiration in equal measure among the French soldiery and general populace. Stories quickly accumulated of miracles she had performed and the Dauphin, suitably impressed, recruited her assistance, providing her with a suit of armour and forces. She became the inspiration of the French army, which with Joan at its head successfully drove the English besiegers from Orléans. She enjoyed further victories at Patay and Troyes. In 1429 she saw Charles crowned king of France in Rheims cathedral, as she had dreamt.

Within a year, however, while attempting to relieve Compiègne, Joan was captured by the Burgundian rivals of

Charles and, abandoned by the Dauphin, was handed over to their allies the English. After nine months in prison she was brought before an ecclesiastical court presided over by the bishop of Beauvais on charges of heresy. Joan's spirited defence failed to persuade the court against imposing the death penalty, and she was burnt at the stake in the market square in Rouen on 31 May 1431 and her ashes thrown into the Seine.

Joan was declared innocent of heresy by papal decree in 1456 and was canonised in 1920, not for dying a martyr's death but for living the life of a godly Christian virgin. Her story has inspired countless works of art and literature. She is honoured as the patron saint of France, soldiers, captives and virgins.

Variants: **Jean**, **Jeanne**, **Siobhan**.

Joanna (f)
[joh-AN-uh] feminine form of *John*.
The wife of Chuza, steward of Herod, who provided for Jesus and his disciples from her own resources. She probably witnessed Jesus' crucifixion and was present when he was laid in the tomb; later she found his tomb empty (Luke 24:10).

Variants: **Jo**, **Joanne**.

Job (m)
[johb] from Hebrew, meaning 'persecuted'.
The main character of the Book of Job. He came from the land of Uz (Job 1:1) which was associated either with Edom or north-west Palestine. Though known among his contemporaries as 'the greatest man among all the people of the East' (1:3), his subsequent experiences of suffering and anguish eventually brought a deeper understanding of God.

Joel (m)
[JOH-el] from Hebrew, meaning 'Yahweh is God'.

The Old Testament prophet who saw a plague of locusts as a portrayal of God's judgement (Joel 1:2–2:12). He called on the people to turn back to God. He prophesied a future blessing that included the outpouring of the Spirit (Joel 2:18–32) which was fulfilled on the Day of Pentecost (Acts 2:16–21).

John (m)
[jon] from Hebrew, meaning 'Yahweh is gracious'.
John, the apostle, who was part of Jesus' inner circle. The nickname 'son of thunder' suggests a lively, possibly aggressive personality, but one who was transformed by his association with Jesus into 'the disciple whom Jesus loved'. He was the only apostle to see the crucifixion and the first to see the empty tomb (John 19:26–27; 20:4–5). Later he became a leader in the Jerusalem and Ephesian churches. Traditionally considered the writer of the fourth Gospel, the Letters of John and Revelation.

John the Baptist. A relative of Jesus who is known chiefly in the New Testament as Jesus' forerunner. His ministry was characterised by the practice of water baptism and by the message of repentance (Mathew 3:1–17). Jesus regarded him as the last and greatest prophet, fulfilling the promise of a second Elijah (Matthew 11:11–14). Despite a successful ministry, he was killed by Herod Antipas for criticising his marriage to his sister-in-law (Matthew 14:1–12).

Variants: **Evan**, **Iain**, **Ian**, **Ivan**, **Jack**, **Jock**, **Johnnie**, **Johnny**, **Juan**, **St John**, **Sean**, **Shaun**, **Shawn**.

Feminine forms: **Jane**, **Janet**, **Janice**, **Jean**, **Jeanne**, **Jeanette**, **Jeannette**, **Joan**, **Joanna**, **Joanne**, **Sheena**, **Shona**, **Sian**.

Jonah (m)
[JOH-nuh] from Hebrew, meaning 'dove'.
An eighth-century BC prophet (2 Kings 14:25) who disobeyed God. Having tried unsuccessfully to avoid God's

call to preach to Nineveh, he spoke about judgment when God wanted him to talk about his love. His escape after being swallowed by a large fish finds some support from documented examples of similar cases.

Variant: **Jonas**.

Jonathan (m)
[JON-uh-thuhn] from Hebrew, meaning 'Yahweh has given'.
King Saul's eldest son, who was a more able soldier and exercised greater faith than his father. He made a covenant of friendship with David, to whom he showed outstanding devotion and loyalty at considerable cost to himself (1 Samuel 18:1–4).

Variants: **Johnnie**, **Johnny**, **Jon**.

127

Jordan (m, f)
[JAW-duhn] from the name of the river.
Israel's major river, flowing southwards from near Mount Hermon through a valley into the Dead Sea. It flows for nearly 200 km through Huleh and the Sea of Galilee, dividing the main part of Israel in the west from Transjordan in the east. It is associated with many important events, such as Israel's entry to the Promised Land on dry ground (Joshua 3–4) and Jesus' baptism (Matthew 3:13–17).

Also *Jordan of Saxony (died 1237), German Dominican leader*. Jordan's considerable leadership qualities were recognised early in his career as a member of the Dominican order. Having joined the order in 1220 he took part in the first general chapter at Bologna and when the order's founder St Dominic died just two years later he was the natural choice to become the Dominicans' second master-general. He then led a great expansion in the Dominican order, winning many converts at the universities where he preached. His disciples included St

Albert the Great. He formed a long and enduring friendship with St Diana d'Andalo and writing numerous letters to her, of which many survive. His other writings included a celebrated biography of St Dominic.

Joseph (m)
[JOH-zif] from Hebrew, meaning 'may he add (another son)'. In the *Old Testament, Joseph, the favourite son of Jacob* and his first son by Rachel, his favourite wife. He was the owner of the famous coat of many colours, though actually it was probably a long-sleeved coat. His story (Genesis 37–50) contrasts the working of God's purpose in his life with his own immaturity, his father's over-indulgence and his brothers' jealousy. Joseph's faith, courage and wisdom eventually preserved his whole family in Egypt (Genesis 45:7–8), but only after much suffering. Joseph was made second only to Pharaoh in Egypt, and though he is not mentioned in existing records, several incidental details about him are confirmed in Egyptian sources, suggesting that the brilliant literary story of Joseph is historically reliable.

In the *New Testament, Joseph, husband of Mary*, who cared for Jesus as though he were his earthly father (Matthew 1:18–2:23). A descendant of David, the silence of the Gospels about him during Jesus' ministry indicates that he died before Jesus reached the age of 30.

Joseph of Arimathea, a secret disciple and member of the Sanhedrin who provided his tomb for Jesus' body to be buried (Matthew 27:57–60). The location of Arimathea is uncertain, but is thought to be Rathamein in Samaria.

Variants: **Joe**, **Joey**, **José**.
Feminine forms: **Josephine**, **Josie**.

Josephine feminine form of **Joseph**.

128

Joshua (m)
[JOSH-ew-uh] from Hebrew, meaning 'Yahweh saves'.
Joshua, son of Nun, Moses' assistant and successor, originally named Hoshea. Because of their outstanding faith, only he and Caleb among the adults who left Egypt actually entered the Promised Land of Canaan (Numbers 13–14). Joshua led Israel's military campaigns during the people's first five years in Canaan. Near the end of his 110-year life, he challenged Israel to renew their covenant with God (Joshua 23–24).

Also the *high priest also known as Joshua*, a high priest who was involved in rebuilding the temple after the exile (Zechariah 3:1–10).

129

Variant: **Josh**.

Josiah (m)
[JOH-zy-uh] from Hebrew, meaning 'may Yahweh heal'.
A king who in his teenage years began a religious reformation that led to the discovery of an old 'Scroll of the law' and resulted in a national covenant renewal ceremony. He was tragically killed by Egyptian forces who were not at war with Judah (2 Kings 22:1–23:30).

Variant: **Josh**.

Josie feminine form of **Joseph**.

Jotham (m)
[JO-thuhm] from Hebrew, meaning 'Yahweh is righteous'.
The youngest of Gideon's sons who escaped the slaughter in which his brothers were killed. Also, the eleventh king of Judah (742–735 BC) (2 Kings 15:32–38; 2 Chronicles 27).

Joy (f) [joy] (ultimately from Latin *gaudere*, 'to rejoice').
The feeling or state of great happiness, e.g. at events such as the birth of a child. In the Bible, joy also often refers to an attitude which comes from an experience of God. It is

a quality of happiness which should characterise every Christian (Philippians 4:4). What particularly distinguishes Christian joy is that it can be experienced even in times of great difficulty (1 Peter 4:13). Throughout the Bible, it is often experienced in worship and in response to signs of God's work in people's lives.

Joyce (f)
[joys] from Breton name *Jodoc*.
Seventh-century hermit, also known as *Jodoc*, *Josse*, *Judoc* or *Judocus*, known for his penance, prayer, meditation and healings. The name gradually became to be given to boys or girls, and then eventually only to girls.
    Variant: **Jocelyn**.

130

Judah (m)
[JEW-duh] from Hebrew, meaning 'praise'.
Jacob's fourth son, and a leader among his brothers, though it seems he did not have high moral or spiritual standards (Genesis 38).

The most important of the tribes of Israel, occupying the southern part of Canaan and gradually absorbing several smaller tribal groups including Simeon and Benjamin. This larger Judah developed a separate identity by the time of the judges. The New Testament refers to Jesus' descent from Judah (Hebrews 7:14; Revelation 5:5).

The kingdom of Judah in southern Canaan lasted from c.922 BC until the fall of Jerusalem in 587 BC (1 Kings 12:17–19; 2 Kings 25:21). It was ruled by David's descendants, apart from the brief reign of Queen Athaliah. Judah's greatest periods were under Uzziah and Hezekiah in the eighth century BC. After the exile, Judah was reduced to the status of a province under the Babylonians and Persians, though for some time it had its own governor of whom the best known are Zerubbabel and Nehemiah

(Nehemiah 5:14). It became the Roman province of Judea in the first century AD.

Judas (m)
[JEW-duhs] Greek form of *Judah*.
Judas Iscariot. The apostles' treasurer, who sometimes helped himself to their funds. He betrayed Jesus for 30 pieces of silver, but committed suicide because of remorse over Jesus' death (Matthew 26:14–16). The name Iscariot probably indicates his place of origin.

Also, *Judas, son of James*. One of the twelve apostles, probably also called Thaddaeus and often identified as being the same apostle as Jude. His only claim to fame is a question asked at the Last Supper (John 14:22).

131

Jude (m)
[jewd] variant of *Judah*.
First-century apostle. Half-brother of Jesus, the brother of James and the author of the Letter of Jude in the New Testament. He is honoured today as the patron saint of hospitals and of lost causes (an association that may have arisen through the similarity between his name and that of Judas Iscariot, as a result of which he is thought less likely to be approached by many petitioners and thus ready to answer even the most hopeless prayer).

Judith (f)
[JEW-dith] from Hebrew, meaning 'woman of Judea', 'Jewess'.
In the Old Testament, the daughter of Beeri the Hittite and wife of Esau (Genesis 26:34). In the apocryphal book of Judith, the enterprising woman who saved the people of Israel by letting the enemy general Holofernes think he was seducing her, and then cutting off his head with his sword.

Variants: **Jodi**, **Jodie**, **Jody**, **Judy**.

Julia (f)
[JEW-lee-uh] feminine form of *Julius*.
The name of several saints, including Julia of Troyes, third-century martyr saint, who was taken prisoner by the Romans. She is said to have been given to a Roman officer named Claudius, whom she led to the Christian faith and they were both beheaded together.

  Variants: **Julie**, **Juliet**.

Julian (m)
[JEW-lee-uhn] variant of *Julius*.
Julian of Norwich (c.1343–c.1423), English mystic. Little is known about this fourteenth-century female recluse, including even her name – she is called Julian of Norwich simply because she lived in a cell adjoining the Benedictine church of St Julian in Conisford, Norwich. Having narrowly survived death from illness at the age of 30 she fell seriously ill once more in 1373 and experienced a series of 16 revelatory visions, mostly concerning the passion of Christ. After her recovery, she meditated on these visions and, being apparently a well-educated woman, went on to record her thoughts in *Revelations of Divine Love*, which was widely read in later centuries.

  Julian the Hospitaller (dates unknown), nobleman. Historical evidence for the existence of Julian the Hospitaller appears to be scant; Julian is identified in tales as a nobleman who mistakenly kills his own mother and father. He is driven by remorse to give up his wealth and live humbly with his wife beside a ford across a river, where he may do penance by tending to the needs of travellers and offering shelter to the poor. When the couple offer a dying leper their own bed to sleep in, they are finally assured that Christ has forgiven them. Julian and his wife duly die soon after. He is also honoured as the patron saint of ferrymen and innkeepers as well as circus performers and other wandering folk.

  Feminine form: **Gillian**.

Juliana (f)

[jew-lee-AH-nuh] feminine form of *Julian*.

Fourth-century Italian martyr. Legend has it that she engaged in a long contest with the devil, who sought to persuade her to give up her vow of virginity and marry as her father and suitor wished. She is thought to have been tortured and beheaded for her stubborn faith.

Also *Juliana Falconieri (1270–1341), Italian foundress*. Born the daughter of wealthy parents in Florence, she declined to marry and instead entered the Servite order as a tertiary. She remained at home, living a godly existence and doing good deeds, for some 20 years before her mother died in 1304 and she moved into a convent of nuns called the Mantellate and became their superior. She eventually secured full recognition for the sisters as members of the Servite order and is consequently remembered as the effective foundress of the Servite nuns.

Variant: **Lianne**.

Julie (f)

[JEW-lee] French form of *Julia*.

Julie Billiart (1751–1816), French foundress. Born into a wealthy family in Picardy, she saw her family gradually slip into poverty but still found time to teach others in religious matters. In 1774, however, her life changed dramatically when someone fired a shot at her father through the window of their house. The shot missed but triggered a mysterious nervous illness in Julie that rendered her a bed-ridden invalid. Undaunted, she continued her religious studies and, with the outbreak of the French Revolution, emerged as a prominent and outspoken opponent of the new state church. She was obliged to go into hiding from those who tried to silence her but she continued to work tirelessly to renew the faith in France, founding the Institute of Notre Dame in Amiens to care for and instruct girls of poor families.

In 1804 a visiting priest commanded her to pray to the Sacred Heart and soon after she found herself able to walk again. She spent the last years of her life establishing a chain of 15 convents throughout the country.

Julitta (f)
[jew-LEE-tuh] variant of *Julia*.
With Cyricus, martyr of Iconium in Lycaonia (Turkey) (died c.304). Julitta was a nobleman's widow who was condemned to death as a Christian at Tarsus under the Emperor Diocletian. When the governor Alexander sought to comfort the woman's three-year-old son Cyricus, the child only scratched his face. The enraged governor threw the child down some steps and the boy was killed. Julitta then went uncomplainingly to her own torture and death. The memory of Cyricus is preserved in a number of place names across Europe and the Near East.

Julius (m)
[JEW-lee-uhs] possibly from Greek, meaning 'hairy' or 'downy'.
The centurion of the Augustan Cohort (Imperial Regiment) who was put in charge of the apostle Paul and other prisoners (Acts 27:1). His kind treatment of Paul is mentioned (Acts 27:3).

Julius I (died 352), Italian pope. Born in Rome, he succeeded St Marcus as pope after a gap of four months in 337. As pope, he presided over the early church during one of its most turbulent periods, having to cope with much theological controversy and dissension between his bishops, who levelled charges of heresy at one another. He gave his support to St Athanasius against the adherents of Arianism and helped secure his return to his see at Alexandria and in so doing asserted the authority of the papacy over the church. Oversaw the expansion of the

Christian community, ordered the building of two basilicas and churches and introduced the first lists of saints' days.

Variants: **Jules**, **Julian**.

Feminine form: **Julia**.

Justin (m)

[JUS-tin] from Latin *Justus*, meaning 'just'.

Greek philosopher and martyr (c.100–165). Born of Greek parentage in Neopolis, the capital of Samaria, he established a reputation as a pagan philosopher before becoming converted to Christianity, finding it a more satisfactory system than those he had previously studied. He went on to devote his considerable gifts as a philosopher to Christian theology, addressing himself in particular to Jews and pagans in the conviction that he could attract many more converts to the faith. He arrived in Rome around 150 and established a school of philosophy in the city, as well as writing books on Christian philosophy, but was soon attacked by pagan critics for his outspoken views and was eventually arrested and beheaded for refusing to make sacrifices to the gods. He is remembered as the first Christian philosopher and is accordingly honoured as the patron saint of philosophers.

135

Feminine form: **Justine**.

Justina (f)

[jus-TEE-nuh] feminine form of *Justin*.

With Cyprian, martyr of Antioch (c.300). According to legend, Cyprian was a sorcerer of Antioch who attempted to win the love of the Christian maiden Justina through his magic. Depressed at his lack of success in this enterprise, Cyprian found himself attracted to the faith his beloved professed and in due course was baptised himself and became a bishop, while Justina became an abbess. They were both martyred at Nicodemia.

Justine feminine form of **Justin**.

Justus (m)
[JUS-tuhs] from Latin, meaning 'just'.
Justus of Beauvais (dates unknown), French martyr.
Legend has it that Justus of Beauvais was a nine-year-old
boy who was put to death by the authorities after he helped
to hide two fellow-Christians (his father and his uncle)
from their Roman pursuers during the persecution carried
out in the reign of Emperor Diocletian. The location of
these events is traditionally placed at Saint-Just-en-
Chaussée between Beauvais and Senlis.

136   Also *Justus of Canterbury (died c.627), English bishop.*
Justus of Canterbury arrived in England with the second
group of Roman missionaries sent by St Gregory the Great
in 601. He became the first bishop of Rochester in 604 and
in this post sought to bring the practice of Irish and British
Christians into line with that of Rome. He was obliged to
flee to Gaul after the death of King Ethelbert but soon
returned and in 624, in recognition of his piety and loyalty
to Rome, was appointed fourth archbishop of Canterbury.

Jutta (f)
[YOO-tuh] variant of *Judith*, meaning 'from Judea, Jewish'.
Noblewoman from Thuringia (died 1260). Happily married
with a family, she was grief-stricken when her husband
died on a pilgrimage to the Holy Land. She moved to
Prussia and lived as a hermit in Kulmsee.

Katherine see **Catherine**.

Kenelm (m)
[KEN-elm] from Old English *cene*, meaning 'bold' and
helm, meaning 'helmet'.
English prince (died c.811). The life of St Kenelm is
shrouded in obscurity, but tradition has it that he was the

son of King Coenwulf of Mercia and was murdered on the orders of his sister Quoenthryth as soon as he succeeded to the throne. Quoenthryth allegedly suffered punishment for the deed when her eyes fell out. Historians suggest that in reality Kenelm probably died before his father, possibly in battle against the Welsh.

Kenneth (m)
[KEN-ith] from Gaelic, meaning 'handsome'.
Irish abbot (c.525–600), originally Canice (otherwise called Cainnech or, in Scotland, Kenneth), was born in County Derry. A companion of St Columba, whom he visited several times on Iona, he appears to have spent some time in the Western Isles, on the Scottish mainland and in Wales before returning to Ireland to found the monastery of Aghaboe in Ossory around 577. He may also have founded another monastery at Kilkenny. His memory is preserved through several Scottish place names.

Variants: **Ken**, **Kenny**.

Kentigern (m)
[KEN-ti-gern] from Celtic, meaning 'chief lord'.
Scottish bishop (c.518–612). Otherwise called Mungo (meaning 'darling'), Kentigern is traditionally supposed to have been born in Lothian, possibly of royal birth. He became a monk, adopting the Celtic practices of self-denial and solitude, and in due course founded a church at Glasgow and was appointed the city's first bishop. He is also said to have worked as a missionary in Cumbria or Wales, possibly founding the monastery at Llanelwy.

Various legends surround Kentigern, including one in which he agreed to assist a queen who had passed a ring the king had given her to her lover, only for the king to retrieve the ring, throw it in the sea and then challenge his wife to present it to him. Kentigern went fishing, found the ring in the stomach of a salmon he caught and was able to return it to the remorseful queen. This tale is thought to be the reason why a ring and a fish appear on the coat of arms of Glasgow, of which he is the patron saint.

Kerenhappuch (f)
[keer-uhn-HAP-uuk] from Hebrew, meaning 'horn of antimony'.
The third daughter born to Job after his restoration (Job 42:13–15). The origin of her name suggests her beauty: antimony was formerly used as an eyeshadow.

Keturah (f)
138
[ke-TEW-ruh] from Hebrew, meaning 'fragrance'.
Abraham's second wife (Genesis 25:1; also called his concubine in 1 Chronicles), who gave birth to several children, including most notably Midian (Genesis 25:4; 1 Chronicles 1:32–33).

Kevin (m)
[KE-vin] from Irish, meaning 'fair or handsome birth'.
Irish abbot (died 618). Born in Leinster, Kevin (or Coemgen) was brought up at the monastery of Kilmanach before living the life of a hermit at Glendalough, picturesquely situated in Wicklow. Here he attracted many disciples and out of this community evolved the famous abbey of Glendalough, which also boasted a celebrated school. Kevin is also said to have made a pilgrimage to Rome, from which he brought back various relics. Though weakened by a life of great austerity, he is said to have lived to the age of 120. He is honoured as the patron saint of Dublin.

Keziah (f)
[kuh-ZY-uh] from Hebrew, meaning 'cassia'.
The second daughter born to him after his restoration (Job 42:13–15).

Kieran (m)

[KEER-uhn] from Irish name *Ciaran*, meaning 'dark-haired'.

Ciaran of Clonmacnoise (c.512–545), Irish abbot. Ciaran (otherwise referred to as Ceran, Kieran or Queran) was born the son of a travelling carpenter in Connacht and educated at the monastery of St Finnian of Clonard. Subsequently he studied as a monk on Inishmore. He settled eventually at Clonmacnoise on the Shannon, in County Meath, establishing a famous monastery there. Although he died within a year of the monastery's foundation, aged only 33, it became hugely influential through the many pupils who studied there.

Kinborough (f)

[KIN-buh-ruh] Old English *Cyneburga*, meaning 'royal fortress'.

A Mercian princess, who married the king of Northumbria, (died c.680). She founded, and was abbess of, the convent at Castor (Northamptonshire).

Kirsty feminine form of **Christian**.

Laban (m)

[LAY-buhn] from Hebrew, meaning 'white'.

Rebekah's brother and Jacob's father-in-law. He was often in conflict with Jacob while the latter stayed with him for 20 years (Genesis 29–31).

Lambert (m)

[LAM-buht] from Old German *land*, meaning 'land' and *beraht*, meaning 'bright'.

Bishop and martyr of Maastricht (c.635–c.705). Born into a noble family of Maastricht, he was educated by the local bishop and eventually succeeded to his post upon the latter's murder in 670. Political opponents forced Lambert into exile in a monastery at Stavelot but after his restoration as bishop he went on to earn an enduring reputation as an energetic missionary, working chiefly in Kempenland and Brabant, which were then largely unconverted to Christianity. He was eventually murdered at Liège, possibly on the orders of Pepin after he took exception to the bishop's criticisms of his adultery with his sister-in-law.

Lamech (m)
[LAY-mek] from Hebrew, meaning 'strong youth'.
The name of two men in the Old Testament. A descendant of Cain who murdered for revenge (Genesis 4:23–24). Also, a son of Methuselah and father of Noah (Genesis 5:25–31).

140

Laura (f)
[LAW-ruh] from Latin name *Laurus*, meaning 'laurel'.
Martyr of Spain born in Cordoba, Spain, she became a nun at Cuteclara. She was scalded to death by the Moors in 864.
   Variants: **Lauren**, **Laurie**, **Loreen**, **Loren**.

Laurence, **Lawrence** (m)
[LO-rens] from Latin name *Laurentius*, meaning 'of Laurentum', from Latin *laurus*, meaning 'laurel'.
Roman martyr (died 258). Lawrence (or Laurence) is traditionally identified as one of the seven deacons of Rome and is believed to have been martyred for his faith. Legend has it that he was put to death by being roasted on a grid after defying an order from Emperor Valerian to surrender the riches of the church, offering him only the poor and the sick of the city. He is supposed to have been buried on the site of the future church of St Lawrence-outside-the-Walls on the road to Tivoli. Lawrence is honoured as the patron saint of cooks, cutlers, glaziers and of Rome and Sri Lanka.
   Also *Lawrence of Brindisi (1559–1619), Italian theologian and preacher.* Born Cesare de' Rossi into a

wealthy family of Brindisi, he joined the Capuchin Franciscans and completed his education at the University of Padua. Subsequently, aided by his mastery of several languages, he established a considerable reputation as an evangelical preacher, speaking before congregations throughout Europe.

Lawrence of Canterbury (died 619), English archbishop. A Roman Benedictine monk who arrived in England on the orders of Pope Gregory the Great in 597, he was a close ally of Augustine of Canterbury and was trusted by him to return to Rome with Augustine's reports on evangelical progress in Britain. He made the journey back to Britain in 601 and was nominated as Augustine's successor as archbishop of Canterbury by Augustine himself. Lawrence accordingly took over the see on the death of his friend and continued in the post in the face of opposition from the pagan king Eadbald, which ended with Eadbald's conversion, but failed to achieve union with the rival Anglo-Saxon bishops.

141

Lawrence Giustiniani (1381–1455), Italian archbishop. Born into a noble family of Venice, he became a canon of the Augustinian monastery of San Giorgio on the island of Alga and there lived the life of a devout but penniless beggar. Admired both for his energy and for his generosity and humility, he was eventually made general of the congregation (1424) and then appointed bishop of Castello (1433). He was later moved to Venice, where he undertook extensive reform and consolidated his reputation for generosity with gifts of food and clothing.

Lawrence O'Toole (c.1128–80), Irish bishop. Born Lorcan ua Tuathail near Castledermot, Lawrence (or Laurence) was the son of a chieftain and at the age of 10 began two years as a hostage of the rival McMurrough clan. Having been accepted as a monk at Glendalough, he distinguished himself by his simple and austere ways and through his devotion to his fellow-man, noted especially for his generosity to the poor. In due course he was appointed abbot at Glendalough and subsequently (1161) archbishop of Dublin.

After the English invaded Ireland in 1170 Lawrence played a prominent part firstly in the resistance movement and then in negotiations between Rory O'Connor, king of Connacht, and Henry II of England. His work as papal legate in Ireland incurred the enmity of Henry II and he was obliged to remain in exile from his homeland until the opportunity finally came for him to meet the king in Normandy and to persuade him to raise the prohibition.

Variants: **Larry, Lars, Lauren, Laurie, Lorenzo**.

142

Lazarus (m)
[LAZ-uh-ruhs] Latin form of *Eleazar*.
Two named individuals in the New Testament. The poor man in one of Jesus' parables (the only character named in his parables) who went to heaven in contrast to his rich neighbour who suffered God's judgement (Luke 16:19–31). Also Mary and Martha's brother who lived in Bethany and whom Jesus miraculously raised from death (John 11).

Leah (f)
[leer] from Hebrew, meaning 'weary'.
Jacob's first wife. She was less favoured than her younger sister Rachel because she was not so attractive, but she bore him seven children (Genesis 29:16–30:21).

Leander (m)
[lee-AN-duh] from Greek, meaning 'lion of a man'.
Spanish bishop (c.550–600). Born the son of the Duke of Cartegana, he was the elder brother of St Isidore and preceded him as bishop of Seville, to which post he was appointed c.584. A confidante of Gregory the Great, whom he first met on a mission to Constantinople in 583, he won admiration for his conversion of the Spanish Visigoths from

Arianism. Another legacy was his introduction of the singing of the Nicene Creed at Mass.

Lemuel (m)
[LEM-yoo-uhl] from Hebrew, meaning 'dedicated to God'. King Lemuel, the author of Proverbs 31:1–9 (also known as 'king of Massa'), occasionally identified as Solomon.

Leo (m)
[LEE-oh] from Latin *leo*, meaning 'lion'.
Leo the Great (died 461), Roman pope. Probably born in Rome, possibly of Tuscan parents, Leo served as a deacon in the city before being elected Pope in 440. As Leo I, he established a reputation as perhaps the greatest of the successors of Peter, widely respected for consolidating the strength of the church at a time of crisis. In 451, at the Council of Chalcedon, he wrote a profoundly influential letter that established the orthodox approach on the nature of Christ, accepting him as both divine and human. A year later he dissuaded Attila the Hun from attacking Rome while, in 455, he prevented a massacre when the Vandals occupied the city. After the Vandals left, he supervised the rebuilding of Rome and promoted the welfare of its citizens, as well as sending aid to Roman prisoners held in Africa.

143

He never wavered in emphasising the authority of Rome over the rest of the church, extending his influence through Spain, Gaul and elsewhere, and set an example for later pontiffs through his piety and determination. Upon his death in Rome he was laid to rest in St Peter's. He was declared a Doctor of the Church in 1754.

Also, the name of several popes, including: *Leo III (died 816), Roman pope.* Of humble birth, Leo rose through the ranks of the church to succeed Hadrian I as Pope in 795. His 20-year reign witnessed opposition from supporters of a rival claimant to the papacy, which became so bitter that he

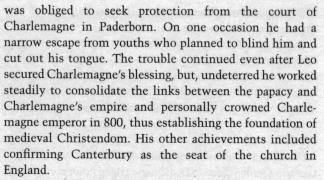

was obliged to seek protection from the court of Charlemagne in Paderborn. On one occasion he had a narrow escape from youths who planned to blind him and cut out his tongue. The trouble continued even after Leo secured Charlemagne's blessing, but, undeterred he worked steadily to consolidate the links between the papacy and Charlemagne's empire and personally crowned Charlemagne emperor in 800, thus establishing the foundation of medieval Christendom. His other achievements included confirming Canterbury as the seat of the church in England.

Leo IX (1002–54), Italian pope. Born into a noble family of Alsace, he distinguished himself as a military leader on behalf of the bishop of Toul and in 1027 succeeded to the bishopric himself. Ultimately he rose to the rank of pope in 1048 and over the next six years did much to restore the battered reputation of the papacy through extensive reform of the church. He combated simony and other abuses among the clergy and also sought to free the church from secular influence. He promoted monasticism and declared that future popes should be elected by the cardinals alone.

Variant: **Leon**.

Leonard (m)
[LEN-uhd] Old German, meaning 'brave lion'.
French hermit (dates unknown). Nothing is known for certain of the life of St Leonard, who may have lived around the sixth century, but legend claims that he was a hermit who founded a monastery at Noblac (later renamed Saint-Léonard) near Limoges. Various miracles were ascribed to him and he became a popular saint in France, England and Germany. He is honoured as the patron saint of captives and pregnant women.

Also, *Leonard of Port Maurice (1676–1751), Italian missioner.* Born Paul Jerome Casanuova at Port Maurice on the Italian Riviera, he was educated by the Jesuits in Rome and joined the strict Franciscan order known as the Riformella, soon emerging as its charismatic leader. Based in Rome and Florence, he established a reputation as an evangelising preacher throughout northern Italy, attracting huge crowds and making thousands of converts over some 40 years.

His sermons, typically held outdoors to accommodate his vast audiences, often referred to the Stations of the Cross and in due course he set up 571 sets of stations throughout the country. He is honoured today as the patron saint of popular missionaries.

Variants: **Len**, **Lennie**, **Lenny**.

Leopold (m)
[LEE-uh-pohld] from Old German, *leudi*, meaning 'people' and *bald*, meaning 'bold'.
Leopold of Austria or Leopold the Good, Leopold III (1075–1136), Austrian duke. Leopold was born at Melk and inherited the dukedom of Austria in 1095. Very little is known of his reign, but he acquired the reputation of a wise and generous ruler who won the love of his people and did much to promote the church. He also contributed towards the First Crusade and presided over the founding of various religious foundations, of which several survive. His humility is seen when he declined to be nominated for the imperial crown. In 1663 he was named patron saint of Austria.

Levi (m)
[LEE-vy] from Hebrew, meaning 'associated'.
In the *Old Testament, Jacob's third son*, who led an attack on Shechem in revenge for his sister's rape (Genesis 34). The tribe descended from Levi were responsible for Israel's worship (Numbers 3). Some were priests, and the rest helped them administratively, fulfilling the roles of musicians, treasurers and gatekeepers (1 Chronicles 23:28–32).

In the *New Testament, one of the apostles*, probably the same person as the tax collector Matthew (Mark 2:14). See **Matthew**.

Lilian (f)
[LI-lee-uhn] from Latin, meaning 'lily'.
Name given to honour the Blessed Virgin Mary, whose symbol is a white lily, to represent her purity.
 Variants: **Lillian, Lilly, Lily**.

Linus (m)
[LY-nuhs] from Greek name *Linos*, meaning 'flax'.
Roman pope (died c.80). Possibly born in Tuscany, Linus is remembered as the second pope, following St Peter as bishop of Rome. Nothing more is known of the details of his life beyond the tradition that, after about 12 years as pope, he died a martyr's death and was buried beside Peter at the foot of Vatican Hill in Rome. He is sometimes tentatively identified with the Linus referred to in 2 Timothy 4:21.

146

Lois (f)
[LOH-is] from Greek, meaning 'pleasing' or 'desirable'.
The devout grandmother of Timothy, and mother of Eunice (2 Timothy 1:5) who exerted a godly influence on Timothy (2 Timothy 3:14–16).

Lot (m)
[lot] from Hebrew, possibly meaning 'veiled'.
Abraham's nephew who lacked his uncle's faith. He and his family were only rescued from Sodom through Abraham's prayer, though Lot's wife became a pillar of salt. Lot became the ancestor of the Moabites and Ammonites in unsavoury circumstances (Genesis 19).

Louis (m)
[LOO-i, LOO-is] from Germanic name, meaning 'famous warrior'.

Louis IX (1214–70), king of France. Born in Poissy, Louis succeeded to the French throne at the age of 12 in 1226. He married Margaret of Provence seven years later and in due course took over the government of the country. Louis proved a wise and capable ruler with a profound religious faith and a sincere belief in the ideals of medieval chivalry.

As well as winning respect as a military leader, defeating the English at Taillebourg in 1242, he built the Sainte-Chapelle in Paris and established a reputation both as a statesman and defender of the rights of the individual noted for his impartiality in dispensing justice. He was also noted for his dislike of profane or blasphemous language. He is honoured as the patron saint of barbers, builders, distillers, embroiderers, the French monarchy, grooms, haberdashers, hairdressers, kings, masons, needleworkers, prisoners, sculptors, the sick and soldiers, among others.

Also *Louis Bertrand (1526–81), Spanish friar.* Born at Valencia, he joined the Dominicans and is remembered chiefly for the missionary work he undertook in Colombia in the years 1562–68. He is credited with having secured thousands of converts among the native inhabitants of the area during this period, despite the fact that he could not speak their language and had to communicate through an interpreter. He is honoured today as the patron saint of Colombia.

Louis Grignion de Montfort (1673–1716), French missioner. Born in Montfort in Brittany, Louis studied at the Jesuit College of St Thomas Becket in Rennes before starting training as a priest at the Seminary of St Sulpice in Paris in 1692. He was ordained in 1700 and appointed chaplain at the hospital in Poitiers. Recruiting the women administrators of the poorhouse in Poitiers, he went on to found a congregation known as the Daughters of Divine

147

Wisdom before moving to Paris and there similarly devoting himself to the care of the inmates of a poorhouse. A fiery and difficult man, he was loved by the poor but provoked considerable criticism from his superiors and eventually left Paris for Rome, where he became a missionary apostolic under Pope Clement XI.

Variants: **Aloysius**, **Lewis**, **Lou**, **Louie, Ludovic**, **Luis**,
Feminine forms: **Louisa**, **Louise**.

Louisa, Louise feminine forms of **Louis**.

Louise (f)
[lew-EEZ] feminine form of *Louis*.
Louise de Marillac, French foundress of the Sisters of Charity, (1591–1660). Born into a wealthy aristocratic country family, probably at Ferrières-en-Brie, she hoped to become a Capuchin nun but instead, in 1613 at the age of 22, began 12 years of married life to a royal official.

After her husband's death from illness, she resumed her religious inclinations and came under the influence of St Vincent de Paul, who was then seeking assistants for his charitable work from among the wealthy women of Paris. Impressed by Louise above all his other recruits, Vincent put her in charge of the Ladies of Charity, which he had founded. Modest yet practical, Louise proved the perfect choice for this work and a highly capable administrator.

In 1633 she opened her own home for the training of social workers and from this evolved the Sisters or Daughters of Charity of St Paul, who within 25 years had some 40 convents throughout Europe. Throughout, she continued in close alliance with Vincent de Paul and hundreds of letters exchanged between the two saints survive. She is honoured as the patron saint of social workers.

148

Love (f)

[luv] Old English *lufu*.

Love is central to the message of the Bible, which is about the nature of God who is love (1 John 4:8). God expresses love within himself, as the three Persons of the Trinity are united in love for one another (Mark 1:10–11). The Father's love for Jesus is the basis of God's love for human beings (John 17:23). Even in the Old Testament, love is God's most important characteristic, for he is 'the compassionate and gracious God, slow to anger, abounding in love and faithfulness, maintaining love to thousands and forgiving wickedness, rebellion and sin' (Exodus 34:6–7).

The Old Testament shows that God is deeply affected by the lives of human beings. He refuses to deal with Israel's sin as they deserve because he loves them (Hosea 11:1–9). God's love is fully revealed in the life and death of Jesus. Paul's definition of God's love is, 'While we were still sinners, Christ died for us' (Romans 5:8). John similarly speaks of God's action in sending Jesus to die for the world as the supreme example of love (John 3:16–17).

Because love is central to what God has done in Jesus Christ, it is also meant to be central to Christian experience. It is the most important characteristic of the Christian life, involving a Christian's relationship with God, with fellow believers and with the unbelieving world. Jesus made it the subject of his new commandment (John 13:34; 1 Corinthians 13).

Lucian (m)

[LOO-see-uhn] from the Roman name *Lucianus*, possibly from Latin *lux*, meaning 'light'.

Lucian of Antioch (died 312), Syrian-born martyr. Born at Samasata in Syria, he became a priest of Antioch, where he founded an influential theological school. He revised the Greek versions of the Old Testament and of the four Gospels before being imprisoned at Nicomedia during the persecution ordered by Emperor Diocletian. Refusing to deny his faith, he spent nine years behind bars and was eventually killed with a sword; others say he was starved to death.

Feminine form: **Luciana**.

Luciana feminine form of **Lucian**.

Lucifer (m)
[LOO-si-fuh] from Latin *lux*, meaning 'light' and *ferre*, meaning 'to bring'.
The Latin word referred originally to the planet Venus. The Hebrew word from which the Latin comes is found in Isaiah 14:12, translated as 'morning star' or 'Day Star'. This came to be used as a name because this verse is applied to Satan. Its use in *Paradise Lost* by John Milton led to its popular application as a name for Satan.

Lucius (m)
[LOO-see-uhs] from Latin *lux*, meaning 'light'.
With Montanus (died 259), Carthaginian martyrs. Lucius and Montanus were prominent members of a group of martyrs who were arrested during the reign of Valerian on charges of plotting rebellion against the procurator at Carthage. During their lengthy imprisonment, Montanus had visions that revealed to him the extent of his human frailties, revelations which he shared with the others. After several months the group all confessed their Christian faith and were duly condemned to death. Lucius went first, being in poor health, while the sturdier Montanus spoke on behalf of them all when he vigorously attacked all heretics and those who made sacrifices to the gods and pleaded with those present to repent their sinful ways. He and the others were then beheaded.

150

Lucy (f)
[LOO-see] from Latin *lux*, meaning 'light'.
Sicilian virgin martyr (d. c.304). The substance of the life of St Lucy is largely a matter of legend, according to which she was a virgin put to death in Syracuse after being exposed as a Christian by her rejected suitor. When she was ordered into a brothel it proved impossible to move her and she was similarly miraculously protected from execution by fire. Because there is a story that her eyes were miraculously restored after being torn out, she is associated with diseases of the eyes. She is honoured as the patron saint of the blind, of authors and of glaziers and salesmen, among others.

   Variants: **Lucette**, **Lucia**, **Lucie**, **Lucinda**, **Lulu**.

Luke (m)
[look] from Greek, from Latin *Lucanus*, meaning 'a man from Lucania (in southern Italy)'.
Possibly born in Antioch of Gentile Greek parentage in the first century, Luke was a medical doctor according to the New Testament. He accompanied the apostle Paul on his missionary journeys and was with him when their ship was wrecked off Malta. Paul describes Luke as his only companion in Rome and another source claims he eventually returned to Greece and died unmarried there aged 84. Another tradition suggests he died a martyr's death. He was the author of the third Gospel and the Acts of the Apostles. He is honoured as the patron saint of physicians, surgeons, butchers and artists.

Luther (m)
[LOO-thuh] from surname of Martin *Luther*, from Germanic name *liut*, meaning 'people' and *heri*, meaning 'army'.
German church reformer, founder of Protestantism (1483–1546). From 1508 he taught theology at Wittenberg and attacked the sale of indulgences (forgiveness of sin). He

refused to withdraw his attacks and was tried for heresy. Excommunicated by the Pope and outlawed by the emperor, he led the cause for Reformation, establishing the Bible as the only source of religious authority and salvation as a gift of God that is received by repentance and trust in Christ, without the mediation of the church. His protests and the drawing up of the Augsburg Confession in 1530 led to the founding of Protestantism.

The name was brought further into the public eye by Martin Luther King (1929–68), the black US civil-rights campaigner, famous for his 'I have a dream' speech.

152 **Lydia** (f) [LI-dee-uh] Greek, meaning 'from Lydia' (region in Asia Minor).
A wealthy Jewish proselyte who was Paul's first convert in Europe at Philippi (Acts 16:14–15). Her home became an early house church (Acts 16:40).

Madeleine see **Magdalene**.

Madonna (f)
[muh-DON-uh] Italian, meaning 'my lady'.
A designation of the Blessed Virgin Mary, popularised by the actress and singer Madonna (born 1958).

Magdalene (f)
[MAG-duh-lin] from Hebrew, meaning 'woman of Magdala' (village on the Sea of Galilee).
Mary Magdalene, a woman whom Jesus delivered from evil spirits and who was one of the first people to see the risen Lord (Luke 8:2; John 20:1–18). From medieval times, the name was used in England in its French forms *Madeleine*, *Madeline* and the variant *Maudlin*, now only used in the form *maudlin* to mean 'weak and sentimental', from depictions in art of Mary Magdalene as a tearful penitent.
Variant: **Madeleine**.

Malachi (m)
[MA-luh-ky] from Hebrew, meaning 'my messenger'.
Prophet whose prophecies are recorded in the last book in the Old Testament, written in Judah during the time after the exile. Malachi's prophecies centre on religions and social improprieties; he called on the people to turn back to God.

Malachy (m)
[MA-luh-kee] Irish variant of *Malachi*.
Irish archbishop (c.1094–1148). Also known by the name Mael Maedoc, he was born the son of a schoolteacher at Armagh and ordained a priest in 1119. A committed and energetic Gregorian reformer, he progressed rapidly from the rank of priest to that of bishop of the diocese of Connor and Down (1124). He proved a dedicated servant of the church and in 1129 was rewarded with the archbishopric of Armagh, which had formerly been an hereditary position. This appointment provoked fierce opposition from those who had expected the post to be inherited in the traditional way and it was only with difficulty that Malachy was persuaded to assert his authority over the see.

153

Under his wise and patient leadership peace was gradually restored to the diocese and in 1137 he agreed a compromise with his opponents, handing over control of Armagh to the abbot of Derry. Two years later he travelled to Rome to obtain papal approval of the reforms he had instituted and there was made papal legate to Ireland by Pope Innocent II. On his return he cofounded the first Cistercian abbey in the whole of Ireland.

Malcolm (m)
[MAL-kuhm] from Gaelic, meaning 'servant or disciple of Columba'.
See **Columba**.
  Variants: **Callum, Calum, Colm, Colum, Mal.**

Manasseh (m)

[muh-NA-se] from Hebrew, meaning 'causing to forget'.

Joseph's eldest son, whose privileges were given to his younger brother Ephraim by their grandfather Jacob (Genesis 48). The tribe descended from him: its people lived in central Palestine east and west of the Jordan.

Also, *Manasseh, king of Judah (c.687–642 BC)*. Judah's longest reigning king but one of its most wicked rulers. He encouraged all kinds of pagan worship, persecuted the prophets and was involved in violence. Though God announced that Judah would go into exile because of his behaviour, reference to his repentance and conversion shows that God listens to the prayers of the worst of sinners (2 Chronicles 33).

Variant: **Manasses**.

Mara, Marah (f)

[MAH-ruh] from Hebrew, meaning 'bitter'.

Ruth's mother-in-law, **Naomi**, who wanted to change her name to *Mara* to convey her sense of desolation.

Marcella (f) [mah-SEL-uh] feminine form of *Marcellus*, diminutive of *Marcus*.

Roman matron (325–410). Born in Rome, she dedicated herself to the religious life after the death of her husband shortly after their marriage. As founder and head of a religious community of women in Rome she offered shelter to her mentor St Jerome and attracted a substantial following among the wealthy women of the city, becoming known both for her personal charm and for her redoubtable character. Jerome himself admired the energetic manner in which she debated religious matters with him, insisting upon proper reasons for his answers.

Marcellus (m)

[mah-SEL-uhs] diminutive of *Marcus*.

Marcellus I (died 309), Roman pope. He was elected pope

in 308 in the wake of the turmoil following the persecutions of Christians instituted under Diocletian and faced a major challenge in regrouping the church. During his short papacy he set about reorganising the church in Rome into parishes, establishing a hierarchy of parish presbyters and only welcoming lapsed Christians back into the fold after they had completed exacting penances, which he enforced with great severity. These measures provoked substantial opposition and Marcellus was ordered out of Rome by Emperor Maxentius, dying in exile shortly afterwards.

Marcellus the Centurion (died 298), Roman martyr. A Roman centurion who declared his Christian faith when ordered to participate in his legion's celebrations of the birthday of Emperor Maximian. Throwing down his badges of allegiance to the emperor he swore that he would refuse to obey any orders but those of God. He was immediately arrested and brought before the deputy prefect at Tangier. Marcellus declined to deny his faith and was sentenced to be put to death by the sword. Tradition has it that one of the officials at his hearing was so impressed by the centurion's demeanour that he too declared his conversion to Christianity and was similarly put to death.

155

Marcus (m)
[MAH-kuhs] probably from Latin *Mars*, Roman god of war. See **Marcella**, **Marcellus**, **Mark**.

Margaret (f)
[MAH-grit, MAH-guh-rit] from Latin *margarita*, from Greek *margaron*, meaning 'pearl'.
Margaret of Antioch (dates unknown), virgin martyr. Margaret (or Marina) of Antioch probably never existed but was included among the popular saints of the medieval period. According to legend, she was the Christian daughter of a pagan priest of Antioch during the reign of Diocletian.

After spurning marriage to the Roman prefect Olybrius, she was denounced by him as a Christian and subjected to horrific torture (which included being swallowed by Satan in the form of a dragon) before finally being beheaded. In many respects her story appears to share much in common with that of Catherine of Alexandria. Over 200 churches throughout England were dedicated to her and she was also revered as the patron saint of childbirth.

Margaret of Hungary (1242–70), Hungarian nun. The beautiful daughter of Bela IV, king of Hungary, she entered a convent for Dominican nuns founded by her father on an island in the Danube near Budapest and determined to remain there for the rest of her life, even defying her father's wishes that she accept marriage to Ottokar, king of Bohemia. She variously impressed and appalled all who knew her with her dedication to her life of prayer and penance, always volunteering for the most menial and unpleasant work about the convent and paying scant regard to feeding or cleaning herself. Being a princess, the other nuns were unable to persuade Margaret to moderate her habits and the austerities of her existence probably contributed to her premature death at the age of 28.

Margaret of Scotland (c.1045–93), Scottish queen. The granddaughter of the English king Edmund Ironside, she was probably born in exile in Hungary and did not come to England until 1057. When the Normans invaded in 1066, she retreated to Scotland and later married the Scottish king Malcolm III. At the time of their marriage, Malcolm was coarse and uncouth in nature, but long exposure to Margaret's refined and educated character gradually reformed him and he is remembered as one of Scotland's most respected rulers. In her godliness Margaret showed considerable generosity towards orphans and others in need as well as exerting a reforming influence upon the Scottish church, founding a number of churches and other religious houses.

She bore her husband eight children and saw to it that they were well brought up: one of them, David of Scotland, similarly acquired the status of saint, while their daughter Matilda married Henry I of England, so becoming an ancestor of the present British royal family. She is the only Scottish saint in the Roman calendar to be universally venerated and is also honoured as a patron saint of Scotland, queens, widows and parents of large families.

Variants: **Greta**, **Gretchen**, **Madge**, **Maggie**, **Maisie**, **Margarita**, **Margery**, **Margot**, **Marguerite**, **Marjorie**, **Meg**, **Megan**, **Peg**, **Peggy**, **Rita**.

Maria see **Mary**.

157

Marian (f)
[MA-ree-uhn] diminutive of *Mary* or derived from *Mary* (or *Marie*) and *Ann*.
Marian and James (died 259) African martyrs. According to tradition, Marian was a church reader and James a deacon who were among the many Christians put to death for their faith at Cirta Iulia in Numidia during the persecutions instituted during the reign of Valerian. Both resisted torture and demands that they renounce their faith and were eventually sentenced to death by the sword.

Variants: **Marianne**, **Marion**.

Mariana (f)
[ma-ree-AN-uh] from *Maria* (*Mary*) and *Anna*.
Peruvian penitent (1614–45). Born Mariana Paredes y Flores into an aristocratic family of Quito (now in modern Ecuador), she displayed a deeply religious nature as a child, her penances including going without food, drink and sleep. When her attempts to enter a convent failed, she resolved to live the life of a recluse, praying and caring for the needy, including native American children, and continuing to exist in conditions of great austerity. When Quito was hit

by earthquakes followed by a serious epidemic she prayed that her life be taken in exchange for the forgiveness of the sins of others and she died soon afterwards, to universal lamentation. Known as the Lily of Quito; in many respects her story resembles that of Rose of Lima.

Variant: **Marianna**.

Marie (f)
[muh-REE, MAH-ri] French form of *Mary*.
Marie of the Incarnation (1599–1672), French missionary. Born Marie Guyard, she was the daughter of a baker in Tours and in due course became the wife of a silk manufacturer, bearing him a son. After her husband died, she entered the Ursuline convent in Tours under the name Marie of the Incarnation and later embarked as a missionary to Canada. She founded the first Ursuline convent in Quebec in 1641 and oversaw its rebuilding after its destruction by fire in 1650. Also known as Marie of the Ursulines, she was particularly active in instructing native American converts in the area and even compiled dictionaries in the Algonquin and Iroquois languages for their benefit. She also became well known for her various mystical visions.

Marina see **Margaret (of Antioch)**.

Mark (m)
[mahk] English form of the name *Marcus*.
John Mark, a cousin of Barnabas and a companion of Paul and Barnabas on their first missionary journey, and the author of Mark's Gospel (the oldest and shortest of the Gospels). He subsequently accompanied Paul and his own cousin Barnabas on their first missionary journey. Mark, however, offended Paul when he turned back after a short time and was consequently not invited to go with Paul on his second missionary journey. Instead, he travelled with

Barnabas to Cyprus to spread the gospel there. He was later reconciled with Paul (Colossians 4:10) and accompanied him to Rome, where he visited Paul in prison following the latter's arrest. It was probably in Rome that Mark wrote his Gospel.

He ended his life evangelising in Alexandria, where one tradition has it that he became the city's first bishop and was ultimately martyred for his faith during the reign of the emperor Trajan. He is honoured today as the patron saint of glaziers, notaries, captives and of the city of Venice (where his relics are supposed to have been taken in the ninth century and preserved in the first church of San Marco).

Martha (f)

[MAH-tha] from Aramaic, meaning 'lady'.

Martha (first century), the sister of Lazarus. According to the biblical account in Luke 10:38–42, Martha and her sister Mary were once visited in their home at Bethany by Christ. While Mary sat listening to Christ's words, Martha busied herself preparing a meal. Martha became angry when her sister did not offer to help, upon which Christ observed that she was so busy doing things that she was losing sight of what was more important in life (apparently commending spending time with Jesus as well as serving him). She reappears in John 11:1–46 at the raising of her brother Lazarus from the dead and at John 12:1–2 it is suggested that once again she served Christ a meal six days before the Passover. She is honoured as the patron saint of housewives, servants and lay sisters.

Martin (m)

[MAH-tin] originally from *Mars*, the Roman god of war.

Martin of Tours (c.316–97), Hungarian-born bishop who became the founder of French monasticism. Born the son of a soldier at Sabaria in Pannonia (in modern Hungary), he was educated in Italy and followed his father into the

Roman army, becoming an officer. After splitting his military cloak in two to share it with a freezing beggar in Amiens, where he was stationed, he experienced a religious revelation and was soon afterwards baptised as a Christian. As his faith now conflicted with his military duties, he requested a discharge from the army in 339 and on securing this (after a term of imprisonment) chose to live the life of a recluse on an island off the coast of Liguria for several years.

In 360 he undertook religious study under St Hilary of Poitiers and went on to found a monastery at Ligugé (the first such institution to be established in western Europe). He was appointed bishop of Tours by popular acclamation around 370 and founded a second monastery nearby. Further monasteries soon followed.

160

While engaged upon evangelical work in pagan areas of his diocese he proved a formidable opponent of pagan leaders, even destroying their shrines, but at the same time disapproved of the death penalty being imposed against pagans and other heretics, so provoking much opposition within the church.

St Martin's unflinching commitment to holiness and compassion, together with the many tales of miracles associated with his name, made him one of the most celebrated figures of his age and his memory is preserved in the names of numerous churches, towns and villages throughout Europe and beyond. Tours itself became a popular centre of pilgrimage. St Martin is honoured today as the patron saint of France, of soldiers, of beggars and of innkeepers.

Also, *Martin I (died 655), Roman pope and martyr.* Born into a noble family of Todi in Umbria, he rose swiftly through the ranks of the church and for a period served as papal nuncio in Constantinople, the capital of the Byzantine empire. He was elected pope in 649, in which year he presided over a council at Rome denouncing the

Monothelite heresy (which denied that Christ had a human will) and two imperial decrees defending it. In response the Byzantine emperor Constans II had Martin arrested and brought to Constantinople, where he was thrown into prison. In 655, after further ill-treatment, he was sent into exile in the Crimea where, weakened by illness and the abuses he had suffered from the emperor, which included starvation and flogging, he died within a short time. After his death he became the last pope to be recognised as a martyr.

Variant: **Martyn**.

Feminine forms: **Martina, Martine**.

Martina, Martine feminine forms of **Martin**.

Mary (f)
[MAI-ree] related to *Miriam* and *Mara*, from a Hebrew root meaning 'bitterness' or 'trouble'.

The name of several women in the New Testament: *Mary, the mother of Jesus Christ*. According to the Bible, Mary was descended from the house of King David, although no information is offered about her immediate parents or her place of birth. Having become betrothed to Joseph, a carpenter of Nazareth, she was visited (at the so-called 'Annunciation') by the angel Gabriel, who informed her that through the power of the Holy Spirit she would give birth to the Messiah, Jesus Christ. Submitting to the will of God, she duly became pregnant. Joseph did not reject her because of the pregnancy and the marriage went ahead.

Mary's baby was born while the couple were in Bethlehem to have their names recorded in the official census, after which they evaded the murderous soldiers of Herod seeking out the new-born Saviour and fled to Egypt. The holy family later returned to Nazareth and little is known of their lives over the next few years.

Mary reappears, however, at the feast of Cana (as related

at John 2:1–10), during which Christ changed the water into wine at his mother's prompting, and finally at his crucifixion (John 19:25–27), at which she was entrusted by Christ to John's care. She prayed with the other apostles at the time of Christ's ascension to heaven (Acts 1:12–14) but is not mentioned again afterwards.

Conflicting traditions claim that she died either in Jerusalem or in Ephesus. Roman Catholics believe that Mary was herself born without sin, the product of an 'Immaculate Conception', and that she remained a virgin throughout her marriage. At the end of her life she did not die in the usual way but was transported body and soul to heaven in what is usually called her 'Assumption'. Mary is variously honoured as the patron saint of numerous countries and organisations and was named patron saint of the entire human race in 1944.

Mary Magdalen (first century), follower of Christ. According to Luke 8:1–2, Mary Magdalen (or Mary of Magdala) was a sinner – by tradition a prostitute – who was tormented by seven demons until Christ drove them from her. Henceforth she served him faithfully wherever he went, even attending at the crucifixion, and became an ideal of the repentant sinner. She was one of the three people who discovered that Christ's tomb was empty and, according to John 20:11–18, it was to her that Christ appeared after his resurrection with a message for the faithful. She is honoured as the patron saint of penitents.

Also *Mary of Bethany. Sister of Martha and brother of Lazarus*. She anointed Jesus for burial in advance and is commended for her choice of priorities and devotion (Luke 10:42; John 11:2). *The wife of Clopas, the mother of James and 'the other Mary'* probably all refer to a woman who saw Jesus' crucifixion and his resurrection (Matthew 27:56; 28:1). *The mother of John Mark* (Acts 12:12), whose home was used by one Jerusalem church.

The name of many saints, including: *Mary of Egypt (fifth century)*, *Egyptian penitent*, a prostitute of Alexandria who underwent a sudden conversion to Christianity while in Jerusalem. Finding herself prevented by an unseen force from entering a church, she realised the error of her ways and called upon Mary to bring her to repentance. In response to this experience she elected to live the life of a hermit in the wilderness on the other side of the River Jordan and remained there for the next 18 years. Her story was particularly popular during the medieval period as an ideal of repentance and a proof of the limitless quality of God's forgiveness.

Mary of the Angels (1661–1717), Italian nun. Born Mary Fontanella at Baldinero near Turin, she entered the Carmelite convent of St Cristina in Turin and there, in response to frequent deep spiritual melancholia, acquired a reputation through her adoption of the most severe forms of penance, which included binding her tongue with an iron ring and suspending herself with ropes. She became novice mistress at the age of 30 and three years later was appointed prioress, in which role she was treated with much respect by all who knew her.

Mary di Rosa (1813–55), Italian foundress. Born in Brescia, she dedicated herself to charitable work among the sick and needy while still a teenager and in defiance of her own physical weakness, seeing this as the best way of serving Christ. In 1840 she founded the Handmaids of Charity of Brescia to promote such work in the region. The charity played a prominent role in alleviating suffering during the war with Austria that subsequently convulsed northern Italy and was also active in treating those infected in the cholera epidemic that followed. Exhausted by her efforts on behalf of others, Mary di Rosa herself died at the age of 42.

Mary MacKillop (1842–1909), Australian foundress. Mary Helen MacKillop was born in Melbourne of Scottish

163

descent and, having decided at an early age to pursue a religious life, was encouraged to found a new charitable community to assist the poor of South Australia. Assisted by Father Julian Woods, she founded the Sisters of Saint Joseph of the Sacred Heart (commonly known as the Josephites) and oversaw the establishment of many schools, orphanages and other charitable institutions. Elected mother-general of the order in 1875, she continued in such work for the rest of her life, often having to show considerable determination and courage in the face of fierce opposition from within the church, including a period of excommunication. She won official papal approval for her work in 1888. She is considered Australia's first native-born saint and was canonised in 1995.

164

Mary Magdalen dei Pazzi (1566–1607), Italian nun. Born Maria Maddalena de' Pazzi into a wealthy family of Florence, she was educated by the Jesuits and at the age of 16 gave up all the advantages of her rank and beauty to enter a Carmelite convent. Shortly after taking the veil in 1584, she was struck down by a combination of life-threatening illness and severe emotional disturbance resulting from temptation and depression. She interpreted these experiences as a sign that she had been allowed to share in the suffering of Christ himself and went on to have daily visions of Christ and regular conversations with him, sometimes retreating into a deep prayerful trance for months at a time. These conversations, which continued until Mary reached the age of 41, were recorded in seven volumes by the other nuns.

After five years of these extraordinary experiences Mary seems to have achieved some resolution to her spiritual turmoil and rose in due course to the positions of novice mistress and subprioress. Her mystical revelations remained unreported outside the convent during her lifetime.

Variants: **Mair**, **Maire**, **Mari**, **Maria**, **Mariah**, **Marian**,

Marie, Mariella, Marietta, Mariette, Marilyn, Marion, Maureen, May, Mimi, Minnie, Moira, Moll, Molly, Moyra, Polly.

Matilda (f)
[muh-TIL-duh] from Germanic, meaning 'strength in battle'.
Wife of the German King Henry I the Fowler, and mother of Emperor Otto I and St Bruno, (895–968). Although badly treated by her sons, she was famous for her devout godliness and her generosity to the poor.
Variants: **Maud, Maude**.

Matthew (m)
[MA-thew] from Hebrew, meaning 'gift of God'.
First-century apostle. Matthew was a Galilean tax collector working for the Romans in Capernaum until Christ summoned him to become one of his disciples, upon which he immediately abandoned his desk and went with him. Also referred to by the name **Levi,** the rest of his life is shrouded in obscurity. He is credited, however, with writing the first Gospel between the years 60 and 90 and with becoming one of the first Christian evangelists.

One tradition claims he died the death of a martyr in Ethiopia or Persia. He is honoured as the patron saint of accountants, bookkeepers, tax collectors, customs officers and security guards.
Variants: **Mat, Matt, Matthias**.

Matthias (m)
[muh-THY-uhs] variant of *Matthew*.
The disciple who was chosen by lot to take Judas Iscariot's place among the apostles after the ascension of Christ and Judas' death (Acts 1:23–26).

Maurice (m)

[MO-ris] from Latin name *Mauritius*, meaning 'a Moor'.

Roman martyr (died *c*.287). Legend has it that Maurice was the name of the Roman officer commanding the so-called Theban Legion comprising Christian soldiers from Egypt who were put to death for their faith while serving in Gaul. The legion is supposed to have mutinied at Agaunum (now renamed Saint-Maurice-en-Valais in Switzerland) either upon being ordered to participate in pagan sacrifices or to repress the Christian population living nearby. As a result every tenth man was executed: when the remainder still refused to obey their orders they too were put to death.

166

Historians suggest that the legend may be based upon a real incident that took place around the end of the third century but that the number of men involved is unlikely to have been as many as an entire legion. The place where the executions were carried out is now the site of an abbey of canons regular. The town of St Moritz in Switzerland is named in his honour.

Maximilian (m)

[mak-si-MIL-ee-uhn] from Latin *maximus*, meaning 'greatest'.

African martyr (died 295). The son of an army veteran living in the vicinity of Tebessa (in Algeria), Maximilian was instructed to join the Roman army by a court order when he was aged 21, the sons of army veterans being obliged by law to serve as soldiers. Being a Christian, he refused to obey, however, arguing that he could serve no one but God. Maximilian's father was told to persuade his son to yield to the court's demands but his father simply replied that he was powerless to change his son's mind. Even the threat of execution had no effect and Maximilian was accordingly condemned and beheaded with a sword.

Variant: **Max**.

Mel (m)
[mel] short form of *Melvin* or *Melanie*.
Late fifth-century nephew of St Patrick whom he helped
with his work; bishop of Ardagh.

Melanie (f)
[MEL-uh-nee] from Greek *melaina*, meaning 'dark'.
(died 439) Melanie (or Melania) was born into a rich family
and she and her husband were also wealthy. When two of
their children died, they gave their wealth to establish
monasteries in places including Europe and Palestine. They
made a pilgrimage to the Holy Land and befriended St
Jerome.
    Variant: **Mel**.

167

Melchior (m)
[MEL-kyaw] possibly from Semitic, meaning 'king city'.
One of the wise men ('Magi') who followed the leading of
the star and came from the East to Jerusalem and then
Bethlehem to worship the baby Jesus (Matthew 2:1–12).
According to tradition, they were three in number and they
were named Balthasar, Casper and Melchoir.

Mercedes (f)
[mer-SAY-deez] from Spanish, meaning 'mercy'.
From the title of the Blessed Virgin Mary, Our Lady of the
Mercies.

Mercy (f)
[MER-see] Latin *merces*, meaning 'reward'.
A quality that is mainly associated with God; one of his
most distinctive characteristics and closely linked with his
love and compassion (James 5:11). God shows his mercy
particularly towards those who turn from their sins. This is
illustrated by David who, though under threat of severe
punishment, preferred to fall into the hands of God rather

than human hands because 'his mercy is great' (2 Samuel 24:14).

People who are in any kind of need frequently call on God's mercy, even when they deserve judgment, because even in his wrath God will 'remember mercy' (Habakkuk 3:2). Jesus perfectly demonstrates God's mercy by responding to those in need, and by forgiving those who had done great wrong (Luke 18:38–42; 23:34). Believers are expected to be merciful in their dealings with other people, because they themselves have received mercy (Luke 6:36).

Micah (m)

168

[MY-kuh] from Hebrew, meaning 'Who is like Yahweh?'.
An eighth-century BC prophet from Judah and a younger contemporary of Isaiah; his message is of God's justice and also of a Saviour who would be born and who would be a shepherd to his people (Micah 5:2).

Also, a man from Ephraim who set up his own shrine and priesthood during the judges period (Judges 17–18). His idols and priest were taken by migrating Danites.

Michael (m)

[MY-kuhl] from Hebrew, meaning 'Who is like God?'
Michael the archangel. The biblical angel who is identified (at Daniel 10:13–21 and 12:1) as the protector of the Israelites and (at Revelation 12:7–9) as the conqueror of the satanic dragon. As chief of all God's angels, Michael was singled out for special praise by the Jews and early Christians and in due course was taken up as a divine protector of the entire Christian church. Numerous churches are dedicated to him and he is also celebrated in many place names, the most notable of which include Mont-Saint-Michel in France and St Michael's Mount in Cornwall, both of which are linked with stories of visions of St Michael witnessed locally. He is also honoured as the patron saint of soldiers, the sick and the city of Brussels.

Variants: **Mick**, **Micky**, **Mike**, **Miles**.
Feminine forms: **Michaela**, **Michele**, **Michelle**.

Michaela feminine form of **Michael**.

Michal (f)
[MEE-kuhl], probably a short form of *Michael*.
David's first wife and Saul's daughter. Her turbulent
marriage with David ended in bitterness and barrenness (1
Samuel 19:11–17; 2 Samuel 6:20–23).

Michele, **Michelle** feminine forms of **Michael**.

169

Milborough (f)
[MIL-buh-ruh] from Old English name *Mildburga*, meaning
'mild fortress'.
From *St Milburga (died c.715) English foundress*. The elder
sister of St Mildred and the daughter of Merewald, king of
Mercia, Milburga (or Mildburh) is remembered as the
foundress of the nunnery of Wenlock in Shropshire around
670. She was credited with various healing powers and was
well known for her godly and saintly way of life.

Mildred (f)
[MIL-druhd] from Old English name, meaning 'gentle
strength'.
English abbess (died *c.*700). Like St Milburga, St Mildred (or
Mildthryth) was a daughter of Merewald, king of Mercia,
and had a convent education in France before becoming a
nun herself, entering the convent her mother had founded
at Minster-in-Thanet. As abbess there she became widely
respected for her kindness and generosity to the poor and
after her death her tomb became a noted place of
pilgrimage.
Variants: **Millie**, **Milly**.

Miriam (f)

[MI-ree-uhm] Hebrew for *Mary*.

Moses' elder sister. She was probably the person who preserved his life when he was a baby (Exodus 2:4–8). She was a noted prophet, who also received healing from the effects of God's punishment (Exodus 15:20–21; Numbers 12).

Modesty (f)

[MO-dis-tee] from Latin *modestus*, meaning 'moderate'.

The quality of not being vain or boastful, and observing traditional proprieties in dress and behaviour.

170

Monica (f)

[MO-ni-kuh] possibly connected with Greek *monos*, meaning 'alone' or Latin *monere*, meaning 'to advise'.

Mother of St Augustine (*c*.331–87). Possibly born at Tagaste in North Africa, she bore her violent-tempered and unfaithful husband Patricius three children before she was widowed when Augustine, her eldest child, was 18. Augustine was unruly as a young man, living with his mistress (who bore him a child) and failing to share his mother's commitment to Christianity, despite the fact she had already managed to secure the conversion of both her husband and her mother-in-law. This intransigence caused St Monica great distress, but her son proved impervious to her prayers as well as to her ceaseless cajoling and weeping on his behalf.

In 383 she stubbornly followed Augustine to Italy, going first to Rome and then to Milan and there came under the influence of St Ambrose. Three years later Augustine finally responded to his mother's unflagging pressure and agreed to be baptised by St Ambrose, to his mother's great joy. Mother and son subsequently decided to return to Africa together, but Monica fell ill and died at the port of Ostia on the Tiber before their departure. She is honoured as the patron saint of alcoholics (having had a serious drinking habit herself in her youth), difficult marriages, mothers, widows and victims of unfaithfulness.

Mordecai (m)
[maw-de-KY] from Hebrew, meaning 'consecrated to Merodach'; Hebrew equivalent of a common Babylonian name derived from the name of the Babylonian god Marduk.

The caring cousin of Queen Esther who helped her frustrate a plot to destroy the Jews in the Persian empire (Esther 4:1–14).

Morwenna (f) [mor-WEN-uh] probably from Welsh *morwyn*, meaning 'maiden'.
Fifth-century Cornish virgin, depicted as teaching reading to children. The Cornish village Morwenstow is named after her.

Variant: **Morwen**.

Moses (m)
[MOH-ziz] from an Egyptian root meaning 'to give birth; to be born'; sounds like Hebrew for 'draw out'.
Moses led Israel out of Egypt to the edge of the Promised Land. He also received the Ten Commandments and was the mediator of the Sinai covenant. He was effectively the founder of the Israelite nation, and for that reason still enjoys a unique status among the Jewish people.

The Bible passes over most of the first part of his life, though his preservation from an Egyptian policy of infanticide and his subsequent adoption by an Egyptian princess are early signs of God's activity. Moses' name is an Egyptian word meaning 'child', and his Egyptian upbringing was an ideal preparation for his later role. However, an attempt to rescue a fellow Israelite from an Egyptian oppressor resulted in him fleeing to Midian, from where God called him at the age of 80 to lead his people out of slavery (Exodus 3).

Moses overcame many challenges in leading Israel to the Promised Land, including confrontations with Pharaoh, bringing about the plagues, crossing the Red Sea, meeting God at Mount Sinai and crossing the Sinai wilderness. He did not succeed in bringing the Israelites into the Promised Land, however, since the people did not believe that God could make it possible. Moses himself was prevented from entering Canaan because he disobeyed God's command (Numbers 20:6–12).

Moses was an extraordinary man who filled a variety of roles. He was Israel's civil leader, he acted as prophet, priest and intercessor, and he was responsible for the system of justice. But he is chiefly known for his friendship with God (Exodus 33:11), and for his role as the mediator of the covenant and its laws. The latter led to his writing at least some of the Pentateuch.

Because Moses is not referred to outside the Bible, some of his activities and occasionally even his existence have been questioned. However, the authenticity of the account of his life is supported by incidental features such as its Egyptian colouring, and reference to Moses' weaknesses is a sign of a realistic rather than an idealistic record. Despite his failings, his achievements are unparalleled, and the New Testament places him as second only to Jesus (John 1:17; Hebrews 3:1–6).

Mungo see **Kentigern**.

Naaman (m)
[NAY-uh-muhn] from Hebrew, meaning 'pleasing'.
A Syrian general who was healed of a serious skin disease. The prophet Elisha and a young Israelite servant girl played key roles in his healing (2 Kings 5).

Nabal (m)
[NAY-bal] from Hebrew, meaning 'fool'.
A rich Israelite landowner, whose sudden death was a punishment from God for belittling David's kindness towards him (1 Samuel 25).

Naboth (m)
[NAY-both] from Hebrew, meaning 'fruit or produce'.
A man whose family property was stolen by Ahab and Jezebel after they had murdered him (1 Kings 21).

Nahum (m)
[NAY-hum, NAY-um] from Hebrew, meaning 'comforting'. Seventh-century Old Testament prophet whose message was the coming judgement against Nineveh (Assyria).

173

Naomi (f)
[NAY-oh-mee] from Hebrew, meaning 'lovely' or 'pleasant'. Ruth's mother-in-law, who wanted to change her name to *Mara*, meaning `bitter', because of the tragedies that she suffered (Ruth 1:20–21).

Naphtali (m)
[NAF-tuh-lee] from Hebrew, meaning 'struggle' or 'wrestling'.
The sixth son of Jacob by Bilhah (Genesis 30:7–8); tribe descended from him that occupied fertile land in eastern and central Galilee. Barak, Deborah's general, was its most famous member. Isaiah predicted great honour for this land, a prophecy that was fulfilled in Jesus' ministry there (Isaiah 9:1; Matthew 4:13–16).

Natalia (f)
[nuh-TAL-ee-uh] from Latin *natale domini*, meaning 'birthday of the Lord'.

Natalia and Adrian (died c.304), martyrs of Nicomedia. According to legend, Adrian was a Roman officer stationed at Nicomedia who was so moved by the courage of the Christians he persecuted that he declared himself to be a Christian also. He was thrown into prison, where he was visited by his Christian wife Natalia. Further visits were barred after Adrian was sentenced to death, but Natalia continued to see him by disguising herself as a boy and bribing the gaoler. She attended her husband's execution and retrieved his remains, which she buried at Argyropolis on the Bosporus. She tended his grave for the rest of her life and at her own death was laid to rest among the martyrs herself.

174

Variants: **Natalie**, **Natasha**.

Nathan (m)
[NAY-thuhn] from Hebrew, meaning 'gift'.
A prophet who challenged David about adultery but who also gave him God's promise that his dynasty would last for ever (2 Samuel 7:1–16; 12:1–14).

Variant: **Nat**.

Nathanael, **Nathaniel**
(m) [nuh-THAN-yel] from Hebrew, meaning 'God has given'.
A disciple mentioned in John's Gospel who is often also identified as Bartholomew who appears in the first three Gospels. He recognised Jesus as the Messiah, and Jesus described him as a person without guile (John 1:43–51). No other details are known of his life, but he is credited with promoting the dissemination of Christianity through the Indian subcontinent. Legend has it that he died a martyr in Armenia. He is honoured as the patron saint of tanners and others who work with skins and leather, such as bookbinders, furriers and cobblers.

Variant: **Nat**.

Nehemiah (m)

[nee-i-MY-uh] from Hebrew, meaning 'Yahweh has compassion'.

A governor of the Jewish community in Judah in the fifth century BC. He was appointed by the Persian king Artaxerxes I, and served for two terms of office which began in 445 BC and 433 BC respectively. Nehemiah was a vigorous man who had a gift of discernment and a special concern for the temple and its worship. He led by example, and was known for his generosity (5:14–16), concern for the poor (5:1–13) and prayerfulness (2:4; 6:9). Together with Ezra 'the priest and scribe', he played a major role in restoring Judaism's viability after the exile.

175

Nicholas, Nicolas (m)

[NIK-uh-lus] from the Greek name *Nikolaos*, meaning 'victory of the people'.

Fourth-century Bishop of Myra. Little is known of the life of St Nicholas beyond the tradition that he was bishop of Myra in Lycia (in modern Turkey) in the fourth century. He is most familiar today as the origin of the modern Santa Claus or Father Christmas, an association derived from his status as patron saint of children. He was revered by Christians as early as the sixth century and there was a church of St Nicholas in Constantinople dating from around that time.

In succeeding centuries, he became one of the most popular of all Christian saints and the central figure in a number of well-known stories. The legend that he saved three girls from prostitution by tossing bags of gold through their open window into the stockings hanging beside their beds is often cited as the source of the present-giving customs of modern Christmas. As well as being honoured as the patron saint of children, he is also identified as the patron saint of sailors, merchants, pawnbrokers, brides, travellers, Greece, Russia and Moscow among other cities.

Nicolas (or Nicolaus) was one of the seven men ('deacons') appointed to help the apostles; he had been a Gentile convert to Judaism before he became a Christian.

Also *Nicholas I (c.820–867), Roman pope.* Born into a noble family of Rome, he served a number of popes before being elected bishop of Rome himself in 858. A wise and diplomatically astute pope, he managed to defend Rome by making strategic alliances and won the love of his own people through his reputation for fair-dealing and generosity. By the time of his death he had won the respect of many contemporaries, particularly for his steadfast defence of the church from interference by secular rulers.

Variants: **Colin**, **Nick**, **Nicko**, **Nicky**, **Nico**, **Nicol**.

Feminine forms: **Colette**, **Nicola**, **Nicole**.

Nicodemus (m)

[nik-uh-DEE-muhs] from Greek, meaning 'conqueror of the people'.

A Jewish leader who learnt about the new birth from Jesus. His support for Jesus in times of need, especially in providing him with a decent burial, suggests he was a secret disciple (John 3:1–21; 19:39–42).

Nicola, **Nicole** feminine forms of **Nicholas**.

Nicolas see **Nicholas**.

Nimrod (m)

[NIM-rod] from Hebrew, meaning 'strong', 'rebel' or 'ruler'.

Son of Cush, descendant of Ham, who became a 'mighty warrior' (Genesis 10:8–9).

Ninian (m)

[NIN-ee-uhn] of uncertain origin.

British missionary bishop (died c.432). Details of the life of Ninian are hazy, but the usual account of his life describes him as having been born in Britain and receiving religious training in Rome. According to Bede, he became a bishop and worked among the southern Picts, in the process becoming the first significant Christian leader to spread the gospel in Scotland.

His base was traditionally identified as a church at Whithorn in Galloway, which subsequently became a site of pilgrimage during the medieval period. This tradition has been supported by archaeological finds in the area. Ninian's memory is preserved in a number of place names in Scotland and northern England.

Noah (m)
[NOH-uh] from Hebrew, meaning 'rest'.
The righteous man who obeyed God's command to build an ark to survive the flood (Genesis 6–9). Because of his faith, he and his immediate family were preserved in the ark. The story is paralleled in other ancient literature, though the name of the chief character varies, and the details elsewhere are less realistic. God made a covenant with Noah (Genesis 9:8–17), and his descendants repopulated the earth after the flood.

177

Noel (m)
[NOH-el] from French *Noël*, meaning 'Christmas', ultimately from Latin *natale domini*, meaning 'birthday of the Lord'.
Name sometimes given to a child who is born on Christmas Day.
  Feminine form: **Noelle**.

Noelle feminine form of **Noel**.

Norbert (m)
[NAW-buht] from Germanic *nord*, meaning 'north' and *berhta*, meaning 'bright'.

German archbishop and founder (c.1080–1134). Born into a noble family of Xanten in the duchy of Cleves, Norbert served as a canon at the cathedral of Xanten but generally lived a carefree life of pleasure at the imperial court until 1115, when he underwent a sudden and profound conversion after narrowly escaping death on being thrown from his horse during a storm. He became a priest and, determined to live as austerely as possible, adopted the life of an itinerant preacher in northern France.

In 1120 he gathered a small group of followers about him and, in the valley of Prémontré near Laon, founded the Canons Regular of Prémontré. Having founded eight abbeys and two convents, he was eventually obliged to hand over leadership when he was raised to the post of archbishop of Magdeburg in 1126. He remained in this position until his death. He is honoured as the patron saint of Magdeburg and Bohemia.

Obadiah (m)

[oh-buh-DY-uh] from Hebrew, meaning 'servant or worshipper of Yahweh'.

The prophet who gave his name to the Book of Obadiah, declaring judgement against Edom but also hope for Israel. Also one of Ahab's leading officials who risked his life to help prophets under persecution (1 Kings 18:3–16).

Odile (f)

[oh-DEEL] from *Ottilia*, from Old German, meaning 'prosperity'.

Odilia (660–720) Abbess of Alsace. Odilia (otherwise known as *Odile* or *Ottilia*) was the daughter of the Duke of Alsace but, being born blind, was initially rejected by him and was brought up in a monastery. It was only after she miraculously recovered her sight on being baptised that father and daughter were eventually reconciled. She went on to found a nunnery in the Vosges mountains and to serve as abbess there. She also founded a second convent at Niedermünster, where she died. She is honoured as the patron saint of Alsace and of the blind.

Variants: **Odette**.

Olaf (m)

[OH-laf] from Old Norse *Anleifr*, meaning 'heir of his ancestors'.

King of Norway (995–1030). The son of a Norwegian noble, Olaf (otherwise referred to as Olave, Ola or Tola) lived the life of a seafaring pirate raider before becoming converted to Christianity in Normandy and fighting for the English king Ethelred II against the Danes in 1013. He returned to Norway two years later, driving out the Swedes and the Danes before claiming the throne of Norway.

As king, he promoted the conversion of Norway to Christianity, inviting priests and monks from England to conduct missionary work among his people. He is honoured today as the patron saint of Norway.

Olga (f)

[OL-guh] Russian form of *Helga*.

Russian noblewoman (c.879–969). The widow of Prince Igor of Kiev, she assumed power following her husband's murder. She was converted to Christianity in Constantinople around 957 and did much to spread the gospel among her people. These efforts met with mixed success, but the work she had begun was eventually picked up and continued by her grandson, St Vladimir.

Olive (f)

[O-liv] from Latin *Oliva*, meaning 'olive', symbol of peace; feminine form of *Oliver*.

Also *Oliva*, *Olivia*; saint honoured for protecting olive crops in Italy.

179

Oliver (m)
[O-liv-uh] Old French form of a Germanic name, possibly from *Olaf*.

Oliver Plunket (1625–81). Irish martyr. Born into a noble family of Loughcrew, County Meath, Oliver Plunket was educated by the Jesuits and became a priest in Rome in 1654. He remained in Rome for 12 years before being appointed archbishop of Armagh and primate of All Ireland. Plunket set about renewing the church along the lines laid down by the Council of Trent, securing the confirmation of some 10,000 of the faithful. Under his leadership the Catholic church in Ireland was substantially revived.

Over the next 10 years he worked to enforce papal authority over the country and to maintain friendly relations between the rival Catholic and Protestant populations. In 1678, however, disaster struck when his name was linked to the so-called Popish Plot supposedly uncovered by Titus Oates in a bid to bring the Catholic community into further disrepute by suggesting its leaders were involved in planning the assassination of Charles II. Plunket was arrested and put on trial in London, where anti-Catholic feeling was intense. After he was found guilty on concocted evidence, he was condemned to death and duly hanged at Tyburn, throughout displaying great courage. He was canonised in 1975.

Variants: **Olivier**, **Ollie**.
Feminine form: **Olive**.

Omar (m)
[OH-mah] from Hebrew, meaning 'speaker', 'eloquent' or 'command'.

Edomite clan chiefs, second son of Eliphaz and grandson of Esau (Genesis 36:11, 15). The origin of this word is unrelated to the Arabic *Omar* (or *Umar*), meaning 'flourishing, long life', the name of the prophet Muhammad's companion and supporter.

Omer (m)
[OH-muh] from Hebrew, meaning 'sheaf of wheat'.
French bishop (d. c.699). Omer (otherwise known as Audomarus) was born near Coutances and spent 20 years as a monk in the monastery of Luxeuil. Around 637 he became a bishop and embarked upon missionary work, earning a considerable reputation as a preacher. Little else is known of his life beyond the facts that he founded the abbey of Sithiu, now the site of the town of Saint-Omer, and he became totally blind in his last years.

Omri (m)
[OM-ree] probably from Hebrew, meaning 'my sheaf'.
King of Israel (c.876–869 BC), and father of Ahab, who founded Samaria and made it the capital of Israel; known also for his evil acts (1 Kings 16:21–28).

181

Onesimus (m)
[o-NES-i-muhs] from Greek, meaning 'useful'.
A slave who became a Christian through contact with Paul in prison. Paul's letter to Onesimus' former master Philemon contains a moving appeal for Onesimus' restoration (Philemon 8–21).

Ophrah (m, f)
[OF-ruh] from Hebrew, meaning 'fawn'.
The son of Meonothai, a descendant of Judah (1 Chronicles 4:14). Also, the name of two places in the Old Testament: a town in the tribe of Benjamin (Joshua 18:23), and a town that was the home of Gideon, in Manasseh (Judges 6:11–9:5).

Oprah see **Orpah**.

Orpah (f)
[AW-puh] from Hebrew, meaning 'neck'.

A Moabite woman, and Naomi's daughter-in-law. After her husband Chilion died, Orpah decided to return with Naomi to Bethlehem, but her mother-in-law urged Orpah to go back to her own family, which she did. However, Naomi's other daughter-in-law, Ruth, remained loyal (Ruth 1:1–14).

The name *Oprah*, made famous by the talk-show host Oprah Winfrey, is a created name; according to one version of events her name was originally *Orpah*, but that name was spelt wrongly on her birth certificate and was continually mispronounced as *Oprah*, so that name became permanent.

182

Osmond (m)
[OZ-muhnd] from Old English *os*, meaning 'god' and *mund*, meaning 'protection'.
English bishop (died 1099). Born into a noble Norman family, Osmund (or Osmond) followed William the Conqueror to England and there served as royal chaplain and later as chancellor. As Bishop of Salisbury he completed construction of the cathedral at Old Sarum; he is credited (possibly incorrectly) with drawing up the version of the Latin liturgy known as the Sarum Use, which became a pattern for other churches throughout the country. He was noted for his love of books, copying and binding many volumes personally; he is thought to have participated in the compilation of the Domesday Book.

Oswald (m)
[OZ-wuhld] from Old English *os*, meaning 'god' and *weald*, meaning 'rule'.
Oswald of Northumbria (c.605–42), English martyr king, the son of King Ethelfrith of Northumbria. He was converted to Christianity while in exile on Iona after his father's murder. He recovered the kingdom of Northumbria after defeating and killing the Welsh king Cadwallon of Gwynedd in battle near Hexham in 633 and at once invited

missionaries from Iona to conduct evangelising work among his people; he then presided over the building of churches and monasteries. These efforts prospered under the leadership of Oswald's close friend and ally St Aidan and for a time Oswald's Christianising influence spread beyond the borders of Northumbria by virtue of his marriage to Cyneburga of Wessex. After eight years, however, Oswald's reign ended with his death in battle against the pagan King Penda of Mercia. As he died he is said to have prayed for the souls of the soldiers who died with him.

Oswald of Worcester (c.925–992), English bishop. Born of military Danish descent, he was related to two archbishops of Canterbury and educated under one of them, his uncle St Odo of Canterbury. He served as a canon in Winchester before becoming a Benedictine monk and completing his education in France and becoming a priest. He was appointed bishop of Worcester by his close friend King Edgar in 962 and, with the king's committed support, worked alongside St Dunstan and St Ethelwold towards the restoration of monastic life in England. He went on to found the monastery of Westbury-on-Trym (near Bristol) and later to establish the major monastery of Ramsey in Huntingdonshire in 971. In addition to the see of Worcester, he was later appointed Archbishop of York in 972.

183

Othniel (m)
[OTH-ni-el] from Hebrew, meaning 'lion of God'.
The first of the judges, who defeated Aramean (Syrian) invaders and ruled the Israelite tribes for 40 years (Judges 3:7–11). He was probably Caleb's nephew and married Caleb's daughter as a reward for capturing Debir, a Canaanite town.

Owen (m)
[OH-uhn] possibly from *Eugene*, from Greek, meaning
'well-born' or from Welsh *oen*, meaning 'lamb'.
Seventh-century monk who worked with St Chad near
Lichfield. He was known for his good deeds and his godly
devotion.

Pascal (m)
[pas-KAL] from French, from Latin *Pascha*, meaning
'Easter', ultimately from Hebrew *pesach*, meaning
'Passover'.
Relating to the Jewish feast of the Passover, which
remembers the exodus from Egypt as an act of God's
deliverance, and the Christian festival of Easter, celebrating
the resurrection of Jesus Christ from the dead.
    Feminine form: **Pascale**.

Pascale feminine form of **Pascal**.

Patience (f)
[PAY-shuhns] ultimately from Latin, meaning 'to suffer'.
The Christian virtue; a special quality of God, who is
frequently described by the distinctive phrase 'slow to
anger' (Exodus 34:6). God is patient towards people, being
willing to forgive those who turn back to him, and even
delaying Christ's return (Romans 2:4; 2 Peter 3:15). God
gives patience to believers, enabling them to cope with
opposition and suffering (James 5:7–11).

Patricia (f)
[puh-TRISH-uh] feminine of Latin *patricius*, meaning
'nobleman'.
Seventh-century saint. Patricia came from a noble
Constantinople family; to avoid marriage she went on a
pilgrimage to Rome where she consecrated herself as a
virgin. She later returned to Constantinople to gain her

inheritance, which she distributed to the poor. She is honoured as a patron saint of Naples.

Variants: **Pat**, **Patsy**, **Pattie**, **Patty**, **Tricia**, **Trish**, **Trisha**.
Masculine form: **Patrick**.

Patrick (m)
[PAT-rik] from Latin *patricius*, meaning 'nobleman'.
Irish archbishop (c.389–461). Born to Christian Roman parents in Bannaventa, an unidentified location on the west coast of Britain, Patrick was kidnapped by Irish sea raiders at the age of 16 and forced to spend the next six years as a slave tending his master's pigs in northern Ireland. Eventually, according to legend, he managed to escape on a cargo ship and travelled widely before returning to Britain by 415.

185

As the result of a vision while he slept he undertook the challenge of taking Christianity to Ireland. He spent several years in preparation for this campaign, undertaking many years of religious study, and in due course was ordained as a deacon and then bishop.

He finally arrived in Ireland in 432 and, having obtained the support of local chieftains, began his evangelical work among the people there, making thousands of converts and founding monasteries and churches from his see in Armagh. Having countered the influence of the Druids and established the Christian church throughout Ireland, he was appointed archbishop in 441.

Among the many legendary tales recorded of Patrick is one to the effect that he banished all snakes from Ireland. His other works included a number of writings, of which three manuscripts survive. These comprise the *Letter to the Soldiers of Coroticus*, a *Confession* and the popular poetic prayer entitled the *Lorica* and otherwise known as 'Patrick's Breastplate' or the 'Deer Cry'.

The effective founder of the church in Ireland, Patrick is thought to have died at Saul on Strangford Lough in County

Down. Called the Apostle of Ireland, he is the country's patron saint.

Variants: **Paddy**, **Pat**.

Feminine form: **Patricia**.

Paul (m)

[pawl] from Latin *paulus*, meaning 'small'.

Paul the apostle (died c.65). Born a Jew and a Roman citizen of Tarsus in Cilicia (in modern Turkey), he was known originally as Saul and was brought up as a strict Pharisee and as a zealous opponent of the first Christians. By trade a maker of tents, he participated enthusiastically in the persecution of Jews who had become Christians, participating in the stoning to death of St Stephen and subsequently seeking and obtaining permission to arrest all the Jewish converts in Damascus.

While on his way to Damascus to persecute the Christians in about 35, he had a vision of the risen Christ, as a result of which he was rendered temporarily blind and became convinced that Christ wished him to be a witness among the Gentiles on his behalf. On his recovery he converted wholeheartedly to Christianity, assumed the name Paul, and spent some time in prayer and solitude in Arabia. Subsequently he dedicated the rest of his life to spreading the Christian gospel to non-Jews, embarking upon the first of three missionary journeys around the year 45.

Over the years that followed he pursued his evangelical mission throughout the Mediterranean and Asia Minor and in the process became the first great missionary in the history of the Christian church. He also wrote extensively and 13 of his hugely influential letters, which helped shape Christian theology for centuries to come, are recorded in the New Testament.

He was twice arrested for his faith, the first time in Jerusalem and the second time in Rome, and was

186

ultimately beheaded on the orders of the emperor Nero. Considered the most important figure in the early history of the Christian church after Christ himself, Paul is honoured as the patron saint of Greece (where he preached) and Malta (where he was shipwrecked on his way to Rome) as well as of tentmakers and saddlers.

Paul Aurelian (sixth century) British bishop. The son of a British (probably Welsh) chieftain, Paul Aurelian – otherwise known as Paul of Léon or Pol de Léon – studied at the monastery of St Illtyd and in due course became a monk and priest. With 12 companions he subsequently settled in Brittany, where he founded a number of churches and became bishop of what became known as Saint-Pol-de-Léon. He established a substantial reputation as an evangelist, around whose name a number of legends accumulated. He died at an advanced age at his monastery on the island of Batz. He is usually identified with the Welsh St Paulinus, who lived the life of a hermit at Llandovery and established a monastery at Llanddeusant.

187

Paul of the Cross (1694–1775), Italian priest. Born Paul Francis Danei into a middle-class family of Ovada in Piedmont, Italy, he served in the Venetian army before being ordained as a priest in Rome alongside his brother and best friend in 1727. After experiencing a vision he went on to found his own order, called the Passionists, dedicated to observing the strictest poverty and preaching to the poor, establishing the first house in Tuscany on the Monte Argentario peninsula. Passionist missions were established throughout Italy and Paul earned a reputation as a powerful preacher, often taking the Cross and the Passion of Christ as his subject. He was also credited with miraculous healing powers and with the gift of prophecy.

Variants: **Pablo**, **Paolo**.

Feminine forms: **Paula**, **Paulette**, **Pauline**.

Paula (f)

[PAW-luh] feminine form of *Paul*.

Roman foundress (347–404). Born into a wealthy Roman family, Paula married well and bore her husband five children before being widowed at the age of 32. Subsequently she dedicated herself to a Christian life and assumed the leadership of a small group of similarly minded Christian women then living in Rome. They became patrons and disciples of St Jerome after he arrived in the city and when Jerome eventually left for Jerusalem, Paula and her daughter went with him, joining him on pilgrimages to various sacred sites in the Holy Land.

188

Jerome and Paula went on to found a monastery for men in Bethlehem, as well as a convent for women and a hospice for pilgrims. Under Paula's guidance the sisters lived in conditions of great poverty and performed charitable work on behalf of the poor and needy.

Paulette, **Pauline** feminine forms of **Paul**.

Peace (f)

[pees] from Latin *pax*.

Peace in the Bible (Hebrew, *shalom*) usually has a spiritual dimension, since true peace is a gift from God. Perfect peace will only be established through the promised Prince of Peace (Isaiah 9:6–7), but in the meantime human beings can have peace with God because the death of Jesus Christ has dealt with the power and consequences of human sin (Romans 5:1–2). God gives believers the inner peace of a clear conscience and the ability to establish new relationships with people who may previously have been their enemies (Ephesians 2:14–18; Philippians 4:7). Believers are also to work and pray for peace in the world (Matthew 5:9; 1 Timothy 2:1–2.

Peregrine (m)

[PE-ruh-grin] from Latin *peregrinus*, meaning 'traveller'.
Name of several saints, including the *seventh-century hermit* who was on a pilgrimage to Jerusalem and decided to live as a hermit near Modena in Italy. Also *thirteenth-century Peregrine Laziosi*, a member of the Ghibelline faction, who, having struck Philip Benizi in the face, was so impressed by the patience and calmness which the latter displayed towards his attacker that he resolved immediately to abandon his previous way of life and became a Servite friar and a saint.

Variant: **Perry**.

Perez (m)

[PE-rez] Hebrew, 'bursting through'.
The eldest son of Judah; a twin brother to Zerah (Genesis 38:27–30). The founder of the Perezite clan, he became the most prominent member of the house of Judah (Numbers 26:20; 1 Chronicles 27:3). He is mentioned in the genealogy of Christ (Matthew 1:3; Luke 3:33).

Perpetua (f)

[per-PET-yew-uh] from Latin *perpetuus*, meaning 'perpetual'.
One of two Carthaginian martyrs, Perpetua and Felicity (died 203). They were prominent among a group of martyrs who were executed as Christians in Carthage on the orders of Septimus Severus. Perpetua was a young married noblewoman with a baby; Felicity was a pregnant slave-girl. They and seven men were arrested as Christians and thrown into prison, where Perpetua had the first of several visionary dreams in which she saw a ladder reaching to heaven. She and other members of the group had further similarly miraculous dreams (including one in which Perpetua wrestled and overthrew the Devil) and interpreted them as divine reassurances that they would be raised to heaven at their deaths.

Peter (m)
[PEE-tuh] from Greek *petras*, meaning 'rock'.
A fisherman who was one of Jesus' three closest disciples.
Originally called Simon, Jesus gave him the name or nickname *Peter* (or *Cephas* in Aramaic), meaning 'rock', probably in reference to Peter's statement that Jesus was the Messiah as the foundation of the church's teaching (Matthew 16:16–18). Peter was a natural leader, but had to learn to overcome an innate impulsiveness, especially through his denial of Jesus (Mark 14:29–31, 66–72) and subsequent restoration (John 21:15–19).

190

He became a leader of the church in Jerusalem, and was one of the first to take the gospel to Gentiles. He suffered for his faith, and seems eventually to have been martyred at Rome (c.64) during Nero's persecution. He is honoured as the patron saint of fishermen, clockmakers, bridge-builders, masons, shipbuilders and the papacy.

Peter of Alcántara (1499–1562), Spanish priest and reformer. Born Peter Garavito, the son of a lawyer of Alcántara in Estremadura, he studied law at Salamanca before joining the Observant Franciscan Order at Majaretes. Noted as a preacher and for his austere and penitent lifestyle, Peter went on to found a friary at Badajoz and was ordained in 1524. In the years that followed he served with missions throughout Spain

Around 1556 he published a *Treatise on Prayer and Meditation*, a highly successful text that was translated into several other languages. He also served as confessor to St Teresa of Avila, whom he first met in 1560, and it was with his encouragement that she set up the first convent of reformed Carmelite nuns in 1562. He is honoured as the patron saint of Brazil, Estremadura and also of night watchmen (a reference to the tradition that for 40 years he slept for just an hour and a half each night, in a sitting position).

Peter of Tarentaise (1102–74), French bishop. Born into a

religious family of Saint-Maurice near Vienne, Peter entered the Cistercian order and in due course rose to the position of abbot of Tamié in the Tarentaise region of Savoy. He was later elected archbishop of Tarentaise and set about reforming the diocese along Cistercian lines.

His good works included the rebuilding of a hospice in the Little St Bernard pass for the benefit of travellers from Italy and Switzerland and the establishment of a charity to provide for impoverished rural communities. He yearned for a solitary life, however, he left his post and went into hiding as a lay brother in a Swiss abbey, where he was not located until a year later.

Peter Chrysologus (c.400–c.450), Italian archbishop. Born at Imola, near Ravenna, Peter Chrysologus (meaning 'golden-worded') was converted to Christianity as an adult and served as a deacon in Ravenna before being appointed bishop of the city. He is remembered for his simply worded sermons, the only examples of his many writings that have survived.

Peter Claver (1580–1654), Spanish missionary. Born at Verdu in Catalonia, Peter studied at the University of Barcelona before entering the Jesuit order at Tarragona. In 1610 he was sent to Cartagena (in what is now modern Colombia), the capital of the slave trade in South America, and there dedicated himself to the fight against the slavery of black Africans. He spent the next 40 years working on their behalf, providing food, clothing and medical treatment for slaves in local plantations and mines, as well as conducting evangelical work among them and securing perhaps as many as 300,000 converts to the Christian faith. He also worked in local hospitals, offered pastoral care to prisoners and was reputed to hear as many as 5000 confessions a year.

His work was hampered from 1650, when he contracted plague and never fully recovered, dying alone and neglected in his simple cell. He is remembered today as the 'slave of the negroes' (a description he gave himself). In 1896 he was named patron saint of missionary activities among Black peoples.

Peter Damian (1007–72), Italian cardinal. Born into a poor family of Ravenna, Peter was orphaned at a young age and was brought up by a brother, who provided him with a good education, as a result of which he became a respected university teacher. He later joined a community of Benedictine hermits at Fonte Avellana, adopting an austere lifestyle of fasting, prayer and religious study. He was elected abbot of the community and went on to found several other similar institutions, earning a reputation as a leading reformer of the church, taking as his inspiration the lives of the early Desert Fathers and determining to counter clerical misconduct and corruption among his contemporaries.

He was appointed bishop of Ostia and raised to the rank of cardinal by Pope Stephen X in 1057 and subsequently served under Popes Nicholas II and Alexander II, being entrusted with various important diplomatic missions and with responsibility for church renewal. At his own request he spent his final years living the life of a simple monk at the monastery at Fonte Avellana (although he still conducted diplomatic missions from time to time). His many writings included sermons, treatises, letters and hymns.

Peter Nolasco (c.1182–1256), Spanish founder. Little is known for certain about the life of Peter Nolasco. He was probably born into a merchant family of Barcelona and in due course distinguished himself as a lay brother for his dedication to the cause of captives seized by the Moorish occupiers of much of Spain. The order to which Peter Nolasco belonged gradually evolved into the Mercedarian Order, of which he is considered the founder. With Peter Nolasco as its master-general, the Mercedarians followed the rule of St Augustine and secured the release of hundreds of Christians through the payment of ransoms.

Variants: **Pedro**, **Pete**, **Pierre**, **Piers**.

Feminine forms: **Petra**, **Petrina**.

Petra, **Petrina** feminine forms of **Peter**.

Philadelphia (f)

[fil-uh-DEL-fee-uh] from Greek, meaning 'brotherly love'.
City of the province of Lydia in west Asia Minor. One of the seven letters in Revelation was addressed to the church in that city, which was praised for its patient endurance.

Philemon (m)

[fy-LEE-muhn] from Greek, meaning 'affectionate'.
The recipient of shortest and most personal of Paul's letters. It was written to Philemon, a leader in the Colossian church, about Philemon's slave Onesimus. Onesimus was probably a runaway slave but had become a Christian after meeting Paul in prison, and Paul appeals to Philemon on the basis of Christian love to welcome him back as a brother rather than as a slave (verse16). This letter shows the revolutionary way in which, even in the first century AD, the Christian gospel undermined slavery.

193

Philip (m)

[FI-lip] from Greek, meaning 'lover of horses'.
One of the apostles, often mentioned alongside Andrew. According to the New Testament, Philip lived in Bethsaida in Galilee before being recruited as a disciple and himself persuading Nathanael (Bartholomew) to join the group. He was present at several of the most important episodes of Christ's ministry, including the feeding of the 5,000 and the Last Supper. After the Crucifixion he is said to have preached the gospel in Phrygia and ultimately to have died at Hierapolis, possibly being martyred for his faith during the reign of Domitian. Today he is honoured as a patron saint of Uruguay.

Also, an evangelist who brought Samaritans and the Ethiopian eunuch to faith in Christ (Acts 8:5–13; 26–38).

The name of several saints, including: *Philip of Heraclea (died 304), bishop and martyr of Heraclea.* Philip of Heraclea in Thrace was an old man at the time of the persecution of Christians instituted during the reign of Diocletian. When the authorities closed his church down, the aged bishop simply conducted services in the open, arguing that God lived in the human heart rather than buildings. When the authorities then demanded that he hand over the religious books of his church, however, he refused. On declining to worship the gods of the Romans, he was scourged and thrown into prison along with his deacon Hermes. Together with another priest, St Severus, the pair were then taken to Adrianople where they were interrogated twice more before being beaten and then burnt to death at the stake.

Philip Benizi (1233–85), Italian friar. Born in Florence, Philip studied medicine and philosophy at the universities of Paris and Padua before enrolling as a lay brother in the Servite order at the monastery of Monte Senario and working as a humble gardener until his talents as a scholar were found out. He went on to become a priest and to win respect as a preacher and was later elected head of the order. He is said to have fled in terror when proposed as a successor to Clement IV as pope in 1268 but attended the general council held at Lyons in 1274 and continued as leader of the Servite friars, who prospered under his guidance.

Philip Neri (1515–95), Italian founder. Born the son of a Florentine notary, he studied under the Dominicans at the convent of San Marco in Florence and worked in his uncle's business for a time before abandoning a secular career in favour of life as a hermit in Rome, studying philosophy and theology. When these studies palled, he dedicated himself instead to charitable work, giving away most of his money to the poor and working particularly on behalf of the young men of the city, trying to persuade them to reject evil ways.

In 1544 he experienced a profound revelation, which not only left him with permanent physical disabilities but also spurred him on to pursue a deeply religious life. In 1548 he founded a confraternity to organise care for the thousands of pilgrims attracted to Rome and was himself ordained a priest in 1551. Living among other priests at San Girolamo della Carita, he built a reputation for his devotion to prayer, hearing confessions and preaching, earning the nickname 'the Apostle of Rome'. He continued to combine his work on behalf of the city's young men with charitable efforts to assist the sick and needy and in time organised his assistants into what became in 1575 the Congregation of the Oratory. The Oratory that he founded spread throughout the world after the death of its founder, numbering among its many adherents such notable names as John Henry Newman. He is honoured today as a patron saint of Rome.

195

Variants: **Phil**, **Pip**.
Feminine forms: **Philippa**, **Pippa**.

Philippa feminine form of **Philip**.

Philomena (f)
[fi-loh-MEE-nuh] from Greek, meaning 'loved'.

Roman martyr (dates unknown). The legend of the virgin martyr Philomena was inspired by the discovery of a set of human bones of a young girl in the catacomb of Priscilla in Rome in 1802. The bones were enshrined in a church at Mugnano near Naples and stimulated a substantial cult following with various miracles being attributed to the so-called St Philomena, despite the lack of detail about her life and death. Mugnano became a place of pilgrimage and numerous churches were dedicated to the saint.

Phinehas (m)

[FIN-ee-uhs] from Hebrew, meaning 'serpent's mouth'.

The name of two men in the Old Testament. A priest and the son of Eleazar and grandson of Aaron (Exodus 6:25), whose zeal for God meant that the plague against the Israelites was stopped (Numbers 25:6–11). Also, one of Eli the priest's two sons whom God punished because of their complete disregard for the responsibilities of the priesthood (1 Samuel 2:12–17).

Phoebe (f)

[FEE-bi] from Greek, meaning 'the shining one'.

A woman mentioned warmly in the greetings in Paul's letter to the Romans; a deacon of the church at Cenchreae (Romans 16:1–2).

Pia feminine form of **Pius**.

Pippa feminine form of **Philip**.

Pius (m)

[PY-uhs] from Latin, meaning 'pious'.

The name of several popes, including: *Italian Pope Pius V (1504–72)*. Born Michael Ghislieri into a humble family of Bosco in Liguria, he joined the Dominican order and, having been ordained in 1528, soon distinguished himself as a preacher and teacher. Noted for his personal piety and concern for the spiritual welfare of others, he became bishop of Nepi and Sutri in 1556 and a year later was raised to the rank of cardinal, and in 1566, he was elected pope. Over the next six years Pius V proved a vigorous defender of Roman Catholicism and a prominent figure of the Counter-Reformation. Specific targets of papal wrath during his reign included the Ottoman empire, corruption among the clergy, prostitution and bull-fighting.

Italian Pope Pius X (1835–1914). Born Giuseppe Sarto

into a poor family in Venetia, he was ordained priest in 1858 and in due course was raised to the rank of canon of Treviso and then to bishop. In 1893 he was made patriarch of Venice and cardinal and finally, after some 45 years serving parish and diocese, was elected pope in 1903 in succession to Leo XIII.

As pope he sought to revitalise the church, reorganising the papal government, chartering a codification of canon law and promoting greater spiritual awareness among the laity. He also encouraged frequent taking of Holy Communion and reading of the Bible and argued in favour of allowing children as young as seven years old to participate in the Eucharist.

His final years were darkened by the failure of his efforts to avert World War I, which broke out days before his own death. Much loved for his simple goodness and for his embracing of poverty and virtue in his personal life. He is honoured as a patron saint of pilgrims.

Feminine form: **Pia**.

Placid (m)
[PLA-sid] from Latin *placere*, meaning 'to please'.
Sixth-century Italian monk. Tradition has it that Placid trained as a monk under St Benedict at Subiaco and only narrowly escaped death by drowning in the lake there when rescued by St Maurus. The events of Placid's later life are shrouded in mystery, although medieval legend claims he subsequently settled in Sicily and there died the death of a martyr along with several companions. He is remembered as a monk of unusual holiness.

Priscilla (f)
[pri-SI-luh] from Latin *prisca*, meaning 'ancient'.
Wife of Aquila; Aquila and Priscilla were close friends of Paul (Acts 18:1–3), who had an influential teaching ministry and travelled widely for the sake of the gospel.

197

Also, c. third-century Roman martyr (also known as *Prisca*). Virtually nothing is known of her life and death beyond the plain fact that she was martyred for her faith in Rome some time in the third century. The church on the Aventine hill is named after her.

Prudence (f)
[PRU-duhns] ultimately from Latin *providere*, meaning 'to provide'.
The quality of wise carefulness and foresight as shown in the ability to discern the most sensible practical course of action to follow.

198

Quintin (m)
[KWIN-tin] or Quentin from *Quintus*, Roman name, meaning 'fifth'.
Third-century Roman martyr. According to Bede, Quentin (or Quintin) was martyred for his Christian faith at Augusta Veromanduorum (now renamed Saint-Quentin) in Gaul late in the third century. He is thought to have been sent to Gaul as a missionary and is said to have earned a considerable reputation as a preacher before being imprisoned on the orders of the Roman prefect Rictiovarus, tortured and beheaded.

Rachel, Rachael (f)
[RAY-chuhl] from Hebrew, meaning 'ewe'.
Jacob's second wife, and Leah's younger sister. Jacob waited 14 years to marry her because he loved her so much, but her life was tinged with sadness (Genesis 29:16–31:35). She died giving birth to her second son Benjamin.

Raphael (m)
[RAF-a-yuhl] from Hebrew, meaning 'God has healed'.
Raphael the Archangel, the biblical angel who is identified (at John 5:1–4) as the angel who moved the waters of the

healing pool at Jerusalem and (in Tobit 2 and 6) as the bearer of healing. Because of his identification as the travelling companion of Tobias he is particularly linked with the making of pilgrimages. His association with healing, and his reputation as the most approachable and sympathetic of the three archangels, is reflected by the veneration of his statue at Lourdes. He is honoured as the patron saint of travellers, the blind and of doctors and nurses.

Raymond, Raymund (m)
[RAY-muhnd] from Old German, meaning 'counsel protection'.

Raymond of Capua (1330–99), Italian priest. Raymond of Capua is remembered for his association with St Catherine of Siena, whom he served as confessor for six years until the latter's death. St Catherine selected Raymond as her confessor after witnessing him celebrating Mass although he only gradually became convinced of the authenticity of her mystical experiences.

199

Such was the impact of St Catherine's revelations that Raymond had to spend many hours each day hearing the confessions of the many converts she had won for the church. He also worked alongside her in treating victims of the plague, contracting the disease himself but allegedly being cured by Catherine's prayers. The two saints also sought to restore peace between the cities of northern Italy and the papacy and tried to heal the schism between the rival popes at Rome and Avignon when it broke out in 1378.

Raymund of Peñafort (c.1180–1275), Spanish friar. Born into a noble family of Peñafort in Catalonia, Raymund worked as a lawyer and scholar in Barcelona and Bologna until he was in his forties, when he opted instead for the life of a Dominican priest and preacher. His preaching did much to encourage Christian resistance to the Moorish occupiers of much of Spain and helped reclaim the country for Christianity. Having been summoned to Rome as confessor to Pope Gregory IX, he composed a book entitled the *Decretals*, a collection of decrees issued by popes and councils, which proved profoundly influential and became a standard source of canon law over the next 700 years. He is honoured as a patron saint of canon lawyers and librarians.

Raymund Nonnatus (1204–40), Spanish cardinal. The life of Raymund Nonnatus is shrouded by legend. His name *Nonnatus* (meaning 'not born') is supposed to relate to the circumstances of his birth, during which he was removed from his mother's womb after her death in labour. Tradition claims that he was received as a member of the Mercedarian order at Barcelona by its founder St Peter Nolasco and that subsequently he offered himself as a slave in Algiers in order to secure the release of others. Legend further claims that he was made a cardinal in Rome. Because of the manner in which Raymund was born he is honoured as a patron saint of midwives.

Rebecca, Rebekah (f)
[ruh-BE-kuh] from Hebrew, the word is associated with an animal noose and when applied to females has the connotation of 'captivating'.

Isaac's wife and the mother of Jacob and Esau. Though she trusted God's guidance in travelling hundreds of miles to marry Isaac, she was primarily responsible for Jacob's deception of her husband and her son over Esau's birthright (Genesis 24:57–67; 27:5–17).

Variants: **Beccy**, **Becky**.

René (m)
[RE-nay] from Latin *renatus*, meaning 'reborn'.
René Goupil (1608–1642) French missionary martyr and assistant to the French missionary and martyr Isaac Jogues. Rene sought to become a Jesuit, but his poor health caused him to abandon the hope of fulfilling such a vocation. He

later studied surgery and went to Canada, serving missionaries, especially the French missionary Isaac Jogues. Tragically, he was killed by Iroquois Indians.

Feminine form: **Renée**.

Renée feminine form of **René**.

Reuben (m)
[ROO-buhn] from Hebrew, meaning 'behold a son'.
Jacob's eldest son. He experienced mixed fortunes, defending Joseph and later his youngest brother Benjamin against the other brothers, but losing his special inheritance for sleeping with his father's concubine (Genesis 37:21–22; 49:3–4). Also the name of the tribe descended from him.

201

Reuel (m)
[ROO-uhl] from Hebrew, meaning 'friend of God'.
The name of several men in the Old Testament, especially the alternative name for **Jethro**; also the first son of Esau and Basemath (Genesis 36:4); the father of Shephatiah and son of Ibnijah (1 Chronicles 9:8).

Rhoda (f)
[ROH-duh] from Greek, meaning 'rose'.
The maid in the house of John Mark's mother, Mary, who came to the door and recognised the voice of the apostle Peter. In her joy, she did not open the door but ran back to tell other believers who had just been praying for Peter's release: their prayers had been answered (Acts 12:13 – 17).

Ricarda feminine form of **Richard**.

Richard (m)
[RICH-uhd] from Old English *Ricehard*, meaning 'strong ruler'.

Richard of Chichester (1197–1253), English bishop. Born Richard Wych, he studied canon law at Oxford, Paris and Bologna and after his return to England was appointed chancellor of Oxford University in 1235. He was then recruited as chancellor to St Edmund of Abingdon at Canterbury and subsequently accompanied the archbishop into exile to France, where he was ordained priest.

Having returned once more to England he was elected bishop of Chichester in 1244, although Henry III refused to accept the appointment for two years. Once in post, Richard was considered a model bishop, a humble man who was capable of generosity and mercy as well as being authoritative as occasions demanded.

Variants: **Dick**, **Dickie**, **Dicky**, **Ricardo**, **Rich**, **Richie**, **Rick**, **Rickie**, **Ricky**.

Feminine forms: **Ricarda**, **Richmal**.

Richmal feminine form of **Richard**.

Rita (f)

[REE-tuh] variant of *Margaret*.

Rita of Cascia (1377–1447), Italian nun. Born in Umbria, Rita obeyed her parents' wishes and married, but had to draw heavily on her religious faith for support after her husband proved both violent and unfaithful. Having borne two sons, she was widowed after 18 years when her husband was murdered in a vendetta. Her two sons fell ill and died before they could avenge their father's death (apparently in answer to their mother's prayer), upon which Rita entered an Augustinian convent at Cascia. Here she distinguished herself not only through her ceaseless praying and mortification but also through the appearance of a wound on her forehead, as though pierced by a crown of thorns. The wound remained open until Rita's death from tuberculosis 15 years later, when her body was reverently placed in an elaborate tomb.

Venerated for her great holiness and for the miracles associated with her name, Rita of Cascia became the focus of a substantial worldwide cult, which continues to attract devotees in large numbers today. She is honoured as a patron saint of desperate cases, especially those of a matrimonial nature.

Robert (m)

[RO-buht] from Old German, meaning 'fame' and 'bright'.

Robert of Molesme (1027–1110), French abbot. Born into a noble family of Troyes, he became a monk and progressed quickly to the rank of prior, serving first at Moûtier-la-Celle and later at Tonnerre before responding to a request to assume the post of abbot. The community moved to Molesme around 1075 but Robert's ambition to see the house develop along strict Benedictine lines was only partially realised and instead he later settled in the forest of Cîteaux near Dijon with several other monks and founded a new community there. He is remembered chiefly as one of the precursors of the Cistercian movement.

Robert Bellarmine (1542–1621), Italian cardinal and theologian. Born Roberto Bellarmino into a noble family in Tuscany, he joined the Jesuits and worked as a teacher of classics before being ordained priest at Ghent. He went on to become the first Jesuit professor at the University of Louvain and to hold prominent posts at the College of Rome before being appointed provincial of Naples and, later theologian to Pope Clement VIII as well as examiner of bishops and consultor of the Holy Office. He was raised to the rank of cardinal in 1599, made archbishop of Capua in 1602 and in 1605 was appointed head of the Vatican Library. He was twice considered for the papacy, but failed to be elected.

Considered a leading theologian in the debate between Roman Catholicism and emerging Protestantism, he played a leading role in a number of church disputes and voiced the church's accusations against Galileo concerning his theories about the movement of the earth around the sun. Of his many influential writings the most significant was his *Controversies of the Christian Faith Against the Heretics of This Time*. Others included two catechisms, treatises and commentaries upon the Bible.

Robert Southwell (1561–95), English martyr. Born in Norfolk, Robert Southwell studied in Douay and Paris before being ordained as a Jesuit priest. He was later sent to England to serve in secret as a priest to the Catholics suffering under official persecution during the reign of Elizabeth I. He was employed as chaplain to Countess Anne of Arundel and worked diligently within the Catholic community until he was betrayed to the authorities and imprisoned. While in prison he was subjected to cruel torture, including being placed on the rack on no less than nine occasions, and was then kept in solitary confinement in the Tower of London. After three years in the Tower he was condemned to death as a traitor and executed at Tyburn.

Variants: **Bob**, **Bobby**, **Rob**, **Robbie**, **Robin**, **Rupert**.

Feminine form: **Roberta**.

Roberta feminine form of **Robert**.

Ronald (m)
[RO-nuhld] Scottish form of *Reginald* and *Reynald*, from Old English *Regenweald*, meaning 'counsel power'.
Twelfth-century chieftain. A warrior in Orkney, Scotland, he founded the cathedral of St Magnus in Kirkwell in 1137. He was known for his godly devotion. He was murdered by a group of rebels in 1158.

Variants: **Reginald**, **Ron**, **Ronnie**.

Rose (f)
[rohz] from the Old German *hrod*, meaning 'fame'; associated with the name of the flower, Latin *rosa*, meaning 'rose'.

The rose is a symbol of the Virgin Mary. Also, Rose of Lima (1586–1617), Peruvian recluse. Born Isabel de Flores y del Olivia in Lima, Peru, she was of impoverished Spanish parentage and spent her early years trying to earn money to augment the family income. Later, despite her personal beauty (which earned her the nickname 'Rose'), she decided against marrying and instead became a Dominican tertiary at the age of 20, taking up residence in a hut in her garden. She became well known for her dedication to prayer and for the excessive penances she inflicted upon herself. She also became celebrated as a mystic and for her charitable work among the sick and the poor as well as among the indigenous American population, winning recognition as a forerunner of the social services in Peru.

When Lima largely survived powerful earthquakes, the presence of 'Rose of Lima' was widely assumed to be the reason that the damage had been limited. Rose died at the age of just 31 and was canonised in 1671: the first canonised saint of the Americas. She is honoured today as the patron saint of South America, Lima and Peru and of florists and gardeners.

Variants: **Rosabel**, **Rosabella**, **Rosetta**, **Rosie**, **Rosina**, **Rosita**, **Rosy**.

Rufus (m)
[ROO-fuhs] from Latin, meaning 'red-haired'.
The name of two men in the New Testament: the son of Simon of Cyrene (who was compelled to carry Jesus' cross) and brother of Alexander (Mark 15:21). Also, one of the Christian believers in Rome that Paul mentions in his greetings (Romans 16:13). The mother of this Rufus had also taken care of Paul.

Also known as *Rufinus*, the name of several saints, including the fifth-century martyr of Capua, Italy, whose relics are enshrined in the cathedral there.

Rupert (m)
[ROO-puht] variant of *Robert*.
Bishop of Salzburg (died c.710). Possibly of Frankish or Irish birth, Rupert served as bishop of Worms for several years before going as a missionary to Regensburg in Bavaria. He extended his evangelical activities over a wide area and established his base at Salzburg, where he founded the monastery of St Peter. He also founded a nunnery at Nonnberg. He is remembered as one of the most important of the early evangelisers of the German peoples.

Ruth (f)
[rooth] related to the Hebrew word for 'friend'.
A young Moabite widow who was one of the ancestors of David and Jesus (Ruth 4:17; Matthew 1:5). Ruth is an outstanding example of a non-Israelite who commits herself to the Lord and to Israel (Ruth 1:16). Her great kindness to her Israelite mother-in-law and respect for the Israelite law of levirate marriage illustrate the depth of her faith.

206

Sabina (f)
[suh-BEE-nuh] from Latin, meaning a woman of Sabine (near Rome).
Converted to Christianity by her servant Serapia, Sabina and Serapia were both put to death for their faith under the persecution of Emperor Hadrian, in about 119.

St John (m)
[SIN-juhn] see **John**.

Salome (f)
[suh-LOH-mee] from Hebrew, meaning 'peace'.
The name of two women in the New Testament: Herodias' daughter, who is not named in the New Testament but was named in this way by Josephus. According to the New

Testament narrative, Salome danced for her stepfather Herod at his birthday feast. Herod then promised on oath that he would give her whatever she asked. Prompted by her mother, she asked for the head of John the Baptist (Matthew 14:6–11). Also, the name of one of the women who saw Jesus' crucifixion from a distance and who after his body had been buried came with some spices to anoint his body (Mark 15:40; 16:1).

Salvador (m)

[sal-vuh-DAW] from Latin *salvator*, meaning 'saviour'.

Saviour is one of the highest titles used to describe Jesus Christ (Titus 1:4). Jesus Christ is the Promised One who would come to save his people from their sins (Matthew 1:21). His work of salvation was accomplished supremely through his death and resurrection. Jesus Christ is the unique Saviour of the world (Acts 4:12; 1 John 4:14). His offer of salvation is received by believing (trusting) in Jesus Christ (Acts 16:30–31).

207

Variant: **Salvatore**.

Samson (m)

[SAM-suhn] from Hebrew, meaning 'sun child' or 'strong; distinguished'.

One of the judges, who led Israel for 20 years (Judges 13–16). He often fought single-handedly against the Philistines, and destroyed 3000 occupants of a Philistine temple at his death. Though he was dedicated to God as a Nazirite and received great strength from God, he seems to have accepted rather than challenged the low spiritual and moral standards of his day. He was betrayed by Delilah, who persuaded him to tell her the secret of his strength, and captured. In his death he brought down the temple of Dagon on the Philistines.

Also *Samson, Welsh bishop (c.490–c.565)*. Born in south Wales, Samson is said to have been educated and ordained in Glamorgan and then gone on to serve as abbot at a monastery on Caldey Island. After a visit to Ireland and a period spent as a hermit on the banks of the Severn, he was made a bishop by St Dyfrig. A wandering Celtic monk-bishop, he next moved to Cornwall as the result of a vision and from there founded monasteries at Dol and Pental in France. He is also thought to have evangelised in the Channel Islands and the Scilly Isles, where one of the islands bears his name. Recognised as the leader of the British colonisers of Brittany, he died at his monastery at Dol. Numerous miracles were attributed to Samson and his memory is preserved in various place names and churches in southwest Britain and Brittany.

208

    Variants: **Sam**, **Sampson**.

Samuel (m)
[SAM-yool] from Hebrew, meaning 'heard by God'.
An important Old Testament prophet and the last of the judges. His chief role was to choose and anoint Israel's first two kings, Saul and David, though as one who brought God's word to Israel, he found himself in opposition to Saul as the latter acted increasingly independently of God. His early life was remarkable for two reasons. His mother Hannah prayed for a son after being barren for many years (1 Samuel 1:1–2:11), and he received his first prophecy while still a child (1 Samuel 3).
    Variants: **Sam**, **Sammy**.

Sandra feminine form of **Alexander**.

Sapphira (f)
[suh-FY-ruh] from Greek, meaning 'beautiful'.
The wife of Ananias. The couple died suddenly in Jerusalem because they lied to the church and to God (Acts 5:1–11).
    Variant: **Sapphire**.

Sarah (f)

[SAIR-uh] from Hebrew, meaning 'princess'.

Abraham's wife and his half-sister, and the mother of Isaac. Her name was changed from Sarai to emphasise her importance as the mother of God's promised child (Genesis 17:15–22). However, she could not believe that she would bear a child when she was 90 years old (Genesis 18:10–15).

Variants: **Sadie**, **Sal**, **Sally**, **Sara**, **Zara**.

Saul (m)

[sawl] from Hebrew, meaning 'asked [of God]'.

The first king of Israel. He was a complex character who was initially chosen by God in response to the people's request for a king, but his reign increasingly collapsed. Because Saul preferred to pursue his own interests rather than trust God, God rejected him as his king while allowing him to remain in power (1 Samuel 15). He was publicly overshadowed by his son-in-law David, privately tormented by depression and was finally killed in battle by the very Philistines God had chosen him to defeat. Saul's is one of the saddest stories in the Bible, showing the consequences of rejecting God's word.

Also the original name of the apostle **Paul**.

209

Sebastian (m)

[suh-BAS-tee-uhn] from Latin *Sebastianus*, meaning 'man of Sebasta (town in Asia Minor)'.

Roman martyr (died *c*.300). Possibly born in Milan, or educated there, Sebastian ranks among the best known of the early martyrs through the many celebrated depictions of his execution by sculptors and painters during the Renaissance. Very little is known for certain about his life beyond the fact that he was put to death for his Christian faith by being shot to death with arrows and buried on the Appian Way in Rome during the reign of Diocletian. Legend has added the tradition that he was born at Narbonne in

Gaul and served as an officer in the Roman Pretorian Guard before being revealed as a Christian, arrested and condemned to death. He is honoured as the patron saint of archers and soldiers.

Variant: **Seb**.

Sergius (m)

[SER-jee-uhs] possibly from Latin, meaning 'servant'.

Sergius Paulus, a Roman proconsul in Paphos on Cyprus (AD 47–48), who asked Barnabas and Paul to visit him because he wanted to hear the word of God (Acts 13:7).

Sergius, an early fourth-century martyr. A Roman officer who was martyred in Syria during the persecution under Emperor Diocletian.

Sergius of Radonezh (1313–92), Russian monk. Born into a noble family of Rostov, he fled his home with his family because of civil war with the Tartars and was brought up in Radonezh, near Moscow, becoming a monk following the death of his parents. At the age of 20 he and his brother adopted the life of hermits in the forest nearby and in due course attracted a number of like-minded companions, who by 1354 formed the basis of the monastery of the Holy Trinity, under the leadership of Sergius.

Sergius then founded around 40 more similar communities and became arguably Russia's most renowned religious figure, celebrated not only for his role as a monastic reformer but also for his personal qualities, which included humility, gentleness and willingness to serve others. He is also credited with having had many visions of the Virgin Mary during his lifetime; he is honoured as patron saint of Moscow and of all Russia.

Variants: **Serge**, **Sergei**.

Seth (m)
[seth] possibly from Hebrew, meaning 'granted' or 'appointed'.
Adam and Eve's third son. He was born after Abel's murder and was an ancestor of Noah (Genesis 5:3).

Seymour (m)
[SEE-maw] from a surname referring to a person from the French town of *Saint Maur*.
St Maur (or *Maurus*) was a sixth-century Italian monk. According to tradition, he was the son of a Roman nobleman but was brought up in the care of St Benedict and chose the life of a monk at the monastery of Subiaco, fulfilling the role of Benedict's personal aide. Nothing is known of the details of his subsequent life apart from a story that he performed a miracle by walking on water in order to save St Placid from drowning.

211

Sharon (f)
[SHA-ron] from the name of the plain.
Sharon is a coastal plain in northern Palestine, stretching for 80 kilometres north of Joppa. Its fertile soil was largely covered with forests in ancient times. The 'rose of Sharon' (Song of Songs 2:1) was distinctive to the region, but its precise identification remains uncertain.

Sheba (f)
[SHEE-buh] from *Bathsheba* or a name in its own right.
A variant of *Bathsheba*. Also the Queen of Sheba (south-west Arabia) visited Solomon with a large and fine retinue to investigate reports of his wisdom and accomplishments and to ask him difficult questions, which he answered satisfactorily. She then praised Solomon and gave him fine and expensive gifts; in exchange Solomon gave her all she wanted and asked for (1 Kings 10:1–14). *Sheba* is also the name of several men in the Old Testament, including a

member of the tribe of Benjamin who led a rebellion against David (2 Samuel 20).

Sheena feminine form of **John**.

Shem (m)
[shem] from Hebrew, meaning 'renown'.
One of Noah's three sons who survived the flood with him and from whom the world was repopulated (Genesis 6:10; 9:18–19).

Shona, **Sian** feminine forms of **John**.

212

Sidony (f)
[SI-duhn-ee] probably from Latin *Sidonia*, meaning 'woman of Sidon (ancient Phoenician city)'. This name may also derive from Greek *sindon*, meaning 'linen', a reference to the shroud in which the body of Christ was wrapped.

Sigfrid (m)
[SIG-freed] variant of *Siegfried*, from Old English 'victory' and 'peace'.
Swedish bishop (died *c.*1045). Tradition claims that Sigfrid was of English birth, serving as a priest in York or Glastonbury before travelling to Scandinavia with two other bishops to conduct missionary work there. Based in southern Sweden, where he built a church, he baptised the Swedish king, Olaf and visited various remote areas in the course of his Christian work. His campaign, which took him as far as Denmark, aroused some opposition and while he was away, his church at Växjo was attacked and his two nephews, who served as his assistants, were murdered. Sigfrid, however, persuaded Olaf to spare the lives of the murderers and set about rebuilding his church at Växjo, where ultimately he died.

Silas (m)

[SY-luhs] variant of *Silvanus*, from the Roman god of trees and forests.

Companion of the apostle Paul (first century). Silas (otherwise referred to as Silvanus) is identified in the Acts of the Apostles and elsewhere as a companion of Paul on some of his missionary journeys and was the secretary called Silvanus mentioned in 1 Thessalonians 1:1 and 1 Peter 5:12.

Silvia see **Sylvia**.

Simeon (m)

[SIM-ee-uhn] from Hebrew, meaning 'hearing'.

In the Old Testament Jacob's second son, who attacked Shechem in revenge for his sister's rape and who was taken as a hostage for Benjamin in Egypt (Genesis 34; 42:24). In the New Testament, a devout old man who gave two prophecies about the baby Jesus, one of which is known as the *Nunc Dimittis* (Luke 2:29–35).

Simeon the Stylite (390–459), Syrian ascetic and first of the pillar hermits. Born the son of a shepherd in Cilicia, Simeon the Stylite adopted a lifestyle of extreme austerity and fasting as a child and went on to spend some 20 years in hermitages and monasteries in northern Syria. The severity of his austerities proved too much for the other monks, however, and after only narrowly recovering from his injuries after binding his arm with a tight noose of rope made from palm leaves he was obliged to live in seclusion in a hut for three years. Finding himself mobbed there by people attracted by his reputation for meeting requests for prayers and advice, he made the decision in 423 to remove himself literally above the world of ordinary men by taking up residence on top of a nine-foot pillar, at Telanissus (Dair Sem'an). He spent the remaining 36 years of his life on a platform on top of a series of pillars, the height of which

213

was gradually raised to around 60 feet. Ironically, his decision to live on a pillar only served to attract even larger crowds of the faithful seeking his advice, from humble pilgrims to emperors. He preached to these throngs of people twice daily, urging them to give up their licentious and unjust ways. By the time of his death Simeon the Stylite had become the most famous of all the ascetics to take up such a mode of life and a monastery and sanctuary were later built over the remains of his columns.

Simeon the New Theologian (949–1022), abbot and mystic. Born in Paphlagonia in Asia Minor, Simeon (or Symeon) was brought up in Constantinople and eventually was admitted as a monk to the monastery of Studius in 984. He found the rule there too lenient, however, and moved to the monastery of St Mamas, where subsequently he served as abbot for 25 years. Eventually criticism of his radical reforms obliged him to go into exile, though ultimately he founded another small monastery at Chrysopolis, where he remained until his death. He is remembered chiefly for his influential writings, such as the *Catechetical Discourses* and *Hymns of Divine Love*.

Variant: **Simon**.

Simon (m)

[SY-muhn] variant of *Simeon*.

The name of several men in the New Testament: *Simon Peter* (see **Peter**). *Simon the Zealot*, one of the twelve apostles (Matthew 10:4; Luke 6:15). The term *Zealot* probably indicates his previous Jewish nationalist tendencies. *Simon, the brother of Jesus* (Matthew 13:55). *Simon, the leper at Bethany*, in whose house Jesus was anointed with oil (Matthew 26:6–13). *Simon, the Pharisee*, in whose house a sinful woman washed Jesus' feet with her tears (Luke 7:36–50). *Simon, the man from Cyrene* who was passing by on his way from the country and who was compelled to carry Jesus' cross (Mark 15:21). *Simon, the*

sorcerer of Samaria who believed and was baptised. When he saw that the gift of the Holy Spirit was given by the laying on of the apostles' hands, he offered money to the apostles so that he too could have this power. He was rebuked by Peter; his request showed his sin and ignorance (Acts 8:9–24). *Simon, the tanner* at whose house in Joppa by the sea Peter stayed (Acts 9:43; 10:6).

Feminine form: **Simone**.

Simone feminine form of **Simon**.

Sinclair masculine form of **Clare**.

Solomon (m)
[SOL-uh-muhn] from Hebrew, meaning 'peace'.
David's successor as king during whose reign Israel enjoyed unparalleled prosperity and peace. His wealth was based largely on trade, and included the use of ocean-going ships, but his greatest achievement was his building activity. This took place in various cities, but was concentrated in Jerusalem with the temple as its centrepiece (1 Kings 5:1–9:28). However, Solomon changed Israel's character for ever by replacing the tribal system with a centralised civil service. Solomon's taxation and conscription policies were unpopular, however, and he was also criticised for the pagan influence of his extensive harem. God therefore announced that Solomon's kingdom would be divided, an event which duly took place within months of his death (1 Kings 11:29–12:24).

Sophia, Sofia (f)
[SO-fee-uh, suh-FY-uh] from Greek, meaning 'wisdom'.
The second-century saint traditionally believed to have died of grief after the martyrdom of her three daughters Faith, Hope and Charity under Hadrian's persecution.

Variant: **Sophie**.

Stanislas (m)

[STAN-is-luhs] from Slavic, meaning 'camp of glory'.

Stanislas of Cracow (1010–79), Polish bishop and martyr. Born into a noble family of Szczepanow in Poland, he was elected bishop of Cracow in 1072 and proved a vigorous reformer, generous to the poor and an energetic preacher. Subsequently, however, he came into conflict with King Boleslav II after finding fault with the king's personal behaviour. When Stanislas had the temerity to excommunicate the king for abducting the wife of one of his nobles after she refused his advances (amid other misdeeds), Boleslav apparently responded by having his bishop assaulted and murdered while conducting Mass – although there is some confusion about what actually happened. One version of the story claims that Boleslav killed the bishop himself after his guards found themselves physically incapable of completing the deed. Whatever the case, Stanislas is venerated today in Poland, Lithuania, Belarus and Ukraine. He is also honoured as the patron saint of both Cracow and Poland.

Stanislas Kostka (1550–68), Jesuit novice. Born into a noble family living in the castle of Rostkovo in Poland, Stanislas Kostka was educated at the Jesuit college in Vienna and in due course, after a life-threatening illness, resolved to become a Jesuit himself (in defiance of his father's wishes and the attempts of his brother Paul to dissuade him). Refused admittance to the order in Vienna, he travelled on foot all the way to Rome, where he was finally allowed in by St Francis Borgia. Despite his wealthy background, Stanislas Kostka proved an ideal recruit with a saintly demeanour and the ability to see visions, but died at the age of 17 after a final vision of the Virgin Mary just nine months into his novitiate.

Stella (f)

[STE-luh] from Latin, meaning 'star'.

Stella Maris (meaning 'star of the sea') is a title of the Blessed Virgin Mary.

Stephen, Steven (m)

[STEE-vuhn] from Greek *Stephanos*, meaning 'wreath' or 'crown'.

The first of the Christian martyrs (died c.35). According to Acts 6:1–8:4, Stephen (probably a Greek-speaking Jew) became the first of the seven deacons to whom the apostles entrusted the care of Greek-speaking Christian widows living in Jerusalem. He proved a powerful preacher and worker of miracles, but soon fell foul of the Jewish authorities, who accused him of blasphemy. When brought before the court he roundly condemned his accusers for having brought about the death of the Messiah and stirred up such indignation that he was dragged out of the city and stoned to death. Among the witnesses to Stephen's martyrdom was Saul, who was subsequently moved to embrace Christianity under the name Paul. He is honoured as the patron saint of deacons, stonemasons and headache sufferers.

Also *Stephen I (died 257), Roman pope*. Born into a noble family of Rome, he served as a priest in the city before succeeding Lucius I as pope in 254. His brief reign of three years is usually remembered for the eruption of the Novatian controversy concerning the validity of baptism when carried out by heretics or apostates (which Stephen stubbornly considered valid). He also emphasised the authority of the papacy over the rest of the Christian church, involving himself in confronting heresy in Gaul and intervening in a religious dispute in Spain.

Stephen of Hungary (c.975–1038), King of Hungary. The son of the duke of the Magyars in Hungary, Stephen (or Istvan) was baptised at an early age, married the sister of the Holy Roman Emperor St Henry II and succeeded to his father's dukedom in 997. He proved a highly capable ruler, restoring law and order throughout the region and going on to be crowned the first king of Hungary in 1001. As king, Stephen actively encouraged the evangelisation of his people, founding monasteries and supporting his bishops as well as doing many works of charity (often incognito). Where he met determined opposition from rival pagans, however, he suppressed it with a firm hand, forbidding, for instance, marriages between Christians and pagans and severely punishing anyone suspected of observing pagan superstitions. He is honoured today as the patron saint of Hungary and kings. Feast Day: 16 August.

Stephen Harding (died 1134), English abbot. Probably born in Dorset, Stephen Harding was educated at Sherborne abbey before going abroad and becoming a monk in Burgundy. In 1098 he moved to Cîteaux and 10 years later succeeded St Alberic as abbot there. Together with Alberic and Robert of Molesme, Stephen Harding is considered one of the three founders of the Cistercian movement. Particularly influential was his formulation of the Charter of Charity (*Carta Caritatis*), which set in place the rules under which the movement was to develop through the generations. Monks joining the order were expected to renounce all luxury and to dedicate themselves to public and private prayer and manual labour. Heads of the all houses of the order were required to meet on a yearly basis and similarly to expect a visit from the abbot of the founding house every 12 months.

Variants: **Steffan**, **Steve**, **Stevie**.

Feminine form: **Stephanie**.

Susannah, Susanna (f)

[sew-ZAN-uh] from Hebrew *Shushannah*, meaning 'lily'.

In the New Testament, one of the women who provided for Christ and his disciples from their own resources. In the apocryphal book of Susanna (chapter 13 of the Greek version of Daniel), Susanna is a moral and beautiful woman who is lusted after by two corrupt Jewish judges. They seize her while she is bathing in her garden, but she screams out rather than give in to their threats. The two judges falsely accuse her of adultery. Susanna is given a show trial by the judges and condemned to death. However, the young Daniel intervenes, re-opens the trial and proves the falsity of the testimony of the judges, who are then put to death.

Variants: **Sue**, **Sukey**, **Susan**, **Susana**, **Susanne**, **Susie**, **Suzanna**, **Suzanne**, **Suzette**, **Suzy**, **Zana**.

Swithin (m)
[SWITH-in] from Old English, meaning 'strong'.
English bishop (died 862). Born in Wessex, Swithun (or Swithin) was educated in Winchester and in due course became chaplain to the Wessex kings Egbert and Ethelwulf. In 852 he was made bishop of Winchester, in which role he proved highly energetic, building several churches and promoting the welfare of the poor. He is usually remembered today for his association with the traditional belief that if it rains on St Swithin's Day (15 July), then it will continue to rain for the following 40 days. This tradition has its origins in a story that describes how attempts made to move the saint's body 100 years after his death from a humble spot in the churchyard to a more prestigious location within Winchester cathedral were delayed by heavy rain which was interpreted as a sign that Swithin preferred to remain where he was.

219

Sylvester, Silvester (m)
[sil-VES-tuh] from Latin, meaning 'of the woods or forest'.
Silvester I (died 335), Roman pope. Born in Rome, Silvester (or Sylvester) succeeded St Miltiades as pope in 314. Few details are known of his life and papacy, although a number of legends became associated with his name. These included the tradition that it was to Silvester that the emperor Constantine granted the papacy supremacy over

all other bishops and secular rulers in Italy. More reliable is the claim that Constantine granted Silvester the Lateran palace, which became St John Lateran, Rome's cathedral church. It was also during Silvester's reign that the first general council of the church was held at Nicaea in 325.

Silvester Gozzoli (1177–1267), Italian abbot. Born at Osimo, Silvester Gozzoli studied law before defying parental opposition and being ordained priest and becoming a canon in the cathedral at Osimo. He remained there until the age of 50, when he found fault with the behaviour of his bishop and resigned from his post. He spent the next four years living as a hermit but in 1231 founded a monastery at Monte Fano, near Fabriano, where he served as abbot. The monastery prospered under his direction, which obliged monks to observe a very strict version of the Benedictine rule, and several more similar so-called Silvestrine houses were established before the time of the founder's death.

Sylvia, Silvia (f)
[SIL-vee-uh] from Latin, meaning '(woman) of the wood'.
The mother of Gregory I, Gregory the Great (c.520–592). She was renowned for her godly devotion and led a solitary, almost monastic life.

Tabitha (f)
[TAB-i-thuh] from Aramaic, meaning 'gazelle'.
A disciple in Joppa who was known for her good works. She died but was brought back to life by the apostle Peter (Acts 9:36–42). She was also known as Dorcas, the Greek word for gazelle.

Talitha (f)
[TAL-i-thuh] from Aramaic, meaning 'little girl'.
Talitha Koum (meaning 'little girl, get up!') were the words Jesus spoke to the 12-year-old daughter of Jairus, the synagogue leader.

Tamar (f)

[TAY-mah] from Hebrew, meaning 'palm tree'.

The name of two women in the Old Testament: the mother of the twins Perez and Zerah by her father-in-law Judah (Genesis 38) and an ancestor of David and Jesus (Matthew 1:3). Also, David's daughter who was raped by her half-brother Amnon (2 Samuel 13:1–22).

Tatiana (f)

[ta-tee-AH-nuh] feminine form of Latin *Tatianus*, from the old Roman family name *Tatius*, of uncertain origin.

Third-century Roman martyr put to death for her faith during the reign of Emperor Alexander Severus. She is venerated especially by the Orthodox Church.

Variants: **Tania**, **Tanya**.

Terence (m)

[TE-ruhns] from the Roman family name *Terentius*.

A third-century martyr killed in Carthage during the persecution of Roman emperor Caius Messius Quintus Trajanus Decius.

Variants: **Tel**, **Terry**.

Teresa, **Theresa** (f)

[tuh-REE-zuh, tuh-RAY-zuh] origin uncertain, possibly from Greek *therizo*, meaning 'to reap', or from *Therasia*, the name of the Greek island in the Aegean Sea.

Teresa of Avila (1515–82), Spanish foundress. Teresa (or Theresa) de Cepeday Ahumada was born into an aristocratic family near Avila in Castile and at the age of 15 was sent to be educated at the local Augustinian convent. Here she decided to become a nun and accordingly entered the Incarnation of the Carmelite nuns in Avila in 1536. As a young woman she suffered several bouts of serious illness, only narrowly surviving, and through this experience discovered the power of prayer. Once recovered, she had the first of many mystical revelations, going into ecstatic raptures. From that time on, she spent much of her time in prayer, often going into deep religious trances. In 1559 she underwent the rare experience of a trans-verberation, in which she felt her heart pierced by an arrow of divine love plunged into her by an angel.

In 1562 she founded the reformed Discalced (meaning 'barefooted') Carmelite order to further her ambition of reforming Carmelite convents throughout Spain, returning to the strict rule under which the order was originally established. Over the years that followed she travelled extensively through the country, founding a total of 17 reformed Carmelite houses.

She was joined in this work by St John of the Cross, whom she first met when she was aged 53. The two became close friends and corresponded regularly, St John under-taking similar reform among friars of the order.

Greatly loved by her nuns, St Teresa was also celebrated for her written works on spiritual matters, which included her autobiography *Life* and the classic mystical treatises *The Interior Castle* and *The Way of Perfection*. In 1970 she became the first woman to be declared a Doctor of the Church. She is also honoured as the patron saint of lacemakers.

Also the *Spanish wife of the French bishop St Paulinus of Nola*.

Also, *Theresa of Lisieux (1873–97) French mystic and nun*. Theresa (or *Thérèse*) of Lisieux was born Marie Françoise Martin in Alençon in Normandy and dreamt initially of becoming a missionary and a martyr. Realising this was unrealistic, she became a Discalced Carmelite nun at Lisieux in 1888, having obtained special permission from the local bishop as she was aged only 15 and so technically too young to enter a convent. Calling herself Thérèse of the Child Jesus, over the next nine years she demonstrated great piety and inexhaustible love of God and impressed all

222

with her simple faith, which she termed her 'little way of spiritual childhood'. In 1896, however, she was diagnosed with tuberculosis and was ordered by her superiors to commit an account of her life to writing before her illness could claim her. This she obediently did before dying at the premature age of 24.

Her thoughts and recollections, together with details of her various mystical experiences, were subsequently published as *The Story of a Soul*, which became one of the most loved of all Catholic bestsellers. She is honoured as the patron saint of France, of foreign missions and of florists, air crews and Aids sufferers.

Also, *Mother Teresa (1910–97)*. Born in Albania, she became a Roman Catholic nun. She founded the Missionaries of Charity in Calcutta in 1950. For over forty years she ministered to the poor, the sick, orphans and the dying, while overseeing the expansion of the work of the Missionaries of Charity, first throughout India and then in other countries. In 1979 she was awarded the Nobel Peace Prize.

Variants: **Terri**, **Tess**, **Tessa**, **Thérèse**, **Tracey**, **Tracy**.

Thaddaeus (m)
[tha-DEE-uhs] possibly from Aramaic for 'heart'.
One of the 12 apostles (Matthew 10:3), probably the same as Judas son of James (Luke 6:16).

Thekla, Thecla (f)
[THEK-luh, TEK-luh] from Greek, meaning 'god' and 'glory'.
Thecla of Iconium (first century), virgin martyr. Details of the life and death of St Thecla (or Tecla) of Iconium depend almost wholly on legend dating from the second century. Tradition claims that she was born in Iconium in Asia Minor and became a follower of the apostle Paul, breaking off her engagement in order to embrace a celibate Christian

223

life. When her conversion was discovered, however, Paul was driven out of Iconium and Thecla herself was condemned to death by burning. When a storm put out the flames that threatened Thecla, she was thrown into the arena to be killed by wild beasts, but the animals refused to go near her. She then managed to escape and was reunited with Paul at Myra.

She spent the remaining 72 years of her life as a hermit in a cave at Seleucia, earning a reputation as a miracle worker. At the age of 90 Thecla was assaulted by pagan rivals but was protected from them when the rock of her cave opened up to surround her and she was never seen again.

224

Theodora feminine form of **Theodore**.

Theodore (m)
[THEE-uh-daw] from Greek, meaning 'gift of God'.
Fourth-century martyr. Little is known about St Theodore beyond the fact that he was a Roman soldier who refused to pay homage to the pagan gods at Amasea in Pontus and then burnt down a temple dedicated to the Mother Goddess, upon which he was tortured and sentenced to death as a Christian. While in prison awaiting execution he is said to have been consoled by visions of heaven.

Theodore of Canterbury (602–90), Greek-born arch-bishop. Born in Tarsus in Cilicia, Theodore of Canterbury was educated at Antioch and Constantinople and lived as a monk first in Greece and then in Rome until he was in his sixties, when he was unexpectedly appointed to the vacant see of Canterbury by Pope Vitalian. Theodore accordingly came to England, accompanied by St Adrian and St Benedict Biscop, and presided over the first synod of the whole English church, held at Hertford. He also appointed bishops to fill vacant sees, set up a celebrated school in Canterbury, negotiated in the argument between St Chad and St Wilfrid over their jurisdiction of the see of York, created a number of new sees and assumed responsibility for unifying the hitherto disorganised English church as one body, effectively laying the foundations for the modern church in England and becoming the first archbishop of Canterbury to enjoy universal authority.

Theodore the Studite (759–826), Greek abbot and theologian. Born the son of a treasury official in Constantinople, he became a monk in the monastery of Sakkoudion in Bithynia, where his uncle was abbot, and was ordained priest in 787. He succeeded to his uncle's post of abbot but incurred imperial wrath shortly afterwards when he criticised the emperor Constantine's adulterous remarriage and was banished for a brief period. He then moved to Constantinople and took over the monastery founded by the Roman consul Studius, going on to make it an influential centre of Byzantine monasticism. He proved a steadfast defender of the church's independence from secular interference and instituted important monastic reforms, although these were not achieved without difficulty. He remains one of the most revered of all saints in the eastern church.

225

Variants: **Teddie**, **Teddy**.

Feminine form: **Theodora**.

Theophania (f)

[thee-o-fuh-NEE-uh] from Greek, meaning 'manifestation of God'.

In the Middle Ages, the name was occasionally given to girls born on the feast of Epiphany, associated with the revelation of Christ to the Magi (wise men), which is celebrated on 6 January.

Variant: **Tiffany**.

Theophilus (m)

[thee-OF-i-luhs] Latin form of Greek, meaning 'loved by God'.

The man Luke dedicated his two books (the Gospel of Luke and the Acts of the Apostles) to.

Theresa see **Teresa**.

Thomas (m)
[TO-muhs] from Aramaic, meaning 'twin'.
One of the twelve apostles, known as Didymus or 'the twin'. Despite Thomas' pessimistic tendencies (John 11:16; 20:24–25), Jesus responded positively to his doubts (hence the expression *a doubting Thomas*) about the resurrection. Thomas' subsequent declaration that Jesus was Lord and God is one of the most succinct New Testament statements concerning Jesus' identity.
    Variants: **Tammy**, **Tom**, **Tommy**.

226

Timothy (m)
[TI-muh-thee] from Greek name *Timotheus*, meaning 'honouring God'.
Born the son of a Gentile father and a Jewish mother of Lystra, Timothy was converted to Christianity by the apostle Paul and became his younger colleague. Timothy entered Christian ministry as a result of a prophecy, and became Paul's representative as well as his assistant (Romans 16:21; Philippians 2:19–23). Despite a timid personality, Timothy led the church at Ephesus (1 Timothy 1:3). He was also imprisoned, but set free for his faith (Hebrews 13:23).

Tina feminine form of **Christian**.

Titus (m)
[TY-tuhs] Latin name of unknown origin and meaning.
A 'partner and fellow-worker' of the apostle Paul (2 Corinthians 8:23). Of Gentile birth, Titus was converted to Christianity by Paul, after which he became one of Paul's

most trusted assistants and companions. He probably travelled with Paul on several of his journeys, was his representative to Corinth and was then given charge of organising the church in Crete as first bishop of the Cretan city of Gortyna. In a letter sent to Titus in Crete Paul recommended a firm hand in conducting his ministry among the Cretans.

Tobias (m)
[tuh-BY-uhs] meaning 'Yahweh is my good': see **Tobit**.
According to the apocryphal book of Tobit, Tobias is Tobit's son, whom his father sends on a journey, which becomes the means by which God answers the prayers of Sarah, whom Tobias meets, falls in love with and marries.
   Variant: **Toby**.

227

Tobit (m) [TOH-bit]
Greek form of Aramaic *Tobi*, a shortening of *Tobiyah*, meaning 'Yahweh is my good'.
According to the apocryphal book that bears his name, Tobit is a Jew from the tribe of Naphtali whose family had been deported by the Assyrians. He is a godly and kind man, who is committed to the Mosaic Law. But he becomes very poor and accidentally becomes blind. He loses all hope and prays to God that he may allow him to die. But God has a better plan for him that involves restoring his eyesight, his wealth and his reputation, and finding a wife for his son Tobias.

Toni feminine form of **Anthony**.

Tryphena (f)
[try-FEE-nuh] from Greek, meaning 'delicacy'.
One of the women greeted by the apostle Paul in his personal greetings in Romans 16 (verse 12), who worked hard in the Lord.

Tychicus (m)
[TY-ki-kuhs] from Greek, meaning 'fortuitous'.
Paul's companion on his journey to Jerusalem and his representative to the churches in Colosse and Ephesus (Ephesians 6:21–22; Colossians 4:7).

Ulric (m)
[UUL-rik] from the Old English name *Wulfric*, meaning 'wolf ruler'.
Ulric of Augsburg (*c.*890–973) Swiss bishop. Born near Zurich, Ulric was educated at the monastery of St Gall and spent time in the household of his uncle Adalbero, bishop of Augsburg. In due course, despite ill-health, he rose to the rank of bishop himself and served in the post for some 50 years, earning a reputation for his dedication to prayer and for his tireless work on behalf of the diocese, which was much traumatised by the effects of war.
Variant: **Ulrich**.
Feminine forms: **Ulrica**, **Ulrike**.

Ulrica, **Ulrike** feminine forms of **Ulric**.

Urban (m)
[ER-buhn] from Latin *urbanus*, from *urbs*, meaning 'city'.
Roman pope and martyr (died 230). Born in Rome, Urban was elected pope in 222 in succession to the martyred St Callistus. Virtually nothing is known about his relatively peaceful papacy, which witnessed steady growth in the Christian community in Rome. The name *Urbanus* is mentioned in the apostle Paul's greetings in Romans 16:9; he is described as a 'co-worker in Christ'.

Uriah (m)
[yuh-RYR] from Hebrew, meaning 'Yahweh is my light'.
Uriah the Hittite, the husband of Bathsheba. David arranged his death while Uriah was fighting on Israel's front

line to cover up his affair with Bathsheba, but God sent the prophet Nathan to confront David with what he had done (2 Samuel 11:6–25; 12:1–10).

Also the name of other Old Testament men, including a priest in the time of Ahaz who built a pagan altar and put it in the temple (2 Kings 16:10–16). The prophet from Kireath-Jearim whose message of judgement offended King Jehoiakim that Jehoiakim murdered him (Jeremiah 26:20–23).

Ursula (f)

[ER-suh-luh, ER-sew-luh] from Latin, meaning 'little bear'. Virgin martyr (dates unknown). The story of St Ursula depends mostly on legend. According to an inscription found on a stone at the church of St Ursula in Cologne and dated from around 400, Ursula was the name of a local virgin who was martyred for her faith together with an unknown number of companions. By the tenth century, however, the legend had become embellished and Ursula was becoming established as one of the most popular saints of the whole medieval period. She was now identified as the daughter of a Christian king in Britain, who asked for and got a postponement to her marriage to a pagan prince in order to make the lengthy journey to Rome, together with 10 ladies-in-waiting and 1000 maidens. The party reached Rome safely, but were all massacred for their faith by Huns on the return trip after Ursula refused to marry their chief.

Another version of the legend identified Ursula as a Cornish princess who was sent together with 11,000 maidens and 60,000 servants to provide wives for British settlers in Armorica, only for their ships to be wrecked and all the women murdered or enslaved.

A third variant describes Ursula and her companions as an army of women who died after fighting a battle. The figure of 11,000 companions is thought to have been arrived at through misinterpretation of the Latin for 11. She is

229

honoured as a patron saint of schoolgirls and young women.

Valentine (m, f)
[VAT-uhn-tyn] from Latin *valens*, meaning 'strong'.
Third-century Roman martyr. According to tradition, he was a priest who was martyred for his faith in Rome during the reign of Claudius II and was subsequently com-memorated by a church on the Flaminian Way. Legend has it that when imprisoned, Valentine converted his gaoler to Christianity by restoring his daughter's eyesight and that when taken out to execution he left a message for the girl signed 'from your Valentine'.

Another tradition claims that he performed secret marriages on behalf of betrothed couples after Claudius II prohibited weddings because he needed more single men as recruits for his army. This Valentine may or may not be the same person as a bishop of Terni called Valentine who was martyred in Rome around 273. It is uncertain why these two historical Valentines (or a third, one Bishop Valentine of Genoa) became so uniquely associated with love and romance, specifically with the sending of 'valentines' in the form of anonymous cards to potential lovers on 14 February.

The custom may be a relic of the Roman festival of Lupercalia, or it may owe more to the fact that the feast day of St Valentine falls on the date when birds were once believed to start seeking mates. St Valentine is honoured as the patron saint of beekeepers, engaged couples, travellers and the young.

Variants: **Val**, **Valentina**.

Valentina feminine form of **Valentine**.

Vashti (f)
[VASH-tee] sounds like the Persian word for 'beautiful woman'.

230

A Queen of Persia who displeased King Xerxes and was replaced by Esther (Esther 1:9). Vashti may be another name for Amestris, mentioned in classical sources.

Verena (f)

[vuh-RAY-nuh, ve-REE-nuh] possibly from Latin, meaning 'true'.

A third-century saint who, according to tradition, journeyed with the Theban Legion to Rhaetia (modern Switzerland). When some members of the Theban Legion were martyred, Verena decided to live as a hermit, first at Solothurn and later in a cave near Zurich.

231

Verity (f)

[VE-ri-tee] from Latin *verus*, meaning 'true'.

The quality of truth is founded in God himself, including his faithfulness, reliability, integrity and reality. God is the essence of truth; Jesus Christ himself is 'the way, and the truth, and the life' (John 14:6).

Veronica (f)

[ver-RON-i-kuh] from Latin *vera icon*, meaning 'true image'.

First-century woman of Jerusalem. Veronica is traditionally identified as the woman who was moved by pity to wipe the face of Christ when he fell under the weight of the cross while carrying it to Calvary. She is not mentioned in biblical descriptions of the event, however, and only makes her first appearance in accounts of the Crucifixion dating from around the fifth century. She is sometimes tentatively linked with other biblical characters, including Martha and the unnamed woman whom Christ cured of her bleeding. Another suggestion is that she was the wife of a Roman officer or of a tax collector called Zacchaeus.

Veronica became a focus of great veneration in the medieval period and a cloth supposedly bearing the imprint of Christ's face and known as 'St Veronica's veil' has been preserved at St Peter's in Rome since the eighth century. She is honoured as the patron saint of washerwomen.

Variants: **Vera**, **Véronique**.

Victor (m)
[VIK-tuh] from Latin, meaning 'conqueror'.
Victor of Marseilles (third century), French martyr. According to one tradition, he was a Roman soldier put to death during the reign of Maximian alongside three other guards he had converted to Christianity.

232   **Victoria** (f)
[vik-TAW-ree-uh] from Latin, meaning 'victory'.
Third-century Roman virgin martyr. Victoria refused to marry her pagan fiancé (a Roman nobleman) Eugenius; she also refused to offer sacrifices to pagan gods. She was beheaded for her steadfast faith.

Variants: **Tori**, **Toria**, **Vicki**, **Vickie**, **Vicky**, **Vikki**.

Vincent (m)
[VIN-suhnt] from Latin, meaning conquering'.
Vincent of Saragossa (died 304), Spanish martyr. Vincent of Saragossa (or Vincent of Zaragoza) became a deacon and is known to have died for his faith at Valencia during the reign of Diocletian, although exact details of his life and death are not recorded. Tradition claims that he died after being viciously tortured, his sufferings including being beaten, flayed and roasted on a grid iron. Some say that Vincent of Saragossa was put to death alongside St Valerius of Saragossa (or Valerius of Zaragoza), bishop of Saragossa and Vincent's mentor, although another insists that the elderly Valerius was allowed to die peacefully in exile. Vincent of Saragossa is honoured as patron saint of Portugal.

Vincent of Lérins (died c.450), French monk and theologian. Little is known for certain about his life and career. Of noble birth, Vincent is thought to have lived the life of a soldier before entering the church, remaining a monk and priest in the island monastery of Lérins near Cannes. He is remembered chiefly as a scholar and teacher, his best-known work being a treatise upon the theme of Scripture and orthodoxy.

Vincent de Paul (1581–1660), French founder of the Vincentian (or Lazarist) Congregation and of the Sisters of Charity. Born into a peasant family of Ranquine (now renamed Saint-Vincent-de-Paul) in Gascony, he studied at the universities of Toulouse and Saragossa before joining the Franciscans and being ordained at the young age of 19.

One legend has it that in 1605, while travelling by sea, he was seized by pirates and sold into slavery in Tunis. After two years, however, he managed to escape and was soon back in Paris, where he became tutor and chaplain to the Count of Joigny. Subsequently, he served as pastor of the parish church at Châtillon-les-Dombes in eastern France.

233

Initially he seemed content to settle for a life of relative ease, but under the influence of Peter de Bérulle (who later became a cardinal), he became determined to devote the rest of his life to the service of the poor. He established a reputation for behaving with equal generosity and compassion towards both the rich and powerful and the poor and needy and in particular used his connections to better conditions for prisoners on galleys. Having come under the influence of St Francis de Sales, and with funds provided by a wealthy patron he went on to found the Congregation of the Mission (or Vincentians) to provide help for the vulnerable in rural areas and to establish seminaries to provide better training for the clergy. Priests who joined the order were encouraged to preach simply and directly and to renounce their ambitions of preferment within the church. They became known as Lazarists, when the order was installed in the Paris priory church of Saint-Lazare. He collaborated with St Louise de Marillac in founding the Sisters (or Daughters) of Charity, the first unenclosed order of women dedicated to caring for the poor and sick and now spread worldwide.

One of the most celebrated religious figures of his era, St Vincent de Paul was confined to an armchair through illness in his last years, but continued to participate in charitable works and was also prominent in campaigns against heresy. His name is preserved in the Society of St Vincent de Paul, a lay confraternity founded in Paris in 1833 by Frederick Ozanam. He is honoured as patron saint of all charitable societies.

Vincent Ferrer (1350–1419), Spanish friar and missionary. Born in Valencia of an English father and Spanish mother, he became a Dominican at the age of 17 and subsequently studied and taught in Barcelona, earning a reputation as a powerful preacher. He then moved to Toulouse to serve as papal legate for Cardinal Pedro de Luna, and when the cardinal became the antipope Benedict XIII, Vincent became his confessor and apostolic penitentiary.

He went on to play a crucial role in ending the Great Western Schism that had resulted in the creation of rival popes in Avignon and Rome by withdrawing his support for Benedict after the pope at Rome promised to step down, thus opening the way for the election of a new pope.

In 1398 Vincent fell seriously ill and as the result of a vision of the saints Dominic and Francis de Sales he resolved to spend the rest of his life preaching penance for sin and urging the faithful to prepare themselves for divine judgement. He is honoured as a patron saint of builders.

Virginia (f)
[ver-JIN-ee-uh] from the Roman family name *Verginius*, of uncertain origin, but probably associated with Latin *virgo*, meaning 'maid, virgin'.

Name given in honour of the Blessed Virgin Mary, the mother of Jesus Christ. The first baby born to the New World settlers was named Virginia; the North America colony Virginia was named after Elizabeth I, the 'Virgin Queen'.

Variants: **Gini**, **Ginnie**, **Ginny**.

Walburga (f)
[wawl-BERG-uh] from Old German 'power' and 'fortress'.
English-born abbess of Heidenheim (died 779). The daughter of a West Saxon chief and sister of the saints Willibald and Winebald, she spent her early adulthood as a nun at Wimborne in Dorset, before being recruited to assist St Boniface of Crediton in his missionary campaign in Germany. In 761 she was made head of the double monastery of Heidenheim in succession to Winebald, where she remained for the rest of her life. Virtually nothing is known about her life as abbess, although there is a tradition that she was highly skilled in medicine. After her death her bones were said to exude a miraculous clear fluid that continues to be dispensed by Benedictine nuns to selected patients to this day.

235

Walburga is perhaps most familiar today, however, through *Walpurgisnacht*, the night of 1 May (the date of the removal of her relics to Eichstätt) when witches were formerly reputed to gather on a peak in the Hartz mountains.

Walter (m)
[WAWL-tuh] from Old German *Waldhar*, meaning 'army ruler'.
The name of several saints, including the twelfth-century Benedictine monk and later abbot, noted for his godly holiness.

Variants: **Wally**, **Walt**.

Wesley (m)

[WEZ-lee] ultimately from Old English *wes(t)*, meaning 'west' and *lea* meaning, 'meadow or pasture'.

Honouring the eighteenth-century brothers John and Charles Wesley, two sons of Samuel and Susanna Wesley. John and Charles were leaders of the movement that became the Methodist Church. John Wesley was a preacher who evangelised widely, especially in the open air. His early education was largely undertaken by his mother Susanna, who had a significant influence on her children. At the age of five, John was rescued from the burning rectory where they lived. This escape made a deep impression on his mind and he regarded himself as providentially set apart, as a 'brand plucked from the burning'. Like his younger brother John, Charles was a leader of the Methodist movement. He is remembered chiefly for the many hymns he wrote, a number of which are still regularly sung today.

Wilfred, **Wilfrid** (m)

[WIL-frid] from Old English *Wilfrith*, meaning 'wanting peace'.

Wilfrid (*c.*633–709) English bishop. Born into a noble family of Northumbria, Wilfrid (or Wilfrith) studied at the monastery of Lindisfarne and in Lyons and Rome before returning to England and, his abilities being quickly recognised, being appointed abbot at Ripon. Here he introduced the rule of St Benedict and, at the Synod of Whitby in 664, argued successfully in favour of the Roman dating of Easter as opposed to the Celtic date. He went on to be appointed bishop of York, replacing St Chad in the post. He later came into conflict with St Theodore over the division of the diocese and had to go to Rome to secure papal support for his position. While on this mission he was diverted to Friesland and spent a year there preaching and evangelising, in the process winning thousands of converts

On his return to England he was thrown into prison for nine months by King Egfrith of Northumbria and was subsequently sent into exile in Sussex. Here he organised evangelical missions among the South Saxons and established a monastery at Selsey. He was eventually invited back to the north in 686 but three years later was forced to make another trip to Rome after further disagreements with Egfrith's successor Aldfrith. Forced to retreat to Mercia, he was made bishop of Lichfield and busied himself founding several more monasteries in the Midlands. In 705 he was made bishop of Hexham, a post he retained until his death while visiting a monastery he had founded at Oundle in Northamptonshire.

237

Though his life was dogged by controversy and conflict with both ecclesiastical and secular powers, he is remembered as one of the most courageous and visionary leaders of the early English church and as a key figure in bringing the church in England more into line with the church at Rome.

Wilhelmina feminine form of **William**.

William (m)
[WIL-yuhm] from Old German *Wilhelm*, from *wil*, meaning 'will' and *helm* 'helmet'.
William of Montevergine (1085–1142), Italian founder. Born into a noble family of Vercelli, William of Montevergine was orphaned as a boy and as a young adult settled on life as a hermit. After conducting pilgrimages he spent a period as a hermit at Monte Solicoli but later moved to Montevergine near Benevento, where he erected a cell and a church. Here he was joined by several other hermits, whom he organised into a small community around 1124. Under his guidance, members of this monastic community observed an austere regime, against which they finally rebelled. William then abandoned his monastery and lived an itinerant life throughout southern Italy.

William of Norwich (died 1144), English martyr. The legend of William of Norwich was apparently inspired by the discovery in 1144 of the unburied body of a 12-year-old boy in a wood near Norwich. The rumour spread that the boy (a skinner's apprentice from Norwich) had been crucified by local Jews in ritual mockery of Christ's Crucifixion and, despite the refusal of the authorities to accept this story, William of Norwich acquired the status of a martyr in the locality.

William of Rochester (died 1201), Scottish martyr. William of Rochester was a fisherman of Perth who is said to have lived a devout Christian life as a young man, dedicating himself to charitable works on behalf of orphans and the poor. In 1201 he set out on a pilgrimage to the Holy Land with a young man as his single companion, only to be robbed and murdered by this unnamed individual while they reached Rochester.

William of Roskilde (died 1070), English bishop. Details of his life are sparse, but it appears that he became a priest and in due course served as chaplain to King Canute, accompanying him on his trips to Scandinavia. Realising the need for renewal of Christianity in Denmark, he eventually settled permanently in that country, accepting the post of bishop of Roskilde (Zeeland). He is said to shown great courage in confronting the Danish king Sweyn Estridsen after the latter killed some suspected criminals after they had sought sanctuary in a church. King Sweyn was duly impressed by the bishop's fortitude and from then collaborated closely with him in promoting the gospel throughout that part of the world.

William of York (died 1154), English archbishop. Born into a noble family, William Fitzherbert served as treasurer of York and chaplain to his uncle King Stephen before being appointed archbishop of York in 1140. Unfortunately, his election as archbishop provoked intense opposition from the Cistercians and others, who accused William of simony

238

and immoral behaviour. Pope Innocent II confirmed William's appointment in 1143 but his election remained the cause of continuing resentment. A kindly, easy-going man who was very popular with the common populace, William did not prove a particularly good archbishop, neglecting some of his duties and failing to curb the violence of some of his supporters. After being deposed, he retired to Winchester and remained there for six years, living quietly as a monk, until restored to his arch-bishopric. Once back in his post he won respect for his forgiving attitude to his former rivals but died a few months later, possibly as the result of poisoning.

Variants: **Bill**, **Billie**, **Billy**, **Gwill**, **Gwilym**, **Liam**, **Will**, **Willie**, **Willy**.

239

Feminine forms: **Wilhelmina**, **Wilma**.

Wilma feminine form of **William**.

Winifred (f)
[WIN-i-frid] from Welsh *Gwenfrewi*, from *gwen*, meaning 'blessed' and *frewi*, meaning 'peace, reconciliation'.
Welsh maiden (seventh century). The story of Winifred (otherwise called Gwenfrewi, Wenefred or Winefride) depends almost entirely upon legend. Supposedly a niece of St Beuno, she attracted the amorous attentions of a chieftain's son named Caradoc. When she spurned his advances, the indignant young man struck her head off with his sword, upon which the ground opened beneath his feet and swallowed him up. Beuno replaced Winifred's head and restored her to life and she spent the rest of her days living as a nun at Gwytherin in Derbyshire. The location of these events is traditionally supposed to be Holywell (Treffynnon) in Flintshire and a spring that is said to have burst out at the spot where Winifred's head fell has long been considered a site of miraculous cures, attracting thousands of pilgrims.

Variants: **Freda**, **Win**, **Winnie**.

Wolfgang (m)
[WUULF-gang] from Old German *wulf*, meaning 'wolf' and *gang*, meaning 'path'.

Bishop of Regensburg (c.924–94). Born in Swabia, Wolfgang studied at the abbey of Reichenau on Lake Constance and taught in cathedral schools in Würzburg and Trier before entering the Benedictine monastery at Einsiedeln. After a brief period as a missionary in Pannonia (Hungary) he was made bishop of Regensburg, in which post he did much to promote standards among the clergy and to reform monastic life in the region. He was much loved for his generosity and widely respected for his great wisdom, even serving as tutor to the future Holy Roman Emperor Henry II.

Xavier (m)
[ZAY-vee-er] from the name.

Francis Xavier (1506–22), Spanish Jesuit missionary. Born into a well-connected Spanish Basque family at the castle of Xavier near Sanguesa, Navarre, in Spain, he was educated in Paris and initially taught Aristotelian philosophy at the University of Paris. There he came under the influence of St Ignatius of Loyola and became one of the small group of disciples who took a vow of chastity in 1536 and in due course co-founded the Society of Jesus. He was ordained as a priest in 1537 and spent most of the rest of his life doing missionary work abroad on behalf of the Jesuit order, mostly in India and the Far East, with his base being established in Goa.

Over the years he won many thousands of converts (30,000 in India alone) and effectively laid the foundations for the Christian church in that part of the world. In doing so he earned a lasting personal reputation as the most influential missionary since St Paul. He died while planning to enter China. Today he is honoured as the patron saint of foreign missions.

Yvette, **Yvonne** feminine forms of **Ivo**.

Zacchaeus (m)
[za-KEE-uhs] variant of *Zachariah*.
A Jewish tax-collector whom Jesus described as one of the lost he came to save. He is also noted for his determination to see Jesus, despite being short (Luke 19:1–10).

Zachariah, Zachary (m)
[za-kuh-RY-uh] from Hebrew, meaning 'Yahweh has remembered'.
Spelling in some versions of the Bible of **Zechariah**. Also Zacharias (died 752), Greek-born pope. Born at San Severino in Calabria, Zacharias served as a deacon in Rome before being elected pope in 741. As pope he demonstrated skill as a diplomat, retrieving lands lost to the Lombard king Liutprand through negotiation and establishing friendly relations with the Franks. He also opposed the iconoclasm of the Emperor Constantine Copronymus, sought an end to the trade in Christian slaves and supported the missionary work of St Boniface of Crediton in Germany. Two of his letters to Boniface have survived and he was also the author of a translation into Greek of the Dialogues of St Gregory the Great.

Variants: **Zacchaeus**, **Zacharias**, **Zachery**, **Zack**, **Zackery**, **Zak**, **Zechariah**.

241

Zadok (m)
[ZAY-dok] from Hebrew, meaning 'righteous'.
The name of several men in the Old Testament, especially a priest who was loyal to David. He became high priest towards the end of David's reign and anointed Solomon as king (1 Kings 1:7–8, 32–40). After the exile, only his family were allowed to act as priests because they were faithful to God (Ezekiel 44:15–16).

Zebedee (m)
[ZEB-uh-dee] from Hebrew, meaning 'gift of the Lord'.
The father of two of Jesus' disciples, James and John
(Matthew 4:21 –22).

Zebulun (m)
[ZEB-yoo-luhn] from Hebrew, meaning 'honour'.
The tenth son of Jacob by Leah (Genesis 30:20); the tribe
descended from Zebulun, who lived in a fertile area of
southern Galilee, and made its most significant
contribution in the Judges period (Judges 5:18; 6:35), but
was overrun by the Assyrians in the eighth century BC
(Isaiah 9:1). Nazareth, where Jesus grew up, was in its
traditional area.

Zechariah (m)
[zek-uh-RY-uh] variant of *Zachariah*.
The name of several men in the Bible. Father of John the
Baptist: a priest who was struck dumb when an angel told
him his barren wife would have a son. He only began to
speak again when he called the child John (the Baptist)
(Luke 1:5–25, 57–66). Zechariah's song is sometimes called
the Benedictus (Luke 1:67–79). *Zechariah, king of Israel
(c.746–745 BC), the son of Jeroboam II* (2 Kings 15:8–12).
Zechariah, son of Jehoiada: a priest who was murdered by
order of Joash king of Judah because he gave an unpopular
prophecy. Matthew 23:35 probably refers to the incident,
which is recorded in 2 Chronicles 24:20–22. *Zechariah the
prophet*, a late-sixth-century BC prophet who motivated the
Jews to rebuild the temple (Ezra 5:1–2; Zechariah 3:6–7;
4:8–9).

Zedekiah (m)
[zed-uh-KY-uh] from Hebrew, meaning 'Yahweh is my
righteousness'.
King of Judah (597–587 BC). The last king of Judah, who was

really a puppet king of the Babylonians after the first deportation of Jews to Babylon in 597 BC (2 Kings 24:18–25:26). Though he showed some sympathy for the prophet Jeremiah, he was a weak character who finally rebelled against the Babylonians. His sons were executed in front of him before he was blinded and taken to Babylon.

Zephaniah (m)
[zef-uh-NY-uh] from Hebrew, meaning 'Yahweh hides'.
A seventh-century BC Jewish prophet and nobleman. The theme of his prophecy is the coming day of the Lord, with the two aspects of God's judgement and the restoration of his blessing.

243

Zillah (f)
[ZIL-uh] from Hebrew, meaning 'shadow'.
One of the wives of Lamech (Genesis 4:19, 22–23).

Zita (f)
[ZEE-tuh] from Italian, meaning 'little girl'.
Italian maidservant (1218–72). Zita (otherwise referred to as Citha or Sitha) was born into a poor family near Lucca and spent her life as a maidservant in the house of a wealthy weaver of Lucca. Hardworking and generous to those worse off than herself, she proved initially unpopular with the other servants but gradually won everyone over with her goodness. Many tales were told of her charitable acts and she came to be credited with various miraculous powers. It was commonly said that when she stayed too long at her prayers in church (which she often did) her household chores were performed by angels. She is honoured as the patron saint of maidservants.

Zoe, Zoë (f)
[ZOH-i] from Greek, meaning 'life'; a Greek translation of the Hebrew equivalent of **Eve**.

The name of two martyrs, one in the second century martyred under the persecution of Emperor Hadrian and one in the third century martyred under the persecution of Emperor Diocletian.

Zuleika (f)
[zoo-LAY-kuh] probably from Persian, meaning 'brilliant beauty'.
Believed by some to be the name of Potiphar's wife. She made sexual advances to Joseph. Joseph refused her and so she falsely accused him of wanting to sleep with her. When her husband heard his wife's account of the events, he had Joseph put in prison (Genesis 39).

244